beadsimple

150 designs for earrings, necklaces, bracelets, embellishments, and more

susan beal

essential techniques for making jewelry just the way you want it

The Taunton Press

The Taunton Press, Inc., 63 South Main Street, PO Box 5506, Newtown, CT 06470-5506
e-mail: tp@taunton.com

Editor: Erica Sanders-Foege
Copy editor: Diane Sinitsky
Indexer: Lynda Stannard
Jacket/Cover design: Dania Davey
Interior design: Susan Fazekas
Layout: Susan Fazekas
Illustrator: Alexis Hartman
Photographers: Burcu Avsar and Zach DeSart

Library of Congress Cataloging-in-Publication Data
Beal, Susan.
Bead simple : essential techniques for making jewelry just the way you want it / Susan Beal.
p. cm.
Includes bibliographical references and index.
ISBN 978-1-56158-953-1 (alk. paper)
1. Beadwork. 2. Jewelry making. I. Title.
TT860.B333856 2008
745.594'2--dc22

2007030239

Printed in Singapore
10 9 8 7 6 5 4 3 2 1

To Andrew

I'm so lucky to have such amazing family and friends. A special thank you to my mom, for always wearing my jewelry and loving it so much, and to my nephew Julian, for keeping me on my toes as we shopped for beads in New York and came up with so many new ideas together. Making jewelry with a five-year-old really gives you a fresh perspective! Thank you to David and Dawn for everything (especially for letting me borrow Jules as often as possible!), and to Paul and Nancy for all their help, advice, and support along the way. Thank you to my agent, Stacey Glick, who's been flawless from start to finish, and to my editor, Erica Sanders-Foege, for all of her fresh ideas and thoughtful guidance, as well as the perfect title for the book. Thanks so much to Janel, Nicole, Pam, Diane, Katie, Susan, Wendi, Dania, Carol, and everyone else at The Taunton Press; I'm thrilled to be working with you.

Thank you, Burcu and Zach, for the luminous photographs you created together, and thank you, Alexis, for the exquisitely detailed illustrations (and for taking me on my first of many trips to the Rose Bowl flea market for vintage beads and buttons). Thank you to Gayle and Chuck, my first jewelry teachers, for opening my eyes to this whole world. Thanks to my lovely crafty friends everywhere for constantly inspiring me. And thank you to my susanstars customers—online, at shops, and at craft fairs—for supporting my handmade business over the last eight years, and to all my West Coast Crafty readers, who make writing about crafts such a pleasure.

I appreciate my guest designers, who so generously shared their talents by creating such cool, striking pieces for this collection, more than I can say. Thank you to my dear Torie, Diane, Tanja, Nicola, Rebecca, Bethe, and Caitlin in Portland; my Los Angeles crafty girls, Jessica, Cathy, Jenny, Stacy, Wendy, Alexis, and Laura; my Bay Area ladies, Meredith, Nicole, Nancy, Natalie, and Tricia; my New York crafties, Julian, Kayte, Jenn, Linda, Jennifer, Jessica, and Megan; and Leah, Jennifer, Kathy, Faythe, Shannon, Fiona, Emilie, Jessica, Jessee, Betsy, Sarah, Christy, and Kelly everywhere else.

And finally, a heartfelt thank you to my husband, Andrew, for his constant love and support for me in all my endeavors, crafty and otherwise. From looking over my very first design ideas to celebrating when the final chapter was officially in, I couldn't possibly have done it without you.

Contents

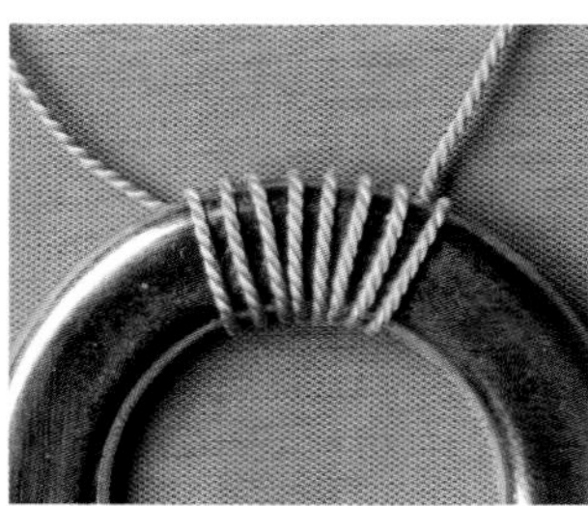

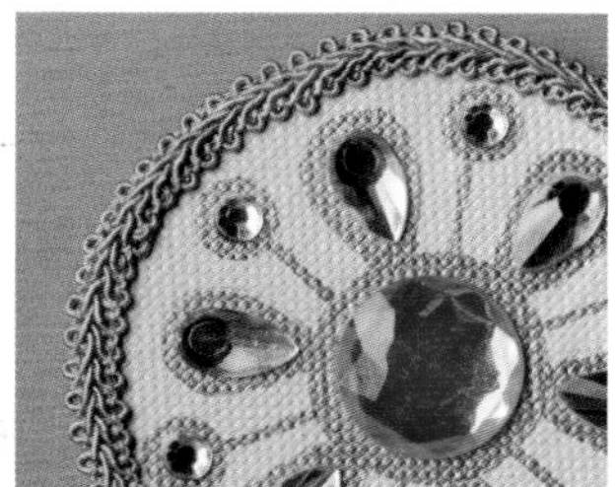

Simply Beautiful

I've always loved jewelry. When I was little, all the paper dolls I drew wore dangling earrings and shiny rings. When I was in high school, I'd take an old necklace apart or endlessly rework a vintage bracelet so I'd have something new and sparkly to wear the next day. And when I kept designing my own pieces after college, I decided to move cross-country to go to jewelry school, where I learned casting, fabrication, and gem-setting. Then I picked up my pliers and started my own jewelry line, susanstars, a collection of vintage-gone-modern pieces, from wood drop earrings to splashy Lucite® pendants.

And in all this time, I never found just the right beading book, with projects I wanted to make—a book with both accessible and gorgeously complicated designs in the mix to keep things interesting … but full of ideas for remaking vintage, secondhand, and hardware pieces into fashion-forward sparklers so you don't have to spend so much at the bead store every time you want to make yourself a little something… and not just jewelry, actually, but also accessories, household stuff, and gifts. So now I've written that book myself! I hope it inspires you to make just the jewelry you want.

Creativity is so personal, and with the right techniques and a little inspiration, the sky is the limit jewelry-wise. For *Bead Simple*, I came up with 50 projects, from earrings to embellished clothing, and made two variations on each for a total of 150 designs. And along the way, 40 of my favorite designers each contributed a spin-off piece, taking my ideas in some amazing directions. No matter what your style is, there's plenty to choose from, and of course you can change the colors, the length, or the design elements to come up with something that's a little more you—like a cookbook, you can either follow these recipes exactly or improvise to suit your taste.

I've also created a website, beadsimple.com, to complement the book. It has short videos of the techniques included here, plus even more resources, a design gallery, and updates on new ideas. You can contact me or post photos of your own designs there—I'd absolutely love to see what you make!

Here's to making jewelry that makes you feel gorgeous.

—Susan Beal

1

Getting Started

Here's everything you'll need to get started designing your own gorgeous jewelry—basic tools, materials, and techniques.

Tools

A set of three **jewelry pliers** are essential for making your own pieces with wire:

Flat-nose pliers (also called chain-nose pliers) are perfect for flattening or forming sharp angles.

Round-nose pliers form smooth loops and curves. They are graduated in size, so you can form tiny loops around the narrow tips or larger ones farther back on the jaws.

Wire cutters are great for neatly clipping wires and cords.

Other pliers that are useful to have are **crimping pliers** and **flattening pliers**, which have flat, plastic-lined jaws for wire straightening.

You can buy inexpensive pliers for about $6 each, which often come in a set, or higher-quality German-made pliers for about $20 each. The more expensive pliers have springs in the handles, which make them both easier to use and much more durable. You can always buy inexpensive tools first and upgrade to better-quality pieces later.

It's always nice to have sharp **scissors** on hand for cutting nonwire materials. And for clipping memory wire, you'll need a special **memory wire cutter**—memory wire is too hard and resistant to cut with normal scissors or pliers. For knotting, you can use long, skinny-tipped **tweezers** to grip the cord right where you want your knot to go.

You'll also use **glue** in some projects, especially to reinforce or embellish. Instant-drying glue (recommended brand: Super Glue) is an easy way to create a quick join—but don't use it on anything that will take weight or wear, since it can be brittle. Cement glue (recommended brand: Bond 527) is perfect for anchoring small findings, like a tip at the

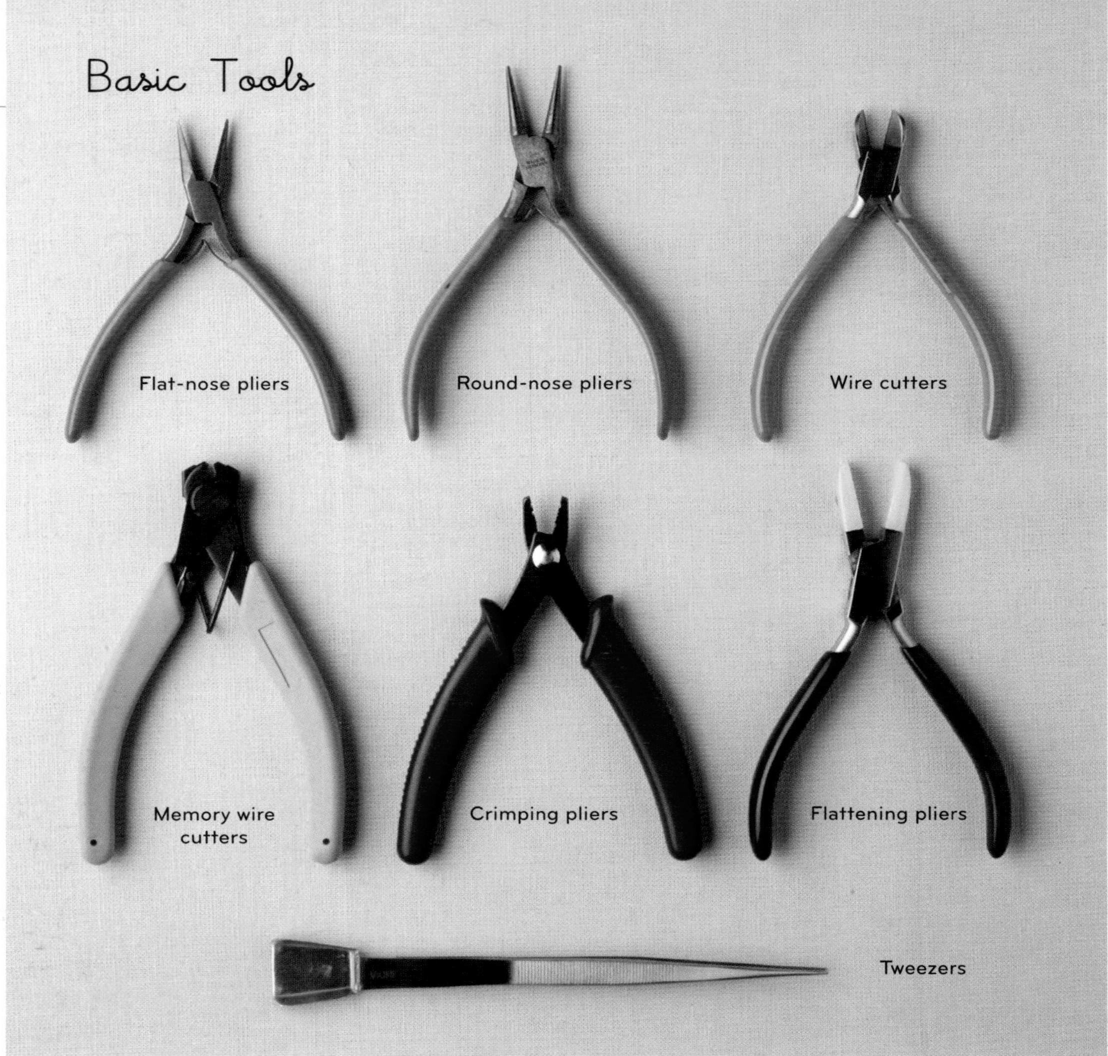

WIRE GAUGES

16: heavy clasps or connectors

18: heavy clasps, sturdy jump rings

20: jump rings, plain loops, wrapped loops, stud-earring posts, heavy earring wires

22: earring wires, basic wire wrapping

24: earring wires, basic wire wrapping (wrapped loops), looping

26: delicate wirework (wrapped loops), lightweight loops

28 and so forth: delicate wrapping and loops, threading

end of a piece of memory wire. Craft glue (recommended brand: Aleene's® Original Tacky Glue®) is ideal for attaching small, lightweight pieces to flat surfaces and will not damage the color or backing of a rhinestone. A hot-glue gun is great for joining larger or varied pieces to a base or to each other, and industrial-strength glue (recommended brand: E6000®) is the strongest bond of all, but make sure you use plenty of ventilation when you're gluing with it.

Materials

Here are some of the materials that are most useful for beading and making your own jewelry. You can find most of them fairly inexpensively, and you can build up a collection as you go. Keep your work materials neatly organized in a fishing tackle box, small shelves or drawers, or plastic bins and bead boxes with snap-tight lids.

Wire and findings

Wire comes in different gauges, or thicknesses. The higher the gauge number, the thinner the wire. For many projects, **20- and 24-gauge wire** are perfect. The 20-gauge wire is thick enough to make earring wires, and the 24 is thin enough to use small beads with but is still durable. Heavier gauges like 16 are ideal for doing structural pieces, while more delicate gauges like 28–32 are so thin that they're almost like thread.

CRAFT WIRE is inexpensive and perfect for beginners to practice with. It comes in a variety of colors—metallics like silver, gold, and copper, as well as a rainbow of hues. Craft wire is generally a bit softer and more pliable than precious-metal wires; it's made of base metal, which is an alloy, or mixture, of different materials. Two things to keep in mind are that some people are sensitive to the nickel in base metal and may do better with sterling, and that the dull gray layer underneath the shiny surface may eventually show through over time.

STERLING SILVER WIRE is wonderful to work with. It comes in different hardnesses—I like **half-hard** wire, which has more strength and body than **dead soft**. Every sterling piece is marked 0.925, which means that it is at least 92.5 percent pure silver, with a few other metals to strengthen it. **Fine silver** is 100 percent pure, but it is softer and not suitable for some wirework projects.

GOLD-FILLED WIRE combines pure gold with a base metal (typically 12K or 14K), since pure gold is very soft. It usually doesn't cause the kind of allergic reactions that base metals can trigger. Both gold and silver fluctuate in price, so the cost of wire often changes with the market, but sterling silver is more affordable than gold.

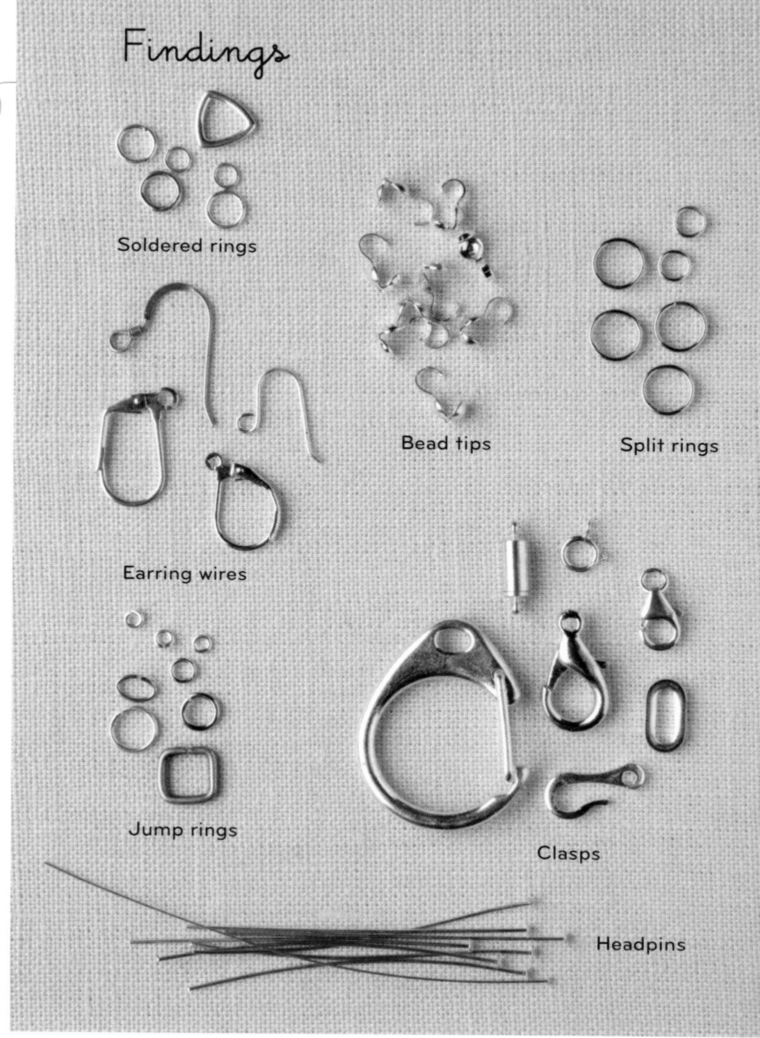

CHAIN comes in all sizes and weight, from delicate and lacy to thick and masculine. When you buy it in bulk (by the foot or on a spool, for example), it's considerably cheaper than buying finished chains, and it's a breeze to put the clasps and finishers on yourself for a necklace that's exactly the length and style you want. You can also make a chain by joining jump rings in a continuous strand. (See p. 24 for more information on chain making.)

JUMP RINGS are useful for joining two pieces together, like chains to clasps. A jump ring is just a circle of wire that isn't sealed shut—it can be opened with pliers and then closed again. They come in a range of sizes, from about 3mm (a small ring that's great for attaching a clasp to a thin chain) to 10mm (a sizable ring for joining large pieces) and larger. In general, 22-gauge rings are useful for most projects.

SOLDERED RINGS are solid, with no openings. They're ideal for using with clasps and are available in the same sizes as jump rings.

SPLIT RINGS are like key rings—you open one side and slip the ring onto a loop or chain. They're more secure than jump rings but harder to put on.

HEADPINS, which are straight pieces of wire with a stopper at one end, are perfect for making earrings, pendants, and other dangles.

EYEPINS have a small loop at the end to serve as the stopper instead of a flat "head," so you can use a jump ring or another loop to join a dangle to your piece. You can easily make your own eyepins, too (as shown on p. 24).

Beads

You can buy beads in every shape, size, color, and material, and in every price range, too, at local bead stores and shops online. You can also look for costume jewelry at yard sales or thrift stores—take it apart and use the vintage beads to make your own unique designs. Buttons and rhinestones are fun to mix in, too.

Bead sizes are usually measured in millimeters. A 3mm bead is tiny, an 8mm bead is about the size of a pea, a 12mm or 14mm bead is on the small side of marble size, and so on. (See the chart on p. 10.)

SEED BEADS are tiny, typically solid-colored glass beads that are useful for creating space between bigger beads or stopping a larger piece from slipping over a thin headpin or small loop. They come in different sizes as well—as in wire-gauge measurements, the larger the number, the smaller the bead size. Use 11/0s for delicate projects, 8/0s for medium-size pieces, and 6/0s for crafting or embellishing.

DELICAS are a high-quality seed bead with a precise, consistent size, while the less expensive versions have some differences in size and shape.

GLASS beads come in all colors, sizes, and shapes. Look for smooth or faceted beads to add sparkle and shine in your designs. Glass is relatively heavy, so don't use larger pieces for earrings or string them on delicate material for necklaces or bracelets.

METAL beads can range from tiny spacers to larger round and other shapes (which are often hollow). They can have a tarnished patina or a super-shiny finish. Metal beads and charms look great mixed with other materials—they add a lovely contrast to bright or dark colors. Like other findings, you can choose from sterling and gold/gold-filled as well as base metals (copper, brass, and silver colors).

ACRYLIC/PLASTIC/LUCITE beads are shiny and lightweight—perfect for adding tons of pop without a lot of weight. Look for vintage beads in smooth or faceted finishes, or new beads in stripes or solids—there are so many styles of this versatile material.

WOOD beads range in size, shape, and color but give a natural, stylish look within a design. Since wood typically isn't especially heavy, you can use larger pieces within a necklace or pendant without adding a lot of weight.

BEAD SIZES IN MILLIMETERS

rounds

2mm 3mm 4mm 5mm 6mm 7mm 8mm 9mm

10mm 12mm 14mm 16mm 18mm 20mm

BONE AND SHELL beads can be found dyed or natural in color. Imitation bone, which is often plastic, comes in many styles, too.

SEMIPRECIOUS beads are wonderful to work with, and there are dozens of stones to choose from.

Some of my favorites are agates (like carnelian or black agate), which have a beautiful glossy tone; jades, in milky whites and greens; amethyst, in cloudy or translucent purples; citrines and ambers, in warm tones; turquoise, in blues, greens, or acid yellows; and pearls, ranging from smooth rounds to long, jagged points. Look for rounds, ovals, briolettes, cylinders, chunky abstract shapes, and tiny beads. Buying semiprecious beads on strands is usually the most economical way to go, but if you buy individual beads you can pick and choose exactly. Semiprecious beads are typically heavy, so use them sparingly as earrings and on thinner chains.

Other Findings

EARRING WIRES are sold commercially in dozens of styles, from simple drops and hooks to more elaborate leverbacks. Like wire, they're available in gold-filled, sterling silver, and base metal, plus other materials like surgical steel and niobium.

CLASPS come in many forms, too, from plain to ornate—S-shapes, lobster claws, barrels, and toggles, to name just a few. (You'll learn how to make your own earring wires and clasps in the wirework section of the Techniques chapter on pp. 24–25). One clasp that's great to use (especially for bracelets) is a magnetic style—so easy to open and close.

Stringing

FLEXIBLE BEADING WIRE (like Soft Flex®) is a coated wire that comes in many thicknesses, from super-thin to heavy, depending on what you're stringing. It's durable, supple, and great for heavier beads or pendants—and the bonus is that you don't need to use a needle to make your designs.

MEMORY WIRE is stiff wire you can bead directly on to that holds a "memory" of its shape, so it doesn't uncoil or change. It is sold in round shapes suitable for making coil bracelets or rings. Make sure you use special shears to cut it—it can ruin wire clippers.

ELASTIC CORD is an easy way to string bracelets or necklaces without using a clasp. It also comes in different thicknesses and strengths. Use a twisted-wire **flexible beading needle** with it for easy threading. You can use heavier elastic without a needle if it is rigid enough to slip through beads (such as the silver cord in the Swingy Sparkle Necklace on p. 86).

CRIMP BEADS can be used to finish the ends of your flexible wire or elastic pieces. Smooth sterling silver or gold-filled crimp beads are much higher quality than base metal, which has rough edges that can damage your cord over time.

BEADING NEEDLES can be used with elastic, silk, and other cords. There are dozens of kinds and brands.

SILK OR COTTON BEADING CORD in various thicknesses is perfect for knotting between beads.

BEADING BOARDS AND TRAYS make creating your own pieces so much easier—you can look at beads, charms, and materials in different combinations before making your final choices.

A VELVET JEWELRY NECK DISPLAY is something I love designing necklaces and pendants on. This lets you see how a piece will drape or hang on a 3-D surface. You can use straight pins to hold a chain or a bead strand in place while you work around it or add to it.

Needles

Use a twisted wire or beading needle with most thin cord or thread. Remember, you'll need to use a needle with an eye that can accommodate your cord but can also pass through the smallest beads you're using. Twisted wire needles are handy because the eye collapses as you pass it through a bead, and they're available in thin or thicker weights depending on your other materials.

Some silk (and other) cords come prethreaded with a twisted wire needle, which is a nice touch.

A few designer's essentials arranged on a jewelry display and beading board (clockwise from top): a plastic canvas mesh round, blank hairband, hair clips, pendant bails, paint, pin backs, bobby pin blanks, plastic bags, and a measuring tape.

Cords, wires, and threads

Here are some stringing materials.

SILK CORD is wonderful to knot on, especially for softer or smoother beads, like pearls, glass, or less brittle semiprecious. It has a lovely drape in a finished piece. Always stretch it before using since

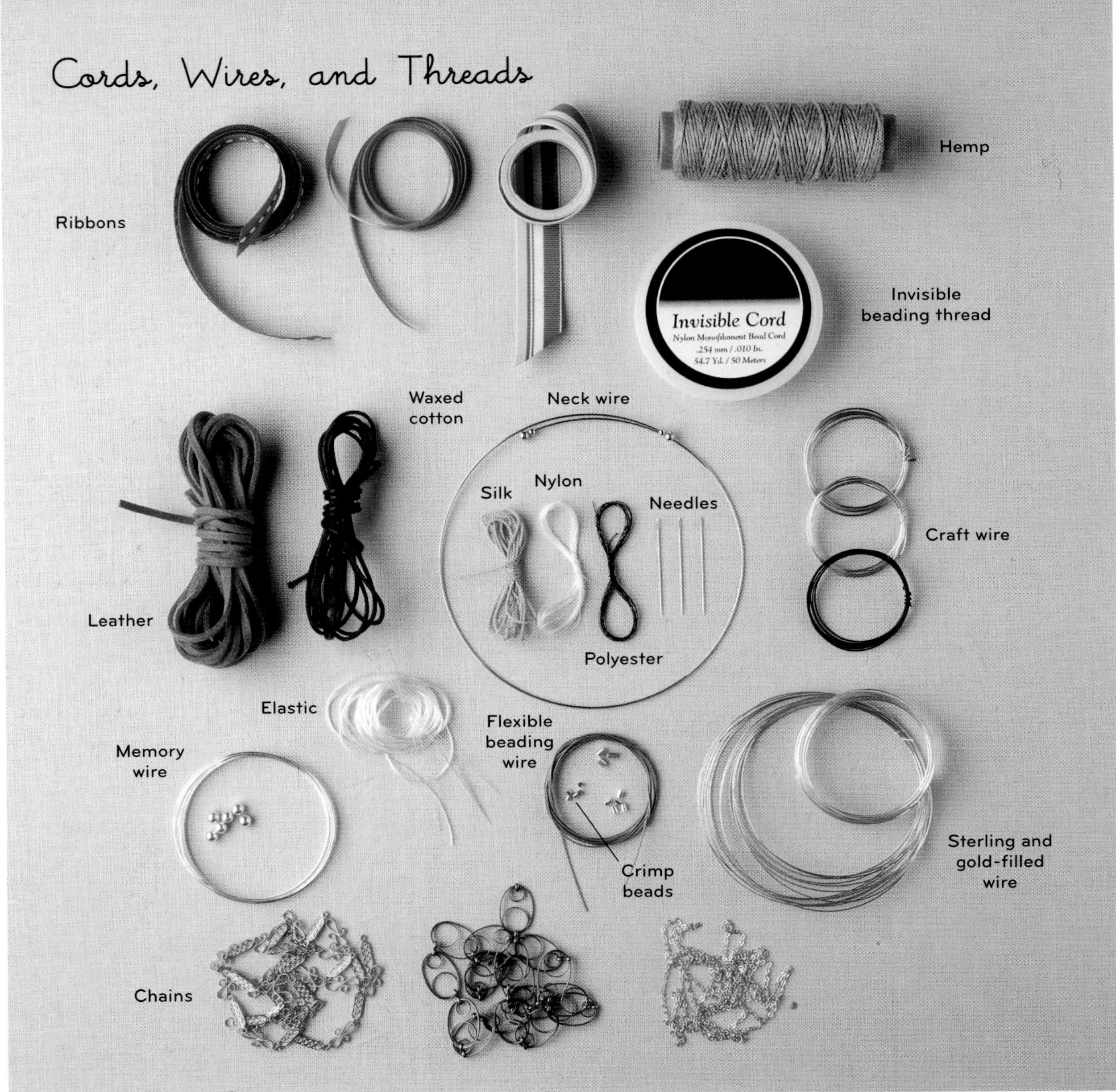

it will give later if you don't. If you choose the kind that comes on a card and there are noticeable kinks and folds, dampen it, then hang it over a hook or door overnight so it will dry straight. Silk cord comes in a range of thicknesses—make sure if you're knotting that you choose one that will easily go through your bead holes but will create a stopper when knotted to keep beads in place.

HEMP is a durable, ropelike material that knots wonderfully. It reacts to and absorbs water, though, and will lose its crispness after wear and use, but it will stay consistently strong.

NYLON and other artificial threads are strong and resilient and will not stretch. However, they are slipperier and harder to knot in my experience. Nylon is great for hard gemstones, which can damage softer materials like silk over time.

WAXED COTTON is a nice basic cord for stringing heavier pieces. It is tightly woven for strength but still isn't as durable as artificial cords.

LEATHER OR SUEDE CORDING is great to string on and has a smooth, natural drape. If the leather has a harder, smoother finish, it will likely be colorfast and largely waterproof. Leather and suede generally work well with crimp clasps.

POLYESTER SEWING THREAD is what I suggest for stitching beads onto fabric or another form for embellishment. It is much more durable over time than cotton.

INVISIBLE BEADING THREAD is clear and delicate and works wonderfully when embellishing fabric, too. It does tend to curl up and tangle a bit, so try using a little Thread Heaven Thread Conditioner and Protectant® or other conditioner on it to smooth it out nicely.

ELASTIC comes in many thicknesses and forms. Thin elastic floss is ideal for lightweight projects (like the Candy Shoppe One-Strand Bracelet on p. 160), must be used with a needle, and can be knotted or crimped shut. Thicker cord is great for heavier projects and is thick and rigid enough to bead without a needle. Knot it (as in the Swingy Sparkle Necklace on p. 86) around larger beads easily.

NARROW RIBBON can be lovely to use—it can be easier to slip a bead on if you cut the ribbon at a diagonal so it has a point much like a needle. If it frays after you've beaded with it, just trim it to a point again.

Design

The 150 projects in this book range from beginner-friendly to involved and elaborate, and employ quite a few techniques. Try using different sizes and colors of beads or different materials than the ones pictured for distinctive effects. Here are a few ideas to get you started creating your own unique variations and designs.

- Leaving spaces within your jewelry designs can give a modern look, which is easy to wear with anything from a cocktail dress to a T-shirt and jeans. Space also gives you room to appreciate each component, since they're not jumbled together.

- Busier, more crowded pieces can be striking, too, but tend to dominate what you're wearing.

- Mixing different-size beads within a design can make it really pop, while using the same size throughout lends more of a classic feel—think of your grandmother's pearls.

- A simple but effective rule is to design in threes (or ones, or fives)—odd numbers of beads make a gorgeous, symmetrical design. Think of one large bead in the middle of a necklace between two smaller ones, or five identical beads spaced along a choker.

- If you do use two beads, it can be eye-catching to vary the size or spacing so the beads are offset instead of symmetrical, as in the Duo Earrings (p. 33) and Spaces and Sparkles Pendant (p. 128).

Each project has at least two variations shown to give you ideas for personalizing your own pieces.

A candy-colored trio of bracelets mixes glass, plastic, and vintage beads on elastic cord. For instructions, see p. 160.

COMBINING COLORS

Use bold colors with delicate designs for an unexpected twist, or try sophisticated paler shades to flatter your coloring. Some fun combinations:

- Light blue and brown
- Pink and brown
- Pink and lime green
- Pink and olive green
- Turquoise and olive green
- Turquoise and lime green
- Turquoise and yellow
- Orange and olive green
- Orange and blue
- Dark red and pink
- Dark red and light blue
- Plum and lavender
- Plum and turquoise
- Dark blue and turquoise
- Black and anything (especially pinks, reds, and light blues)
- Clear and anything
- White and anything

Color Wheel

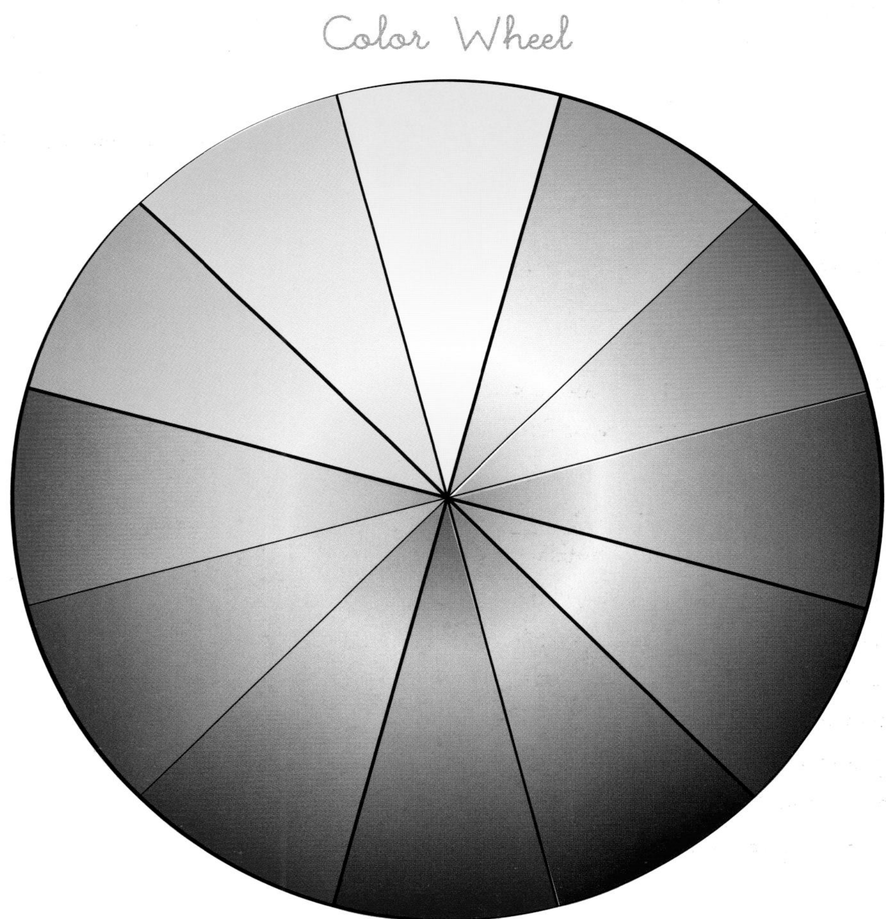

Color

You can create striking color combinations by choosing a color from the color wheel and pairing it with a variation of its opposite. Try using orange with blue or a deep red with an olive green—making the green more neutral will make sure it doesn't look like Christmas!

Colors that are closely related can work well together, too. Create a monochromatic design in different hues, like hot pink next to a lighter pink, or a range of bright and dark blues in a single piece.

Try mixing less-expected pairings or combining two brighter colors with neutrals or metallics for a gorgeous effect. Black or clear beads go with anything, of course. Go a little easier on neons and difficult pairings like yellow and purple.

How to Use This Book

Want to know how easy or advanced a necklace project is, or how long that pair of earrings will take you from start to finish? There are **ICONS** for each project in the book (see the box above right). I've also listed all the **TECHNIQUES** you'll need to use to make a project, boxed as shown at right.

TIPS are quick suggestions on other materials to use, a shortcut, or ideas to change the size or fit of the piece.

PATTERNS are given for some projects, which reference the materials from the list with initials. If a letter is underlined in the pattern (like <u>G</u>), it means either that it's the center of the template (like the Tiered Necklace patterns) or that it's a connector bead, where two strands cross (like the Woven Collar Necklace patterns). It's an easy way to "read" the pattern and orient the design—and don't forget to look at the photos for reference, too!

ICONS

These symbols are easy to follow for clues about what kind of project you're getting into. Look for them at the beginning of each project set.

 = easy or beginner-friendly

 = moderate

 = advanced

 = takes less than an hour to make

 = stash-friendly piece that doesn't use tons of materials

 = inexpensive (less than $15)

TECHNIQUES

- Plain loops
- Wrapped loops
- Jump rings

2

Techniques

Here are the techniques you'll use to create every design in the book. You may need to practice some of them a few times before trying them out on a project, but they get much easier with a little trial and error. If you need help, there are short videos of each of these on beadsimple.com for reference, too.

Bead Stringing

Bead stringing is the most basic way to construct a piece of jewelry like a necklace or bracelet—just thread a needle or pick up a piece of flexible wire, secure the end, and add beads one after another. Depending on what you're using materials-wise and your own taste, there are several ways to construct your piece of jewelry.

Needle beading

1. Before you begin, you may want to add a bead tip (see facing page) to add your clasp or end component.

2. Thread a needle with your thinner material (like elastic, silk cord, or nylon thread), and tie a knot or cover the end with a doubled piece of tape.

3. Add your beads one (or more) at a time, and continue beading until you reach the desired length.

4. Finish with a bead tip or durable knotting (if no clasp is required).

Needle Beading

1

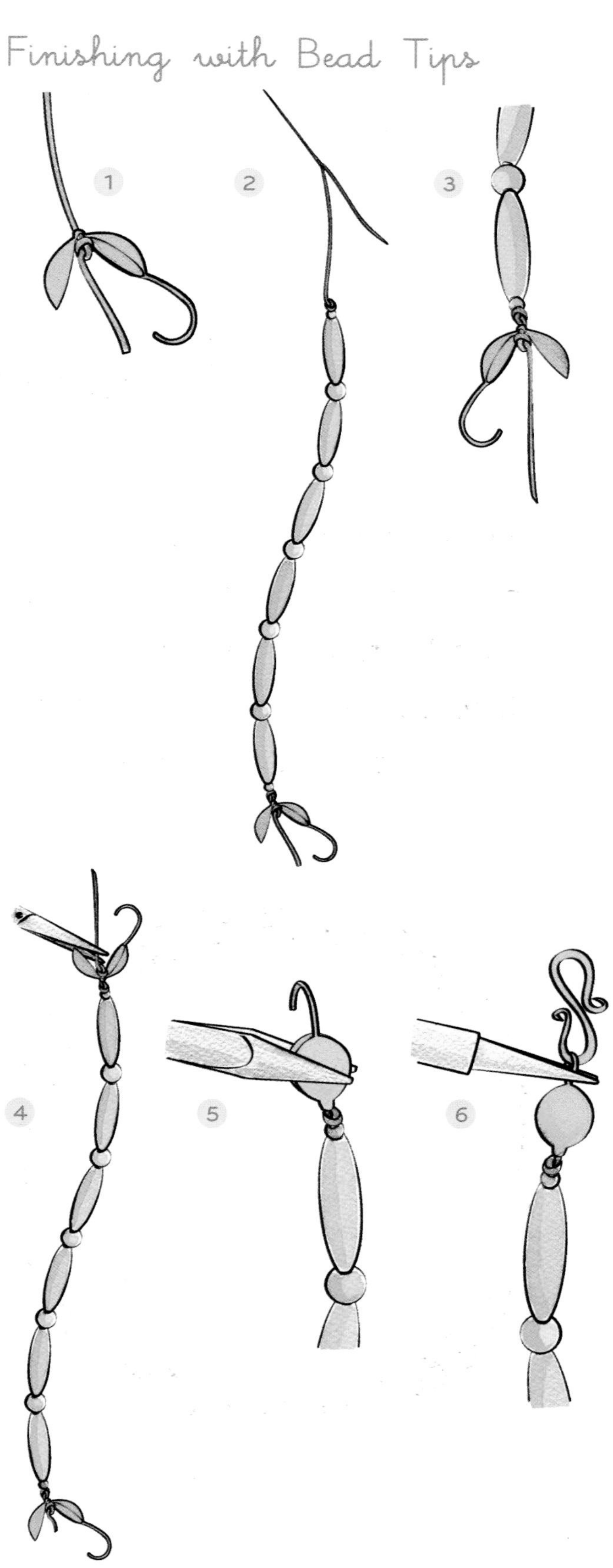

Finishing with bead tips

Bead tips cover a knot at each end of the cord securely, and the curved hook attaches to a finding. See complete instructions for knotting on p. 27.

1. Tie a knot near the beginning of your cord and slip one bead tip onto it, with the two cupping halves facing and enveloping the knot (as shown). Knot again directly above the bead tip to keep it in place.

2. String or knot your beads as you go until you're finished with your piece. Tie a knot at the end.

3. Add a bead tip with the halves facing outward, away from the beads and toward the needle. Using your knotting tweezers to pinpoint the spot, tie a knot inside the tip and pull it taut.

4. Add a drop of glue or Fray Check™ (I often use Fray Check, then glue), and snip the cord ends away just above each knot.

5. Using your flat-nose pliers, press the tips closed around the knots.

6. Using your round-nose pliers, curve the hook around a jump ring or clasp loop.

Flexible beading wire

This thin, durable wire is easy to bead with. Use good-quality materials—it's so worth it! I highly recommend Soft Flex wire, since inexpensive tiger-tail wire kinks and ages poorly.

1. Cut a piece of wire at least 4 to 6 inches longer than the finished length of the piece you're making. Add a doubled piece of clear tape near the end of your wire to hold your design as you string your pieces—it's easy to take off when you're ready to

Flexible Beading Wire

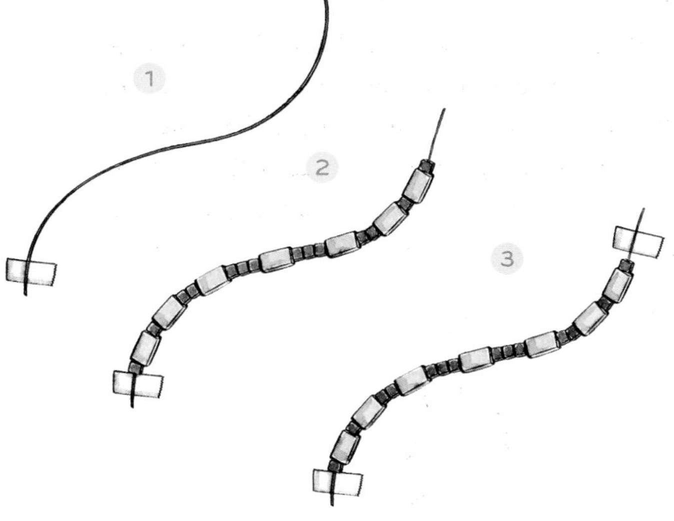

finish the ends but won't kink or untie itself as a knot often does.

2. Begin creating your design from one end, or construct the middle section and move outward—it's up to you. Beads will slip right onto your wire, so you don't need a needle. Just add them in the desired pattern, and remember, you can always tape the working end and switch back to the other side if you want to change your design—it's very flexible.

3. If you need to take a break or don't finish the project right away, just tape both ends of the wire to hold the pattern.

Crimp beads

Finish a Soft Flex or a ribbon piece with crimp beads—small metal cylinders that hold a doubled cord securely when you flatten or crimp them with pliers. They can also be used to hold a bead or piece in place on a single wire or cord, like the Multi-Drop Earrings (p. 43), or as a design element, like the Multi-Drop Pendant (p. 124).

I recommend sterling or gold-filled cylinder-shaped crimp beads, which are easy to work with and finish smoothly. Base metal crimps can be rough at the edge, scratching your skin or cutting through the wire itself.

1. Finish stringing your piece. Place a single crimp bead on the end of the strand and add a clasp.

2. Slip the wire tail back through the crimp bead then through the next several beads.

3. Tug the wire so it's taut, with no gaps between beads or at the end.

4. Firmly crimp the bead closed with your flat-nose pliers.

5. Clip off the end of the wire close to the beads so the end tucks back in and won't scratch your skin.

TIP Use an oversize crimp bead if you are crimping more than two strands at a time, especially if it's a thicker Soft Flex wire.

Crimp Beads

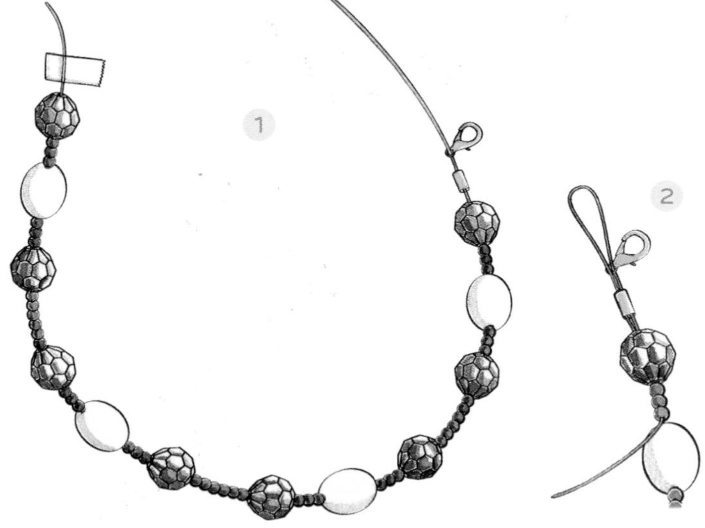

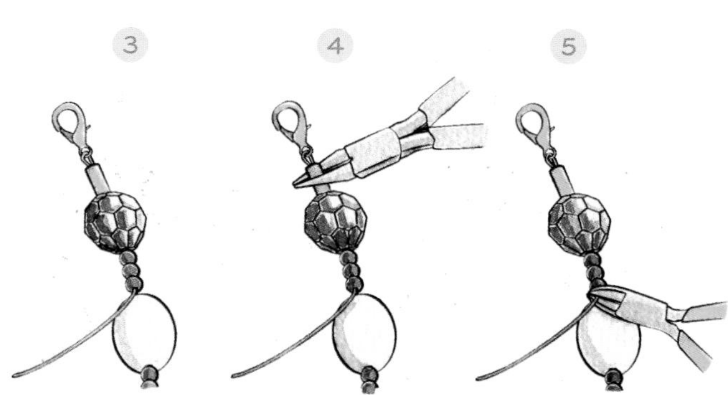

Crimp clasps

You'll attach all-in-one crimp/clasp pieces similarly. Just use your flat-nose pliers to securely flatten the metal crimp around the cord or ribbon (as in the Turquoise Drop Pendant on p. 115). Crimp one side at a time if it's a flap style or the entire thing if it's a cylinder style. You may want to add a drop of glue to your cord before slipping it into the crimp clasp for extra hold.

Double crimp variation

You can also use special crimping pliers to make a double crimp with a tighter, cleaner finish.

1. Follow steps 1–3 for crimp beads, but instead of pressing the crimp bead flat in one motion as in step 4, position it inside the first notch of the crimping pliers (closest to the handles) and gently squeeze it, forming a curved U shape.

2. Place the curved crimp bead into the second notch (closer to the tips), rotate it 90 degrees, and squeeze again, tightening the U shape closed.

3. Finally, flatten the doubled crimp bead completely using the tip of the pliers.

Memory wire

Here's how to start—and finish—a necklace or bracelet made with memory wire.

1. Cut the memory wire round to the length you want it to be. Take a ball- or cube-shaped tip and use a small drop of glue to attach it to the end of the memory wire round on one side. Once it's completely dry, start adding beads.

2. When you finish your bead stringing, you should have a short "tail" of memory wire at the open end. Gripping the tail with your flat-nose pliers, gently shake the memory wire so the beads fall into place with no gaps between them. Place the tip on the end to see if there's any open space once it's on. If there

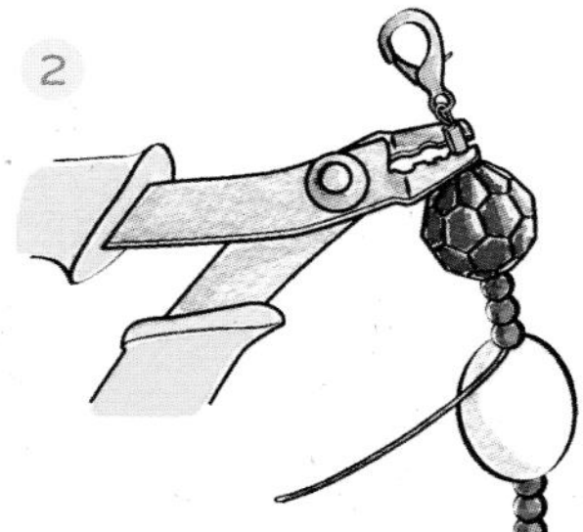

is, cut the tail more closely (you may need to take off a few beads, cut it, and put them back on) or add another seed bead.

3. Glue the last seed bead in place, then carefully glue the second tip onto the tail. Let it dry completely. Note: If you'd rather not glue your last bead, just glue the tip on the end of the wire.

Wirework

These basic techniques—forming plain loops and wrapped loops with your pliers—are easy steps that transform a simple piece of wire into a custom eyepin, earwire, chain link, or pendant. Plain and wrapped loops are the knit and purl stitches of jewelry making—they're invaluable for making just about anything, from simple drop earrings to elaborate wire masterpieces. Once you learn these basics, you'll be able to repair or alter jewelry and create and embellish new pieces.

In these diagrams, the flat-nose pliers are shown with blue handles, the round-nose pliers have red handles, and the wire cutters have black handles.

Plain loops

1. Cut a 4-inch piece of craft wire, then use your flat-nose pliers to bend it at a neat 90-degree angle about ¼ to ½ inch from the end. The longer the wire bend, the larger the loop.

2. Holding the longer part of the wire with your flat-nose pliers, grasp the end of the shorter wire bend with the tip of your round-nose pliers.

3. Twist your wrist so you begin to bring the very end of the wire around to meet the bend, forming a neat circle. You'll essentially be rolling the pliers toward you. It can be easier to do this in two steps, letting go of the wire about halfway through and then grasping it again with your pliers to finish bringing it around. You can adjust or finish the loop after you curve the wire so it's perfectly round.

4. The finished loop should look like a lollipop. If there is any excess wire extending beyond the circle, trim it with wire cutters and gently tweak it back into shape. If your loops are misshapen or crooked, just clip them off and start again.

Wrapped loops

1. Place a bead on the eyepin you've just created. Grasp the wire just above the bead with your round-nose pliers, and make another neat 90-degree angle bend above and over the tips, holding the wire tail with your flat-nose pliers.

2. Next, adjust the round-nose pliers so they are gripping on either side of the wire bend, above and below it. Use your flat-nose pliers to pull the wire tail over the end of the round-nose pliers and all the way around, creating a circle with an extra tail of wire still extending beyond it.

3. Use the flat-nose pliers to hold the circle while you grip the end of the wire tail with your round-nose pliers.

4. Wrap the wire tail around the space above the bead, working from top to bottom to create a neat

1
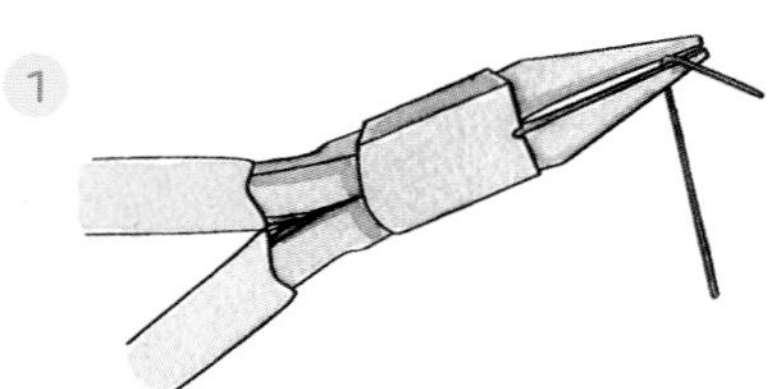

3
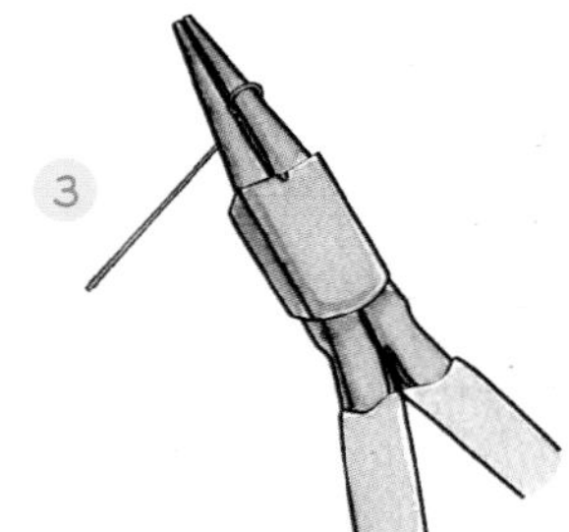

4

Wrapped Loops

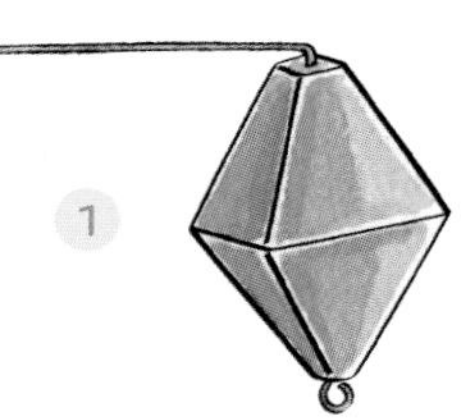

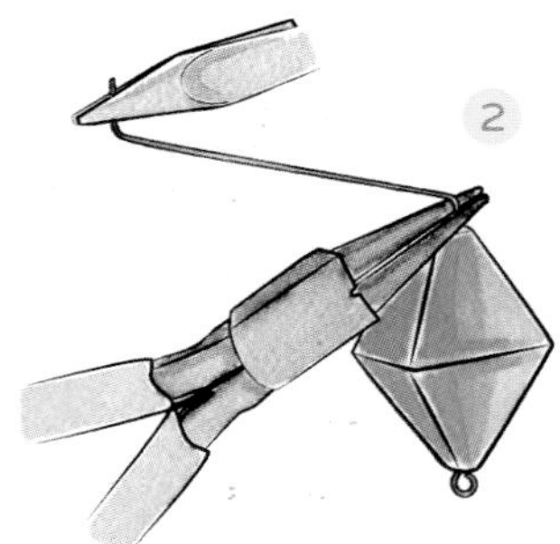

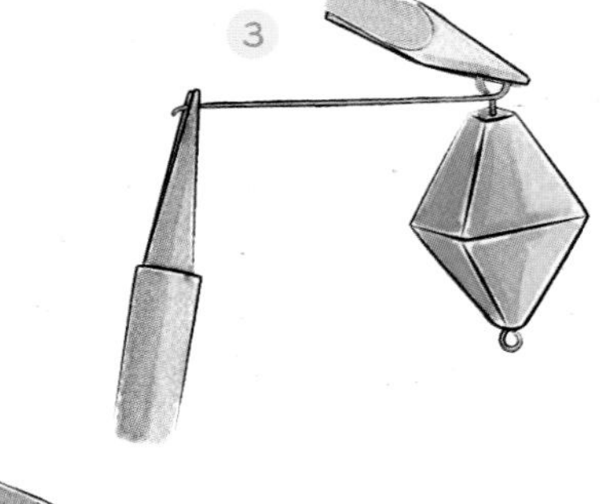

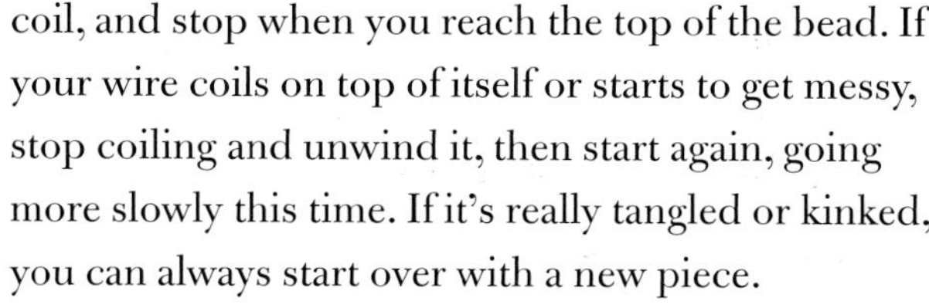

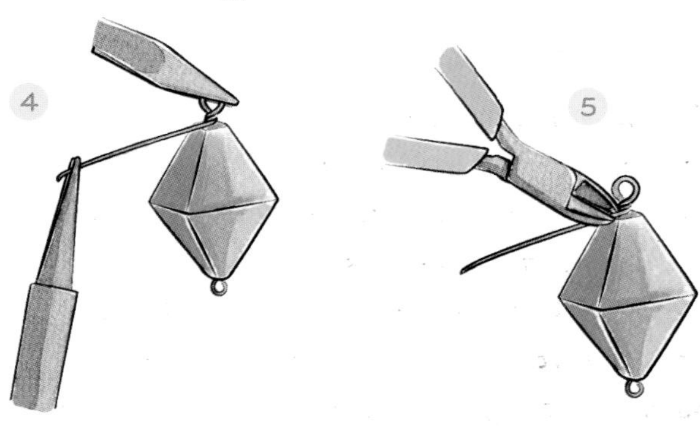

coil, and stop when you reach the top of the bead. If your wire coils on top of itself or starts to get messy, stop coiling and unwind it, then start again, going more slowly this time. If it's really tangled or kinked, you can always start over with a new piece.

5. Clip the end of the wire flush with the coil. Make sure the sharp edge isn't sticking out—if it does, use your flat-nose pliers to flatten and smooth it into the coil.

TIP Practice with inexpensive craft wire until your loops are nice and even.

TIP Plain loops work best with thick wire (such as 20 gauge), while the more secure wrapped loops are good for thinner wire (24 gauge).

BASIC DANGLE Creating a plain loop below a bead and a wrapped loop above it transforms the bead into a dangling charm as illustrated at right.

Alternate way: Use a headpin or eyepin for the base instead of forming the plain loop.

DOUBLE-LOOPED BEAD CONNECTOR Use this process to link a bead into a longer chain or design. Just cut a piece of wire and make a wrapped loop or a plain loop on each side, being sure to join the loops to the chain or design before you close them completely. As always, you'll use a wrapped loop

Flat-Front Plain Loop Variation

For this variation, the plain loop looks like a "P"—the curve of the loop is to the back of, say, a drop pendant. To do this, skip step 1 and grasp the end of the wire. Simply curve it into a loop. The wire will still look straight and smooth in front instead of obviously curved.

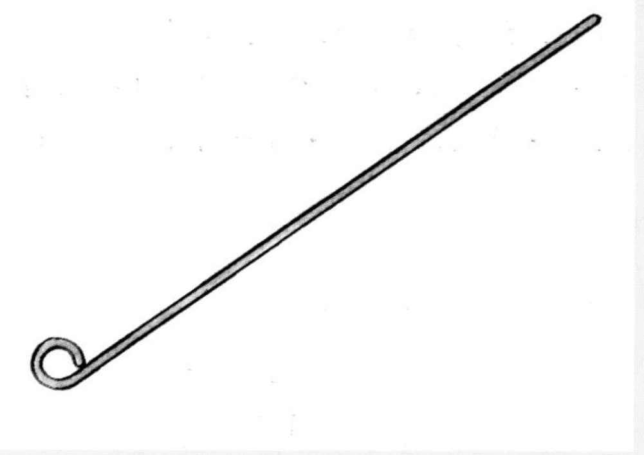

Double-Looped Connectors

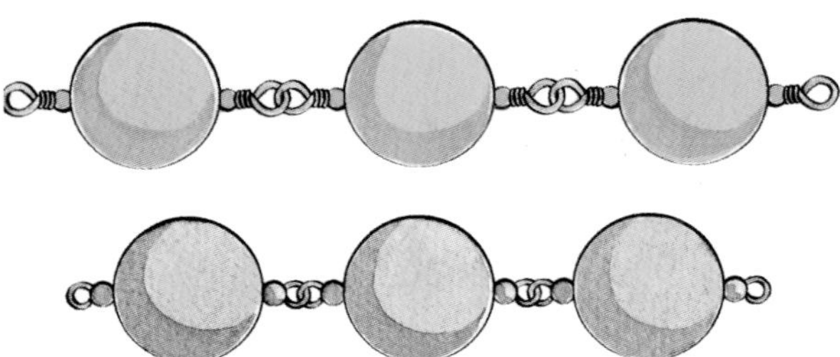

with a thinner-gauge wire (24 and up) and have the option of doing a plain loop with a heavier-gauge wire (20 and below). See the illustrations above.

Briolette wrapping

This technique is great for creating a handmade "hanger" for both horizontally drilled briolettes and pieces with a space in the middle. It's essentially a variation on the double-wrapped loop on the facing page.

1. Cut a 4-inch piece of wire and run it through a briolette, side to side, so one-third of the wire is on one side (A) and two-thirds on the other (B).

2. Fold one then the other wire up into a triangle, following the lines of the bead. The wires will look like an X.

3. Form a sharp angle in wire B so it extends straight above the bead.

4. Grip the wires below the X with flat-nose pliers, and wrap wire A in a coil around wire B. Stop after three coils and clip the wire.

5. Form a loop above the coil. Grip it with flat-nose pliers, using round-nose pliers to make a new coil starting at the top and moving downward.

6. Bring the wire tail around to the side of the coil where the tail from step 4 is and clip it closely. Use your flat-nose pliers to make sure the wire clipping is flush with the coil. This side will be the back of the finished piece, so the neat coiling shows continuously and the raw edges are hidden behind it.

Briolette Wrapping

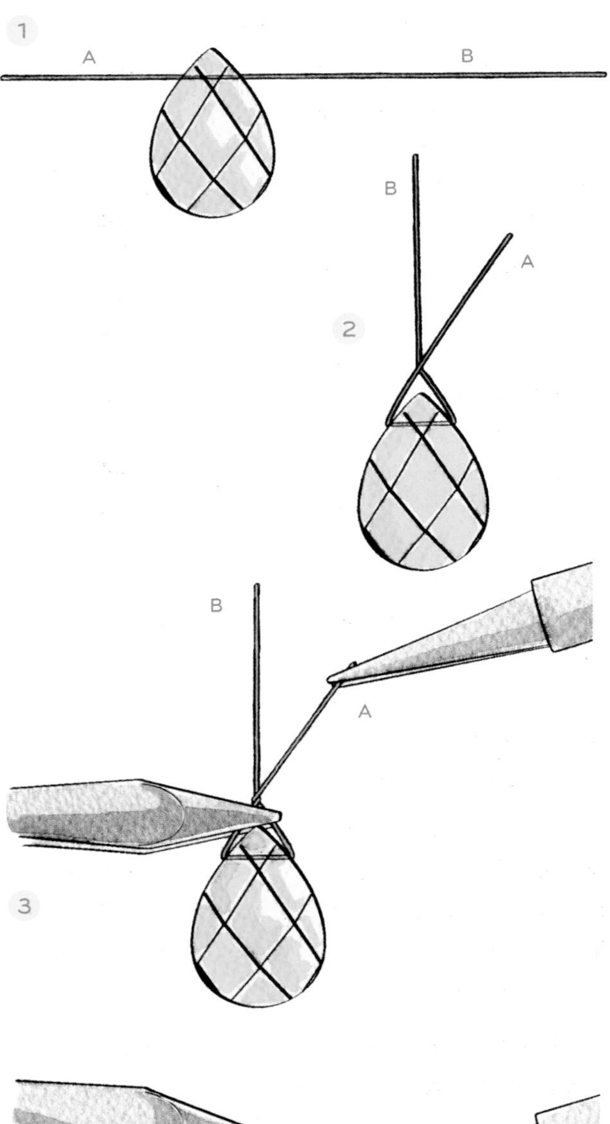

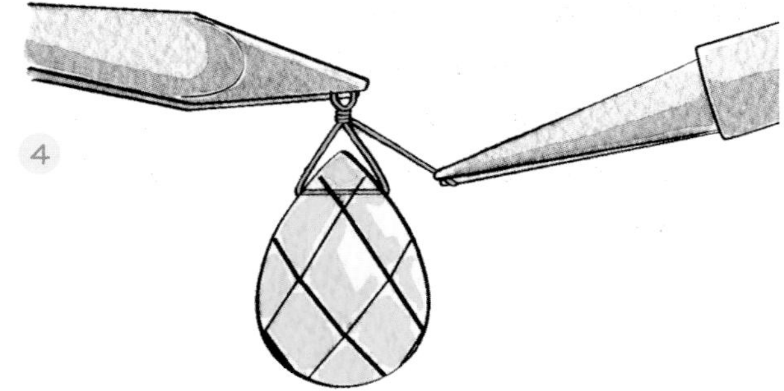

Variation: Side-to-side briolette

Use this version to connect a single briolette to chain or cord on both sides, instead of making a drop to suspend from one strand. Cut a piece of wire and make a wrapped loop on one side, slipping it through the last link of a piece of chain before completing the wrap. Slip the briolette onto the wire and form a second wrapped loop on its other side, again adding it to a last link of chain before completing the wrap (see the drawing above).

You may want to curve the loops upward (as shown in the Teardrop Charming Pendant on p. 112).

Double-wrapped loop

This dual loop wraps around (or through) a charm or piece and the chain or cord to form a double connector or hanger. It's made the same way as a double-looped bead connector without the bead in the middle of the coils.

1. Cut a piece of wire and form a briolette-style hanger around or through the piece, front to back, leaving the top loop open after forming the first half. You'll wrap the coil using the back wire tail, going around the front piece.

2. Slip the open loop onto a chain or cord and complete the wrap, making sure the wire ends are tucked to the back of the coil so they don't show. As you wind the top wrap, the coil will stay neater if you bring the wire around on the opposite side from the first wrap.

Double-Wrapped Loop

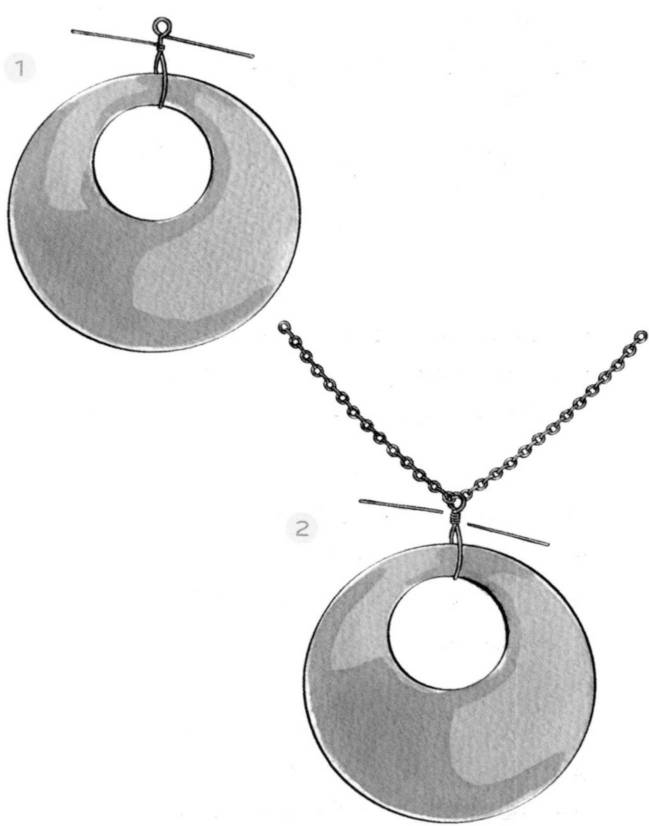

Wire looping

This technique is simple—just use wire to go through a bead once, back to front, bring it around to the back again, and slip it through a second time. It's great for securing small beads or holding larger ones (like the Vintagesque Necklace on p. 71).

1. Slip the bead onto the wire.

2. Bring the wire tail around and through the bead again.

3. Pull it tight so the wire hugs the bead.

Wire Looping

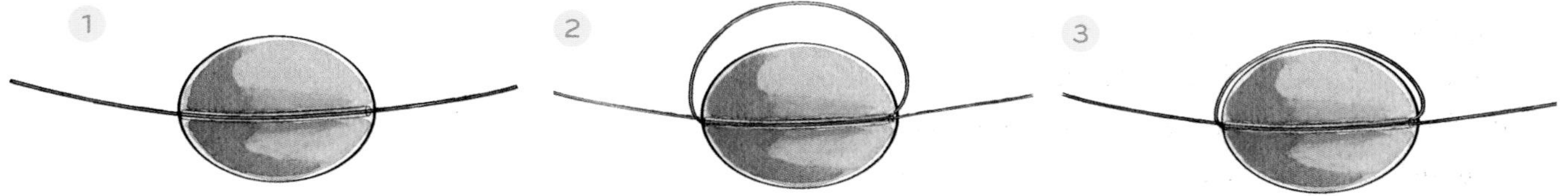

Jump rings

Use jump rings—small circles of wire with an opening—to attach clasps, suspend charms, or form a simple chain.

1. Open a jump ring by gripping the ring on each side with a pair of pliers. Separate the ring by tilting the right side toward you and the left side away from you—don't pull the ring open into a U shape.

2. Close the ring by reversing step 1. The ring should close neatly with no gap where the ends meet. If it doesn't meet neatly on the first try, gently tilt the two sides back and forth past the closed position a few times until the ring "clicks" shut. You can also make sure it's secure by squeezing it shut with the flat-nose pliers.

Jump Rings

1

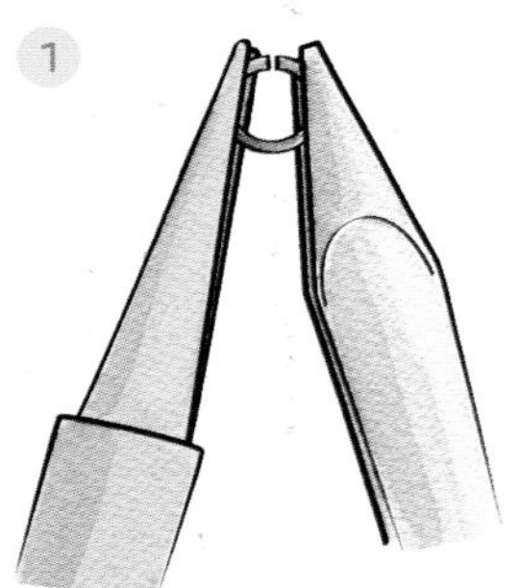

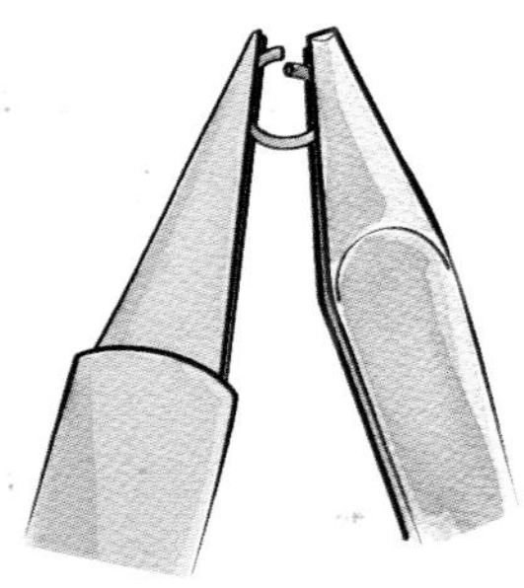

Basic Earring Wires

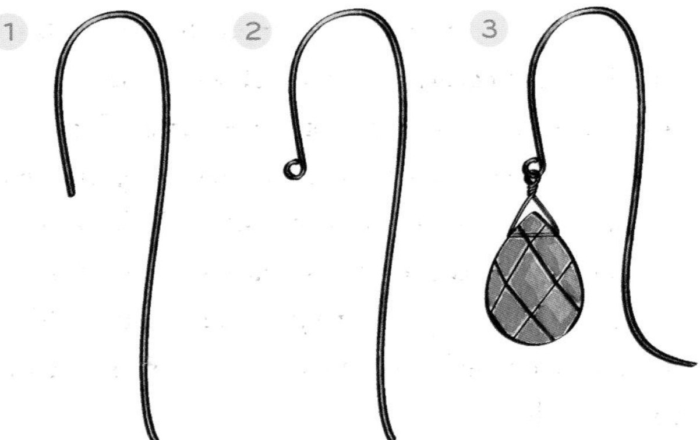

To attach a clasp to a chain, simply slip both the last link in the chain and the clasp (or its ring) onto the open jump ring in step 1. Close it to connect the two, as in step 2.

To attach a charm to a chain, choose the link you want to use and open a jump ring. Slip the charm or dangle onto the ring, then slip one end of the open ring through the link you've chosen. Close it securely.

To create a simple chain, just join a series of jump rings into a long row. Start with two: Open one, join it to the other, and close it. Add a third the same way, and so on until your chain is the desired length.

TIP If your jump ring becomes misshapen or dented from plier marks, just throw it away and start over with a new one.

Basic earring wires

1. Cut a 2½-inch piece of 22-gauge or 24-gauge wire, and form a large, round curve starting about ¾ inch in from the end. If the wire has a natural curve, follow it.

2. Next, create a small flat-front plain loop at the short end. This will be the loop of the earring wire.

3. Use your pliers to make a neat bend on the long end of the wire.

Eyepins

These are ultra-simple—just take a 1-inch to 4-inch piece of straight wire and form a plain loop at one end. That's it!

Clasps

Use your round-nose pliers to bend wire into clasp shapes, much like heavier-gauge versions of the earring wires. Pair these handmade clasps with soldered rings.

TIP Make different sizes of clasps by changing the length of the wire piece you work with. A 1½-inch wire will make an approximately ⅝-inch hook clasp, for example, and a 2-inch wire will make a ¾-inch S-clasp.

Hooks

1. Cut a 1½-inch to 2-inch piece of 16-gauge or 18-gauge wire. Following the natural curve of the wire, bend a curve into it just before the halfway point.

2. Form a small or medium-size plain loop at the shorter end, curving the wire out into a circle. This will be the hook end.

3. Now form a larger plain loop at the longer end. This loop will connect to the cord, chain, or jump ring.

4. Open the larger plain loop just as you would open a jump ring to attach it to your finding or chain.

S-clasp

1. Cut a 2-inch piece of 16-gauge or 18-gauge half-hard wire. Hold the wire about one-third of the way in on one side and make a curve in it, following the natural curve of the wire.

2. Make a second curve about one-third of the way in from the other side. Now you have a basic S shape (as shown).

3. Form a small plain loop at first one end of the S (the flat-front variation is fine, since the thicker wire will be harder to bend) and then the other.

4. Use your pliers to adjust the wire so one side is closed and the other is slightly open—this side will be the hook, and the closed side will be the connector.

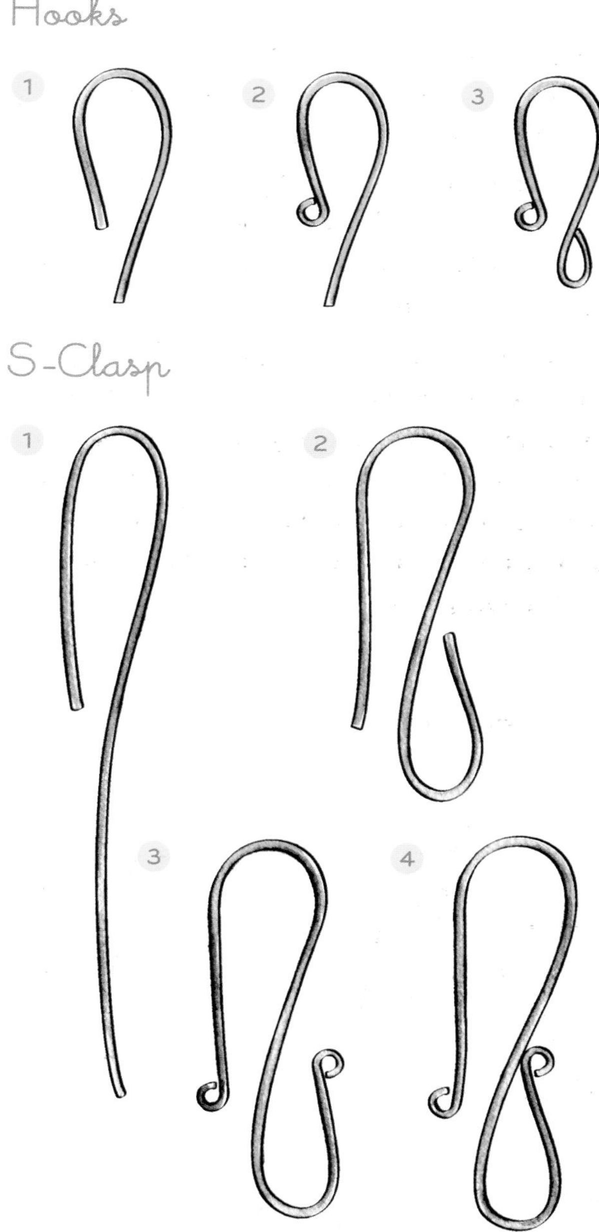

Basic Bead Weaving

Two projects in the collection use this pretty, but very basic, bead-weaving pattern—the Woven Collar Necklace (p. 98) and the Woven Bracelet (p. 175). Once you get the pattern down, it's surprisingly easy: You'll create a repetitive design with beads mirroring each other, and the two wires you weave with will pass through central beads that look like rungs on a ladder.

The main difference between the two projects is that the bracelets are symmetrical, while the necklaces have embellishments on the lower scallops. The necklace sits like a collar, so these projects have an adjustable chain back instead of a simple clasp. Always string this pattern on Soft Flex instead of stiffer wire. For very lightweight beads, you could also use silk or nylon cord with bead tips instead of crimp beads.

Basic Bead Weaving

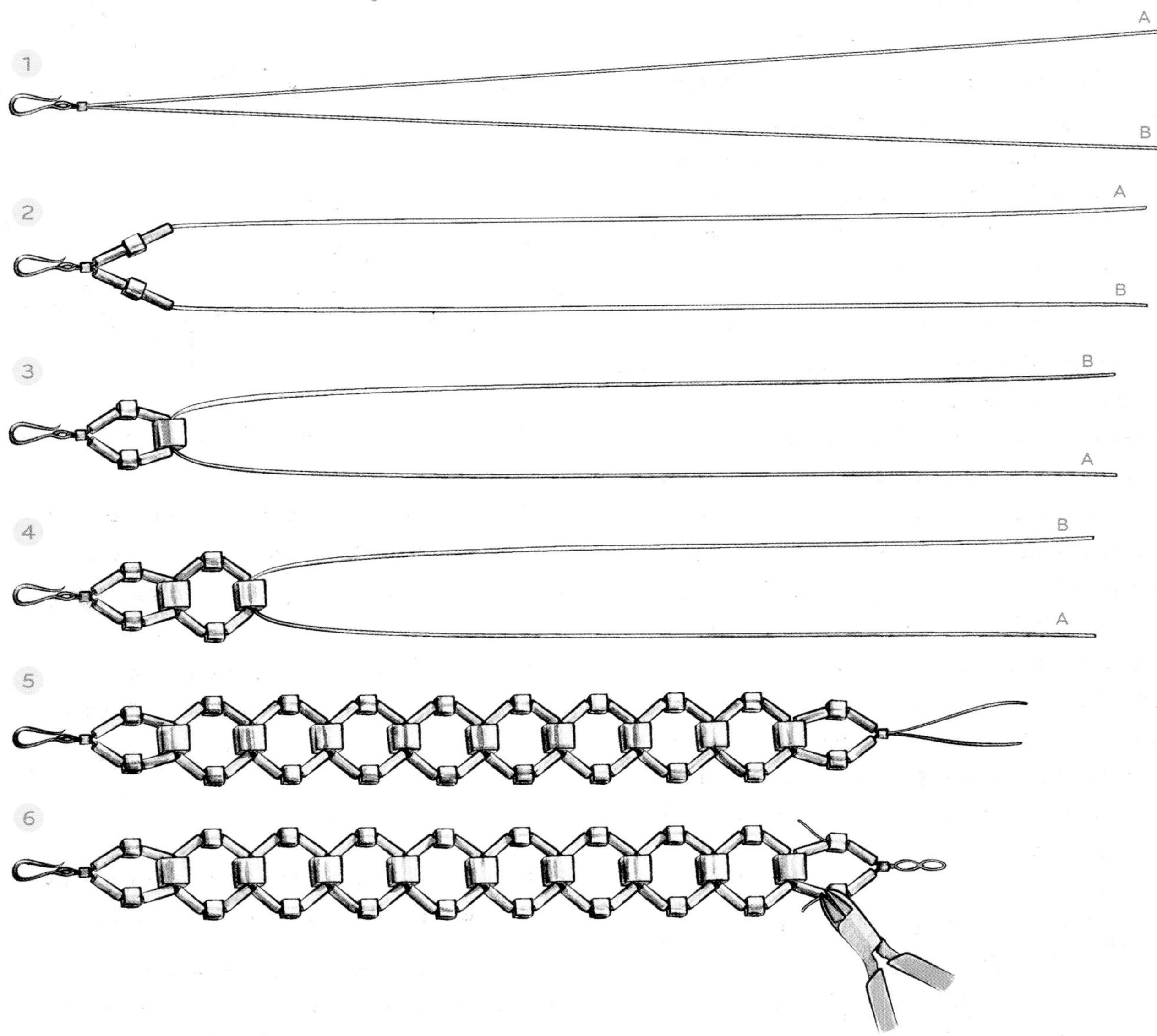

Bracelet/symmetrical style

1. Cut a 3-foot piece of beading wire and slip the clasp onto it. Add a crimp bead over both wire tails, and slip it all the way down the wire so it is just over the clasp or chain. Crimp it closed. You now have two 1½-foot wire tails extending out of the crimp bead to work with.

2. Think of the tail that is currently upper as A and the one that's currently lower as B. Begin your pattern by adding several beads to each strand to form the sides. For this sample pattern, string a bugle, a small bead, and another bugle on each strand.

3. Add a large central bead to A and then slip B through it, coming in the side that A exited. Pull the two tails tight so that the central bead is neatly holding the first few beads in place. A will now be lower and B upper since they have crossed inside the large bead.

4. Add a bugle, a small bead, and another bugle on each strand, then slip both wires through a large bead as you did in steps 2 and 3.

5. Continue until you have nine large beads strung. Add a bugle/small bead/bugle to each strand, then slip a crimp bead over both strands.

6. Slip the other half of your clasp onto both wires, and bring the wires back through the crimp bead. Slip one piece of wire through each of the beaded strands, and pull the tail through so the design is taut and symmetrical. Crimp the bead closed, then trim each of the wire tails.

Necklace/asymmetrical version

This method is very similar to the bracelet, with one major difference: The lower scallops have a drop or embellishment and the upper ones are simpler. There are two things to remember: First, since your wires will weave back and forth, the embellishments will not be strung on the same strand but alternate between A and B. Second, you'll need to balance your embellishments with beads above that have similar width so the pattern hangs well. Follow the same basic directions for making a bracelet style, but construct the necklace with chain on each side so it's adjustable in length, and use a drop ornament on all the odd-numbered segments and a small bead on the evens.

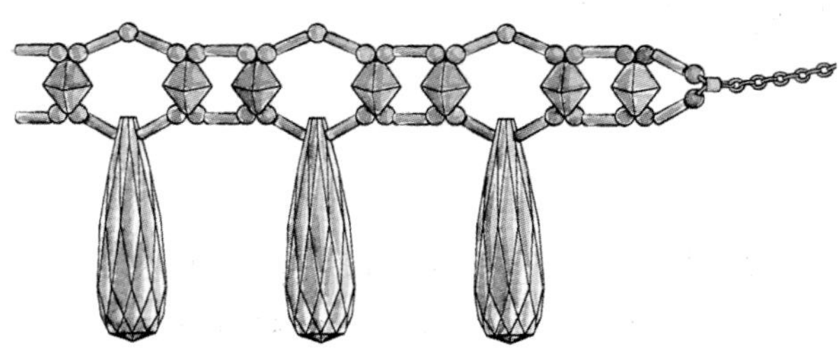

Knotting

Knotting between beads is easy—especially when you use narrow tweezers to pinpoint exactly where you want your knot to go. Use knotting to separate beads (as in the Perfectly Pink Necklace on p. 65) or to create spaces on a cord (as in the Swingy Sparkle Necklace on p. 86).

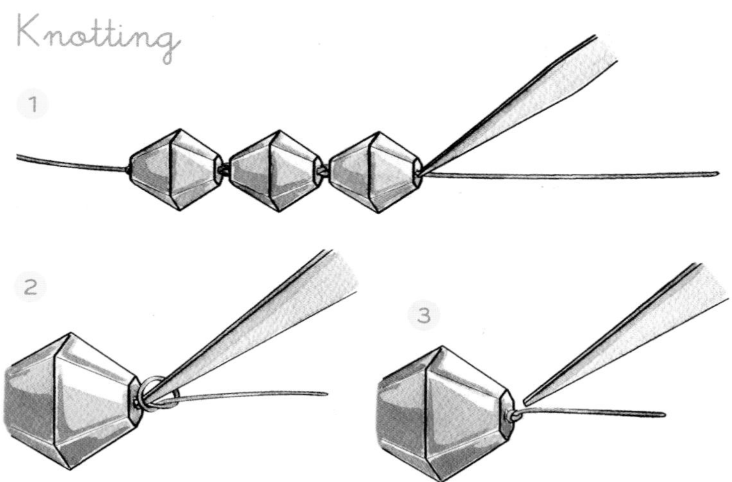

1. Choose where you want your knot to be, and grip that spot firmly with tweezers.

2. Bring your working cord around and over to tie a simple square knot over the tip of the tweezers.

3. Move the tweezers away just as you tighten the knot closed.

You can also use a row of knots (as in the Knotted Circle Deluxe Pendant on p. 122) to hold a larger piece.

Stitching

You can stitch beads, buttons, and charms onto fabric and ribbons as easily as threading a needle.

TIP If you are stitching your beads on with sewing thread (especially nice when you want to match your garment or ribbon's unusual color exactly), be sure to use 100 percent polyester thread instead of cotton, which is much less durable. For added resilience, cut your thread, run it through beeswax twice, and give it a quick iron (on the synthetic setting) to seal it. This process will strengthen your thread considerably. Match your bead weight to the fabric or ribbon you're embellishing—a thin material will sag with heavy beads attached, so use lighter-weight or smaller ones instead.

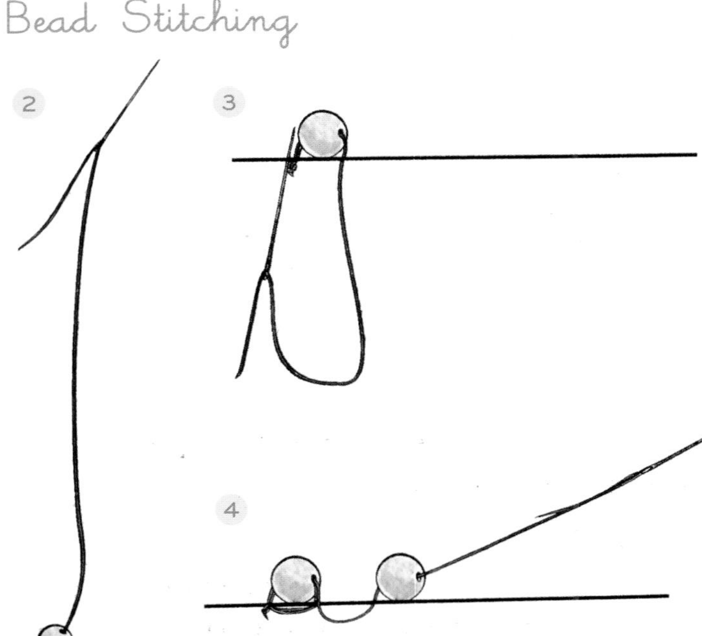

Bead stitching

1. Thread a needle with your thread or cord and double the thread tail. Tie a knot at the end.

2. Choose where you want to place your first bead, then bring the needle up from the wrong side of the fabric there to hide the knot. Slip the bead onto the needle and all the way down the thread. Let the bead lie flat on the fabric, and bring the needle back through the fabric to hold it in place.

3. Bring the thread through the bead twice more for security, always pulling the thread taut as you sew.

4. Place the second bead in your design, and repeat steps 2 and 3 to stitch it down. Continue until all your beads are in place, then knot securely on the back of your work.

Running stitch

This simple forward stitch is the easiest way to join two pieces of fabric or make a broken-line design (as in the Blooms and Vines sweater on p. 190).

1. Thread a needle and bring it up from the back (wrong side) of your fabric through to the front so the knot is on the underside.

2. Next, just stitch ahead, moving your needle forward as shown in the drawing on the facing page, following the pattern of your choice—straight, curved, or angled. You can easily vary the length or distance between your stitches to change the look of them.

Backstitch

This method is a bit more involved, but it creates a much more durable join since it is reinforced by doubling back with each stitch. The stitches on the front of your fabric will look as neat as a running stitch, while the back will have overlapping longer stitches showing.

1. Thread a needle and bring it up from the back (wrong side) of your fabric through to the front so the knot is on the underside.

2. Bring your needle back into the fabric *behind* where it emerged (as shown on the facing page)—you'll double back instead of stitching forward. To begin the second one, bring the needle well out in front of the completed first stitch, then double back again the same way. You can also vary the length or placement of your stitches as with the running stitch, but it works best for a straight line rather than any curve or elaborate pattern.

Jewelry Repair

Let's face it—jewelry can be fragile. Whether it's a new or vintage piece, you can often repair or rework a break or damaged section. Another option is to rework the best of the existing piece into a whole new design—be creative in recycling a single earring or broken brooch into the centerpiece or highlight of an updated piece.

Mending a chain

To mend a broken chain, you'll first need to cut away the damaged links. Sometimes it's easiest to just start over with a new length of chain and add the clasp and other components to it to rebuild your piece.

Running Stitch

Backstitch

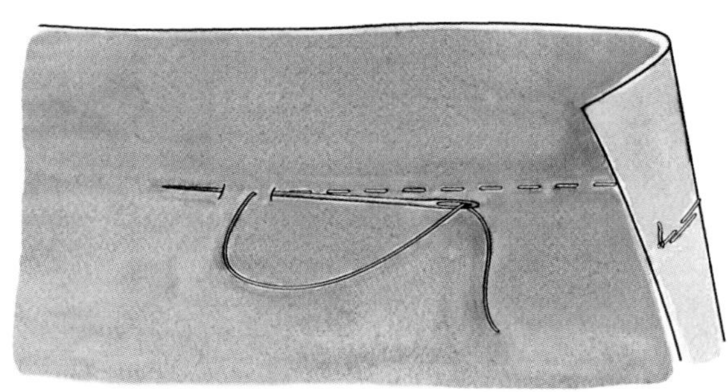

You can often match a jump ring to your chain links for a subtle fix. Another option is to connect your chain using a linked coordinating bead—you can add them symmetrically so the join isn't as obvious once you've added to the design in more than one place.

Replacing a jump ring

This is an easy repair. When a jump ring has deteriorated, simply cut it loose and replace it with a similar new one. If your piece has many (a link bracelet or necklace, for example), carefully examine the others to make sure that they're still in good shape. It's easy to replace one before it gets worn out instead of doing a fix on the fly while you're out and about wearing your jewelry.

Converting a piece into a pendant

You can glue a bail onto the back of a flat-backed button, bead, or pin and wear it as a pendant. Be sure that you attach the bail to a clean, dry surface and that your hardware is heavy enough to support the weight of the pendant.

Reknotting

Unfortunately, this is a complete do-over; you'll have to cut your beads free and reknot them on a new cord from scratch. If you lost any beads in the shuffle and they're hard to match, try adding extras on both sides of the piece so they're less obvious.

Gluing

See the glue descriptions on pp. 5–6 for advice on which one to use for your project. Remember, always let your glue dry completely and make sure the two surfaces you're joining are clean and dry.

Jewelry Repair

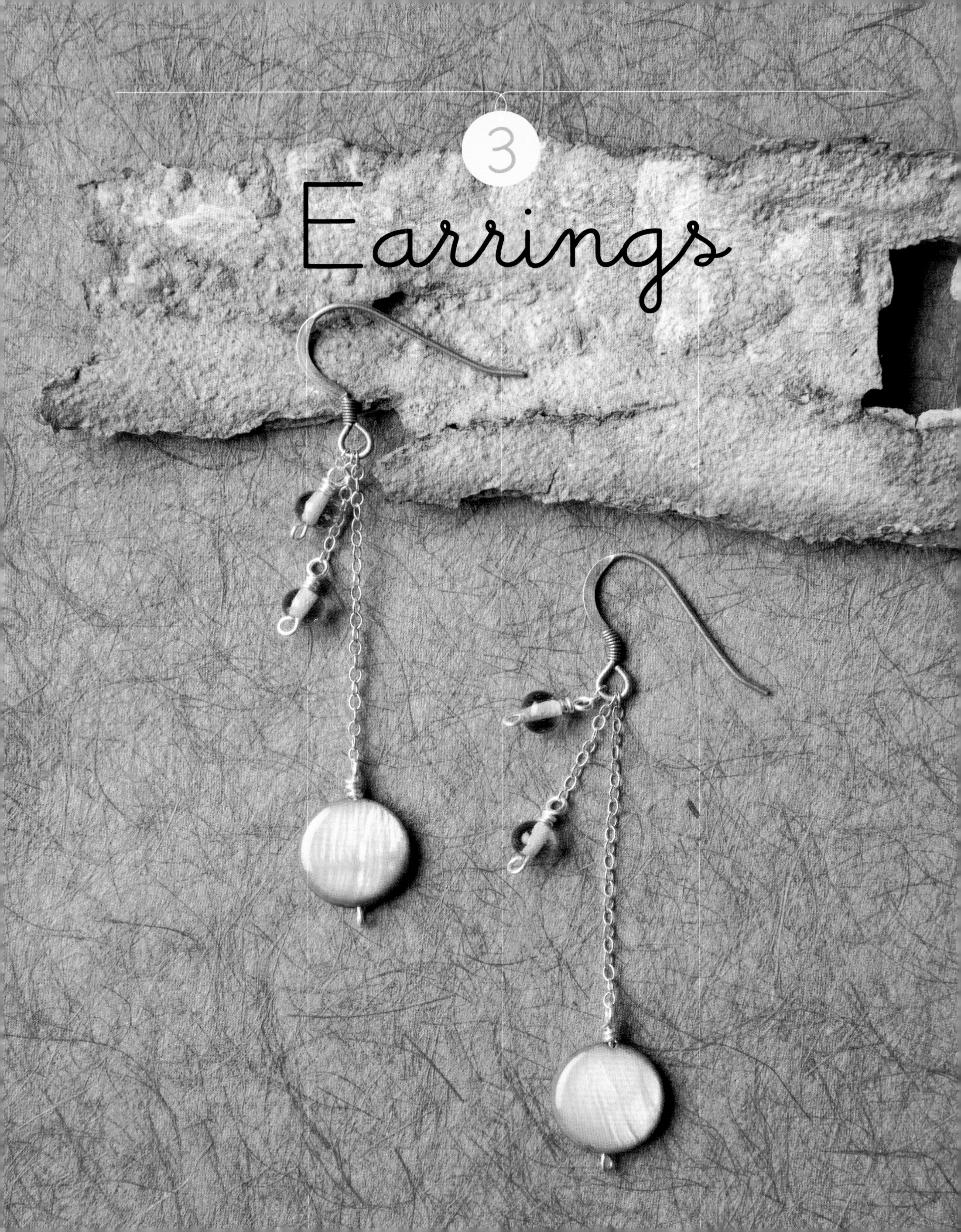

3

Earrings

Solo Earrings

These super-basic earrings are a snap to make—just choose a bead that you especially like and use one of these easy techniques to show it off.

TECHNIQUES

- **Plain loops**
  Skull Drops
- **Bead stringing**
  One Little Sparkle
  Hoops and Circles

TIP Use seed beads above and below a larger bead to hold it steady on its wire if the holes are large.

One Little Sparkle Earrings

Ultra-simple and sweet, these earrings feature a smoky olive bead on sterling wire.

Length: 2¼ inches

YOU'LL NEED

- One pair of hammered paddle-style earring wires
- 2 beads of your choice (I used vintage 16mm faceted olive green Lucite rounds)

Simply slip a bead on the wire (from back to front) until it comes to rest on the wider hammered base. Repeat with the second bead and earwire.

Skull Drops

These spooky skull earrings by crafter-filmmaker Faythe Levine really turn heads.

Length: 1¾ inches

TIP Pick a larger fun bead for a short, dangly earring. It will draw more attention.

YOU'LL NEED

- Pliers
- 24-gauge wire or 2 headpins
- 4 seed beads
- 2 beads of your choice (I used resin skulls)
- Pair of earring wires

1. Cut two 3-inch pieces of wire and form plain loops at the end of each one (or use commercially made headpins). Add one seed bead on each one, then your anchor bead, then a second seed bead.

2. Form a plain loop above each one. Open your earring wires' loops, and slip one dangle onto each one. Close the loops.

Hoops and Circles Earrings

These pretty blue disks hang on sleek silver hoops.

Length: 1½ inches

TIP Make sure your bead or disk of choice slips onto the hoop easily. Other than that consideration, this is a 30-second project.

YOU'LL NEED

- One pair of hoop earrings (I used a ⅝-inch pair of sterling hoops)
- 2 beads of your choice (I used 1-inch faceted blue acrylic disks)

Open the hoops and slip one bead onto each one.

Duo Earrings

This elegant pairing can be long and dramatic or charmingly compact. Just choose beads that complement one another and have fun with the basic design.

TECHNIQUES

- **Wrapped loops**
  All
- **Plain loops**
  All
- **Jump rings**
  Beachy Duo
- **Briolettes**
  Tangled Up in Blues

TIP Try an asymmetrical look (as in the Warm and Sparkly version) to embellish the basic concept. For one earring, add a wrapped loop at the base of bead A, then a small charm.

Warm and Sparkly Duo Earrings

These beautiful brown and gold Lucite beads swing low on chain, with a charming little locket mixed in for good measure.

Length: 4 inches

Warm and Sparkly Duo Earrings

YOU'LL NEED

- Pliers
- Thin chain
- 24-gauge wire
- Seed beads
- 2 pairs of beads (bead A is the faceted one and bead B is the round)
- One small charm
- Leverback earring wires

1. Cut two 3-inch pieces of chain and four 3-inch pieces of wire.

2. Form a plain loop at the end of one of the pieces of wire, and make a basic bead dangle by adding a seed bead, one of the two B beads, and another seed bead. Form the first half of a wrapped loop above it. Repeat with the second piece of wire.

3. Slip one of the bead dangles onto the end of a piece of chain and complete the wrap to join them. Repeat with the second dangle on the second piece of chain.

4. Form a plain loop at the end of the third piece of wire, and add a seed bead, one of the two A beads, and another seed bead. Form the first half of a wrapped loop above it.

5. Take the last piece of wire and form the first half of a wrapped loop on it. Slip the small charm onto the loop and finish the wrap. Now add a seed bead, the other A bead, and another seed bead, and form the first half of a wrapped loop above it.

6. Place each of the two bead-A dangles on the opposite ends of the chains from the bead-B dangles, finishing the wrap to join them.

7. Gently open one of the leverback rings and slip the first chain on, about ½ inch above the bead-A dangle. Close the leverback securely. Repeat with the second leverback and second piece of chain.

Tangled Up in Blues Earrings

Like the Tangled Up in Blues Charming Bracelet on *p. 169**, these earrings spotlight an assortment of fun beads in the same color family. Here, two blue beads are suspended from one costume pearl on sterling.*

Length: 2¾ inches

Beachy Duo Earrings

This summery design by craft writer Nancy Flynn mixes pearls and nautical charms.

Length: 2 inches

YOU'LL NEED

- Pliers
- 24-gauge wire
- Thin chain
- 2 of each of the following beads: small cube (A), round, and top-drilled teardrop (B)
- 2 round pearls
- Earring wires

1. Cut six 3-inch pieces of wire and two ⅝-inch pieces of chain. Form a plain loop at the bottom of two of the pieces of wire and add a cube to each one. Complete a wrapped loop above each piece to make basic bead dangles and set them aside.

2. Using two more pieces of wire, create a double-wrapped loop at the top of each teardrop, but don't close the top half yet. Make sure the top circle faces front on each one. Slip each of the teardrop dangles onto one end of each of the two pieces of chain and complete the wraps to join them.

3. Take the last two pieces of wire and form a wrapped loop at one end on each of them. Add a round pearl to each one, and form the first half of a wrapped loop above them.

4. Take one round dangle and slip the end link of the chain and the loop above the cube dangle into the open loop. Complete the wrap to join them. Repeat with the other three pieces so you have two identical earrings.

5. Open the earring wire loops, and slip the top loops of the rounds onto each one. Close the loops to join them.

TIP Try contrasting the weights of chain you use—many stores offer silver chain that looks like a miniature version of the chains used on ship anchors, which adds to the nautical look.

Beachy Duo Earrings

YOU'LL NEED

- Pliers
- 4 inches fine chain
- 2 inches of slightly thicker chain
- Two 1cm-diameter coin pearls
- 8 fine-gauge silver headpins
- Four 6mm blue faceted glass beads
- Two 6mm clear faceted glass beads
- Four 4mm-diameter jump rings
- 2 small charms
- Leverback earring wires

1. Cut two 2-inch pieces of fine chain and two 1-inch pieces of thicker chain.

2. Thread one pearl on a headpin, and form the first half of a wrapped loop at the top of the pearl. String the half loop through the last link in one 2-inch fine chain piece, and complete the wrapped loop so the pearl hangs at the end of the chain.

3. Thread a blue bead on a second headpin, and form the first half of a wrapped loop. String the half loop two links above the pearl and complete the wrapped loop. Repeat twice, skipping two links above the blue bead to add a clear one, and finishing two links above that with another blue bead.

4. Repeat steps 2 and 3 with the second 2-inch chain piece, pearl, and glass beads.

5. Gently open a jump ring with pliers and use it to join one charm loop and the final link of a 1-inch chain piece. Attach a second jump ring to the other free end of the chain piece. Repeat with the second 1-inch chain piece, charm, and jump rings.

6. Gently open one of the leverback rings and slip on the open end of one 2-inch chain and the jump ring at the non-charm end of one 1-inch piece. Close the leverback securely. Repeat with the second leverback and second set of chains.

Trio Earrings

Trio earrings use three drops in a flurry of different lengths to create a similar but more ornate design. Mix and match size, shape, and material for an eye-catching, swingy piece.

TECHNIQUES

- **Wrapped loops**
  Color Pop
  Glossy Carnelian
- **Jump rings**
  Lacy
- **Hand sewing**
  Lacy

TIP Use beads from your pendant or necklace designs to make complementary earrings.

Glossy Carnelian Trio Earrings

These elegant earrings match the Glossy Carnelian Tiered Necklace on p. 93. Length: 4 inches

YOU'LL NEED

- Pliers
- Thin chain
- 24-gauge sterling wire
- Seed beads
- Two ¾-inch oval beads
- Four 8mm faceted beads
- Leverback earring wires

Glossy Carnelian Trio Earrings

1. Cut two pieces of chain in each length: ½ inch, 1¼ inches, and 2 inches long, for a total of six pieces.

2. Cut two 3-inch pieces and four 2-inch pieces of wire. Form a plain loop at the end of each piece of wire.

3. On the two 3-inch wires, add a seed bead, a ¾-inch oval, and another seed bead. On the four 2-inch wires, add a seed bead, an 8mm bead, and another seed bead. Form the first half of a wrapped loop above each of the six dangles.

4. Join two of the 8mm dangles to the ends of the ½-inch length of chain, completing the wraps. Repeat with the other two 8mm dangles and the 1¼-inch pieces of chain.

5. Join the oval dangles to the 2-inch pieces of chain and complete the wraps.

6. Open one of the leverback rings and slip on one of each length of chain, longest first, then medium, then shortest. Close the leverback.

7. Repeat step 6 to finish the second earring.

Color Pop Trio Earrings

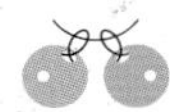   

Lime green mother-of-pearl beads and tiny glass rounds are a fun combination.

Length: 2½ inches

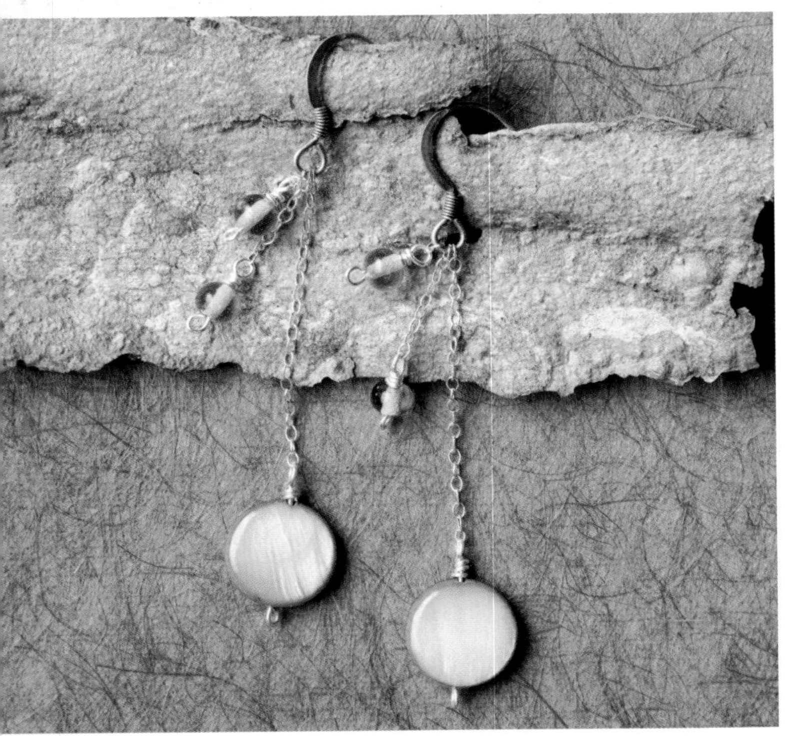

YOU'LL NEED

- Pliers
- 24-gauge wire
- Two 8mm mother-of-pearl lime green flat rounds
- 4 tiny lime green glass rounds
- Thin chain
- 2 earring wires

1. Cut six pieces of wire: two 2 inches long and four 1½ inches long. Form a plain loop at the end of each one.

2. Place the 8mm flat rounds on the longer wire pieces and the smaller beads on the shorter pieces. Form a wrapped loop above each one but don't close any of them yet.

3. Cut six pieces of chain: two that are only two links long, two that are ½ inch long, and two that are 1 inch long. Add one of the small beads to each of the shorter pieces of chain and complete the wrapped loops. Now add the two 8mm beads to the two 1-inch pieces of chain and complete the loops.

4. Open one of the earring wires and slip one of each chain length onto its loop, shortest to longest from front to back.

5. Repeat with the second earring wire and close both of them securely.

Lacy Trio Earrings

Designed by Kayte Terry of Love Forever, these delicate earrings include lace, floral beads, and sequins. Length: 3 inches

TIP Kayte suggests "Save lace scraps from sewing projects for making these earrings. I've scored lots of these floral decal beads on eBay®, but you can find new ones at jewelry-supply stores, too."

YOU'LL NEED

- Fabric scissors
- Paintbrush
- Fabric stiffener
- Waxed paper
- Sewing needle and thread
- Pliers and wire cutters

- Small pieces of lace
- Assorted sequins and small pearls
- Thin gold chain
- Four 3mm jump rings
- 4 teardrop-shaped floral decal beads (or any other drop beads)
- Two 5mm jump rings
- 4 small white beads
- 2 headpins
- Earring wires

1. Cut two shapes out of lace using small fabric scissors.

2. Brush fabric stiffener onto the lace pieces, and lay them out on waxed paper to dry. Let the lace completely dry, then repeat on the other side.

3. Once the lace pieces are dry, sew on sequins and small pearls using a needle and thread. Sew them in the same place on both sides so the stitches won't be seen. Make a small knot at the end of each and hide it behind a bead or pearl.

4. Cut two pieces of chain in each length: 2 inches, 1 inch, and ½ inch.

5. Attach the lace pieces to the 2-inch-long chains with a 3mm jump ring. Attach two teardrop-shaped beads to each of the 1-inch-long chains with a 5mm jump ring.

6. Add two small beads each to the two headpins. Form a small, plain loop and cut the excess wire with wire cutters, but do not close the loop. Slip the ½-inch length of chain onto each of the loops and close the wire.

7. Open a 3mm jump ring and slide on one earring wire, followed by one of each length of chain, longest first, then medium, then shortest. Close the jump ring.

8. Repeat step 7 to finish the second earring.

Modern Drop Earrings

These drop earrings are gorgeously simple and easy to wear, either with coordinating pendant designs or on their own. Clean lines and organic materials like wood and semiprecious stones lend a stylish sensibility.

TECHNIQUES

- **Wrapped loops**
  Wood
  Amber
- **Plain loops**
  Scrolled Wood
  Amber
- **Briolette/top wrapping**
  Wood

TIP Long, vertical drops draw the eye, while more compact designs are easy to wear with other jewelry. Try an asymmetrical set for fun!

Wood Drop Earrings

These mod wood drops are paired with carnelian bits for stylish simplicity.

Length: 4 inches

YOU'LL NEED

- Pliers
- Thin chain
- 24-gauge wire
- 2 elongated wood drops (horizontally drilled)
- 4 small semiprecious round beads
- Earring wires

1. Cut six ⅜-inch-long pieces of chain, two 4-inch pieces of wire, and four 3-inch pieces of wire. Wrap each wood drop briolette-style with a 4-inch piece, completing the coil above the bead. Then create the first half of a wrapped loop above the coil.
2. Slip the loop above one wood drop into the last link of a piece of chain, and complete the loop.
3. Using the first 3-inch piece of wire, form the first half of a wrapped loop and slip it onto the last link of one of the ⅜-inch pieces of chain, completing the wrap.

4. Place a small round bead on the wire and form the first half of a wrapped loop above it. Slip it onto the last link of the second ⅜-inch piece of chain, and complete the wrap.

5. Repeat steps 3 and 4 to create a second wrapped bead, linking the second and third pieces of chain.

6. Next, slip the earring wire loop into the last link at one end of the beaded chain you created.

7. Repeat the steps to complete the second earring.

Scrolled Wood Drop Earrings

These gorgeous sawed wood drops were designed by artist Caitlin Troutman.

Length: 3½ inches

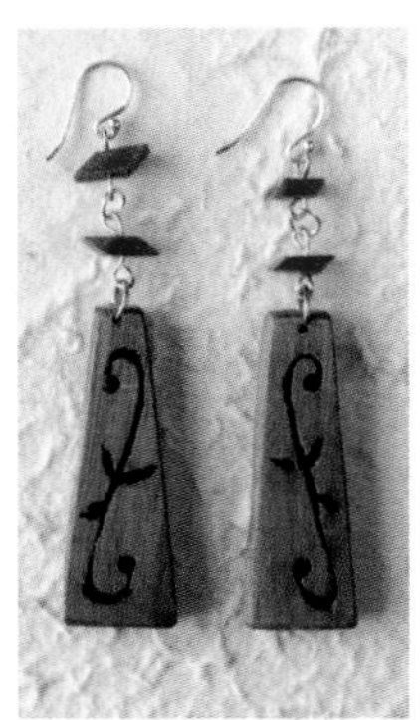

YOU'LL NEED

- Scroll saw
- Drill press
- Fine sandpaper
- Linseed oil and turpentine (half-and-half mixture)
- Pliers
- 2 elongated wood drops (¼-inch-thick hobby wood; I used walnut)
- 2 large jump rings
- 22-gauge wire
- 4 small angular wood beads
- Two 5mm jump rings
- Earring wires

1. Draw a pattern (like the one shown) on two pieces of hobby wood with a pencil. Cut out the pattern with a scroll saw, or have a hardware store do custom cuts.

2. Drill a hole near the top of each wood shape (as shown). Sand all the cut-out areas on all sides until they're smooth, going with the grain.

3. Dip the wood shapes into the oil-turpentine mixture and immediately remove, wiping the excess oil with a rag. Let dry.

4. Now assemble your earrings. Attach the large jump rings to the wood drops through the holes you drilled in step 2. Cut four ¾-inch-long pieces of wire, and form plain loops around each of the four angular wood beads. Use the 5mm jump rings to connect two sets of beads—this will be the middle of the earrings.

5. Gently open one of the bead set's outer plain loops, and connect it to the large jump ring in the wood. Repeat with the second beads and second wood piece.

6. Open the earring wires' loops and slip one of the outer bead loops onto each one.

Amber Drop Earrings

Large amber/resin ovals hang on circle chain.

Length: 4¼ inches

YOU'LL NEED

- Pliers
- 3 inches of oversize circle chain
- 20-gauge wire
- 2 large vertically drilled semiprecious beads (I used amber)
- Earring wires

1. Cut your chain into two 1½-inch halves. Next, cut two 4-inch pieces of wire and make a basic dangle with the two large beads, leaving the top loop open. Slip each dangle onto the end of a piece of chain and complete the wrap.

2. Open both earring wires and slip the chains onto the loops. Close them securely.

Multi-Drop Earrings

Spiky drops in a sleek configuration really spotlight the beads you choose. Choose the most eye-popping ones in your stash to make yours stand out.

TECHNIQUES

- **Plain loops**
  Amber Bits, Pink
- **Wrapped loops**
  Pink
- **Crimp beads**
  Pink
  Stripes and Cubes

TIP Try asymmetrical lengths in different combinations of short, medium, and long with identical beads on each drop. You can also convert earring wires to forward-facing loops by gripping them with flat-nose pliers and gently twisting them 45 degrees.

TIP Make your earrings identical or mirror images of each other—it's up to you.

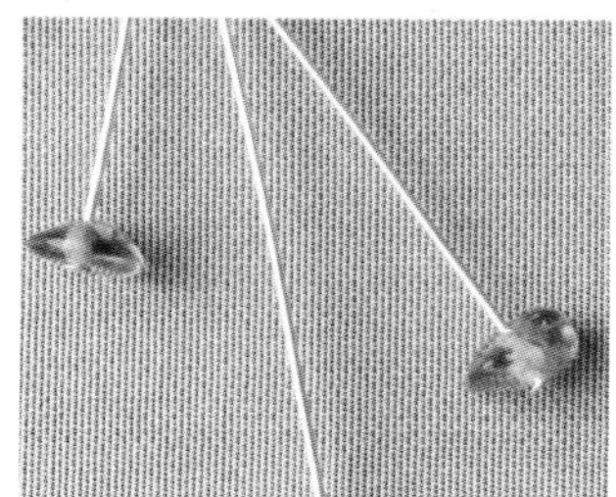
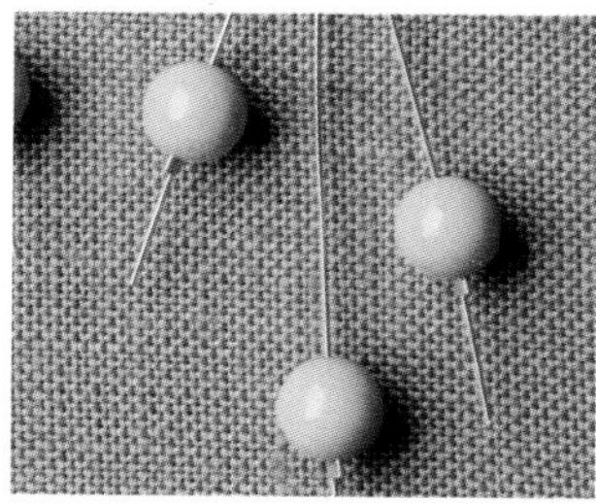

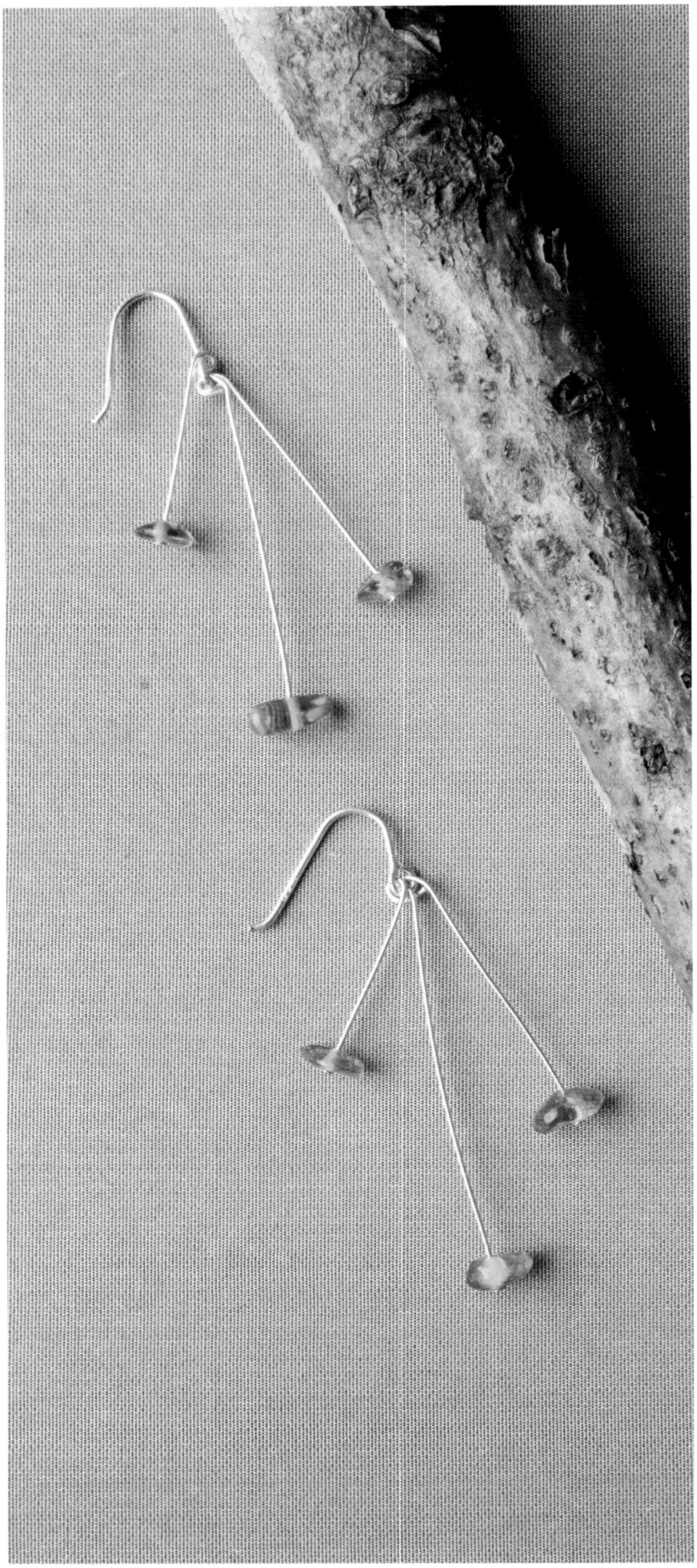

Amber Bits Multi-Drop Earrings

Three amber bits swing on sterling wire.

Length: 2 inches

YOU'LL NEED

- Pliers
- Six 24-gauge headpins
- 6 small vertically drilled oval beads (like these asymmetrical amber pieces)
- Earring wires with forward-facing rings

1. Cut two of the headpins to 7/8 inch (S), two to 1 1/4 inches (M), and two to 1 3/4 inches (L) long.
2. Slip one bead onto each headpin, and form a flat-front plain loop at the top of each. Open your earring wire loops.
3. Take one headpin of each length and slip them onto an earring wire in this order (left to right): S, L, M. Close the earring wire.
4. Repeat step 3 to make the second earring.

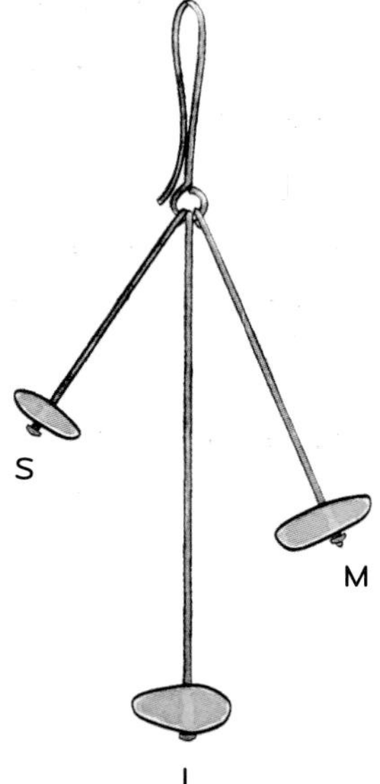

Pink Multi-Drop Earrings

These pretty-in-pink rounds are suspended on spiky gold wires.

Length: 4½ inches

YOU'LL NEED

- Pliers
- Glue
- 24-gauge wire
- 8 lightweight round beads
- Six 22-gauge headpins
- 6 tiny crimp beads
- Oversize earring wires

1. Cut two 2-inch pieces of wire and form a wrapped loop at one end of each piece. Place a round bead on each one, and form a large wrapped loop above it. Set aside.

2. Cut the headpins to these lengths (two of each): 1⅞ inches (S), 2½ inches (M), and 3 inches (L). Make sure you cut off the end with the "head" so you have six spiky, perfectly straight wires.

3. Place a crimp bead ⅜ inch from the end of each wire, and firmly crimp it closed with your flat-nose pliers. Add a tiny drop of glue to each one to secure it. Let it dry completely.

4. Place a round bead on each wire, above the crimps, then form a flat-front plain loop at the top of each wire. Gently open each plain loop.

5. Place the bead dangles you made in step 1 on the earring wires, attaching them with the smaller loop.

6. Take one of each length of wire and slip them on the large (lower) loop of one earring, under the bead dangle, in this order (left to right): S, L, M. Gently close each plain loop to secure them.

7. Repeat step 6 with your last three wires to finish the second earring.

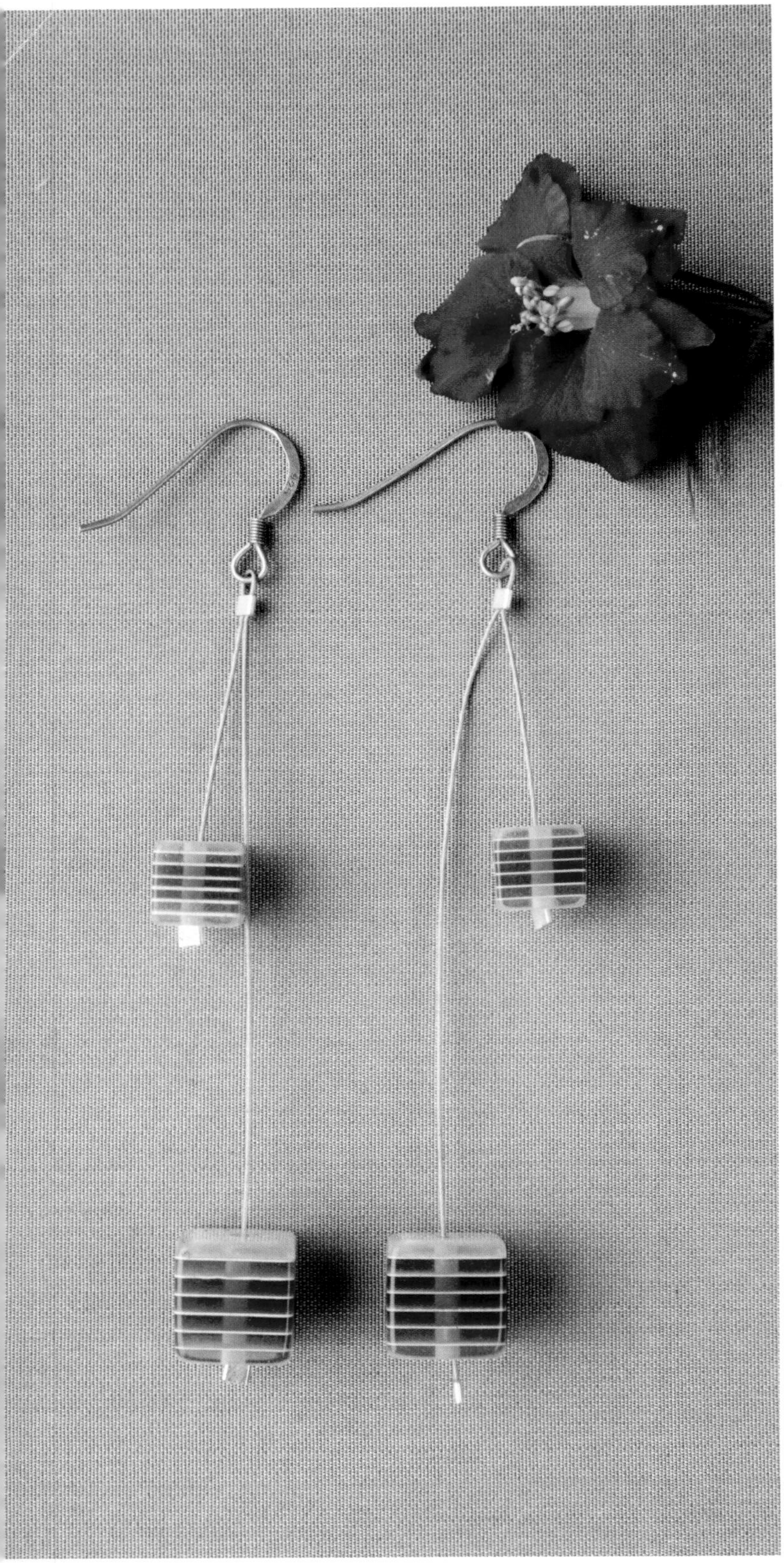

Stripes and Cubes Multi-Drop Earrings

Try out mod style with these geometric striped cubes on Soft Flex.

Length: 3¾ inches

YOU'LL NEED

- Pliers
- Soft Flex wire
- 6 medium-size crimp beads
- Two 6mm cubes
- Two 10mm cubes
- Earring wires

1. Cut two 5-inch pieces of Soft Flex.
2. Measure 1½ inches from one end of the first wire and make a fold there, holding it between your thumb and index fingers.
3. Slip a crimp bead onto the long end and slide it all the way up to the fold, over the short piece as well, so it's nearly to the doubled wire. Use your flat-nose pliers to crimp it securely so the shorter wire and longer wire aren't crossed but hang down at angles.
4. Place one of the smaller cubes on the shorter wire and add a crimp bead at the very bottom of the wire. Flatten it securely with your pliers.
5. Add one of the larger cubes to the longer piece of wire and secure the bottom with a crimp bead as well.
6. Repeat steps 2–5 to create the second earring.
7. Open the earring wires and slip one piece on each one. Close the wires to secure them.

Vintage Button Earrings

Pretty vintage buttons can be transformed into super-fun earrings so easily—they're perfect for suspending as swingy rounds or just adding to an ultra-simple hoop. And if your stash is precious, the nice thing is that it only takes two to create your new set of earrings.

TECHNIQUES

- **Wrapped loops**
  Pink Button Drops
  Red Pop
- **Briolette/top style**
  Pink Button Drops
  Red Pop

TIP Try making a pair to complement the Vintage Button Necklace on p. 88—or use two completely different buttons for a set that's totally unmatchy.

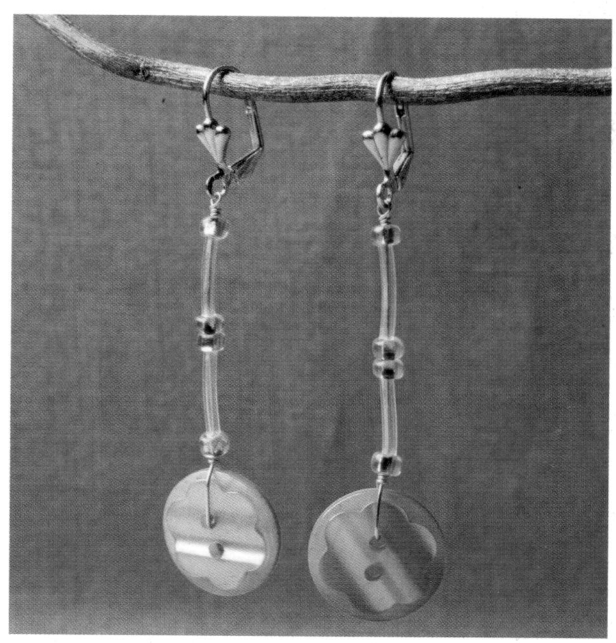

Pink Button Drops Earrings

Try an unexpected combination—shiny pink buttons with plain plastic tubing. Length: 3 inches

YOU'LL NEED

- Pliers
- 24-gauge wire
- 2 buttons
- Seed beads
- 4 pieces of plastic tubing
- Leverback earring wires

Pink Button Drops Earrings

1. Cut two 5-inch pieces of wire, and form a wrapped loop briolette-style above each button, passing the wire through one of the holes. Place a single seed bead on each one above the coil.

2. Take one button drop and place a seed bead, a piece of tubing, two seed beads, another piece of tubing, and finally another seed bead on the wire above it. Form a wrapped loop above the vertical dangle.

3. Repeat step 2 to form the second earring dangle.

4. Open the leverback circles and slip one dangle onto each one. Gently close each one securely.

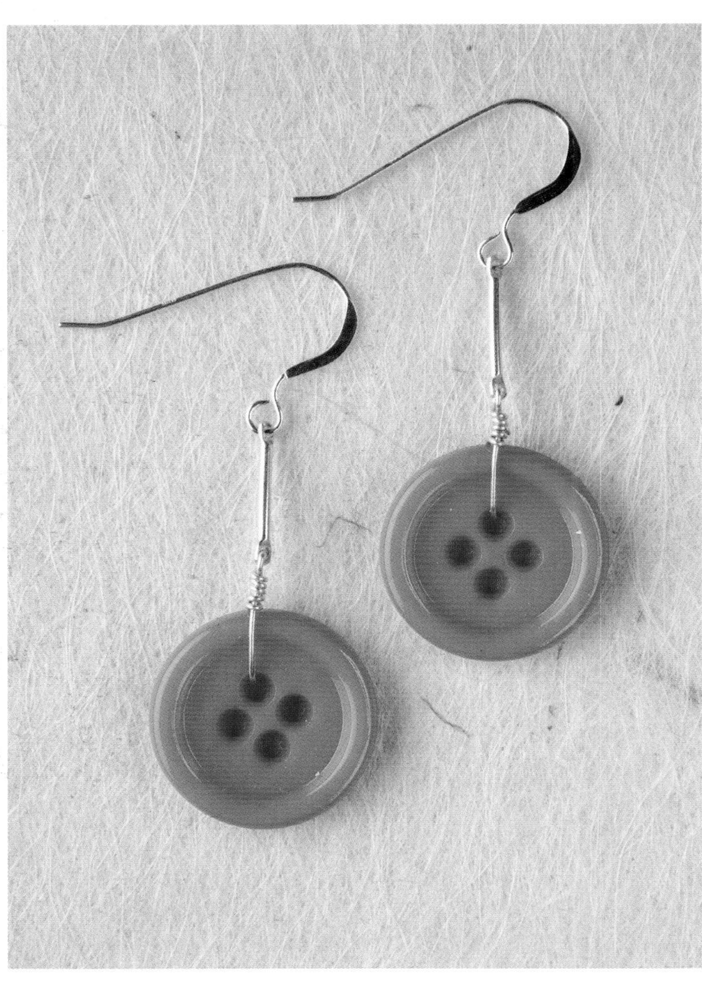

Red Pop Button Earrings

Nothing could be simpler than these red buttons suspended from a single elongated link of chain.

Length: 2 inches

YOU'LL NEED

- Pliers
- 24-gauge sterling wire
- Two 4-hole buttons
- 2 links of elongated chain (mine measured ½ inch each)
- Earring wires

1. Cut two 3-inch pieces of wire, and create a double-wrapped loop through one hole on each button, making sure the upper loop faces to the side—but don't close it yet.

2. Slip one link of chain onto each open loop, then complete the wrap.

3. Open both earring wires and slip the other end of the chain link onto the loops. Close them securely.

Vintage Button Hoop Earrings

Rebecca Pearcy of Queen Bee Creations designed these vintage red-and-white button hoops. She suggests, "Mix and match old buttons depending on how dainty or bold you want them to look. They are also extremely easy and quick to make—and great for a last-minute gift."

Length: 2 inches

YOU'LL NEED

- Pliers
- Buttons of your choice
- Premade hoops from a bead/jewelry-supply store

1. Choose the buttons you would like to use. I used mismatched white pearl earrings in front and back of one big, intricate red button. You could use lots of tiny buttons, one big button, or anything in between.

2. Place the buttons on the hoop in the order that you'd like them.

3. Using the pliers, slightly bend both ends of the hoop upward to ensure a secure closure.

Circle Deluxe Earrings

This earring concept ranges from elaborate embellished double circles to simpler mod singles—but one thing they all have in common is eye-catching style.

TECHNIQUES

- **Jump rings**
  Sparkling Star
  Wood
- **Briolette/top style**
  Wood
- **Wire looping**
  Sparkling Star
- **Plain loops**
  Red Rounds
- **Double-wrapped loops**
  Wood

TIP Try making a coordinating pair to match a Circle Deluxe Pendant on p. 120.

Sparkling Star Circle Deluxe Earrings

These starry circle-within-a-circle earrings are just the thing to wear with the Perfect Clarity Necklace on p. 106.

Length: 3 inches

YOU'LL NEED

- Pliers
- 24-gauge wire
- 12 small faceted beads
- Two star charms
- Six 3mm jump rings
- Two 1¼-inch circle drops
- Two 2-inch circle drops
- A short piece of thin chain
- Earring wires

1. You'll start by creating the embellished outer circle. Cut two 12-inch pieces of 24-gauge wire and begin wrapping the first circle, with the tail to the back, at the top of one circle. Wrap it closely until you've covered about a ½ inch of the hoop, then slip one faceted bead onto your wire tail. Wrap it securely so it sits on the front side of the circle, and continue your wraps the same way.

2. Add the other five beads in the same way, ½ inch apart—if the circle were a clock face, you'd place the beads at the 1, 3, 5, 7, 9, and 11 o'clock spots. Wrap the wire securely to end the embellishment when you reach the other side of the top.

3. Embellish the second outer circle the same way.

4. Suspend one star charm inside each of the two smaller circles using jump rings.

5. Connect one of the smaller circle drops inside one of the larger ones using a jump ring. Repeat with the other two circles.

6. Cut two very short lengths of the chain, making sure that you use an odd number of links so the earring will hang correctly—I used three links for each of mine, which were about ⅛ inch long. Connect one piece of chain above each of the circles using jump rings.

7. Open the earring wires, and slip the top loop of each chain into each one, making sure the earrings are facing front. Close them securely.

Red Rounds Circle Deluxe Earrings

This version is another double circle, capturing trios of red beads.

Length: 1¾ inches

Red Rounds Circle Deluxe Earrings

YOU'LL NEED

- Pliers
- 22-gauge wire
- 12 oversize seed beads
- Two 5mm soldered rings
- Earring wires

1. Cut two pieces of wire that are 1½ inches long and two pieces 3 inches long. Form a plain loop at the end of each piece.
2. String three beads on each piece of wire, and form a plain loop at the opposite end of each piece.
3. Take one of the shorter pieces and open both plain loops. Gently curve it into a circle shape. The wire will resist, but just hold it in place for a moment.
4. Slip the open loops onto the first soldered ring, then close them.
5. Repeat steps 3 and 4 to attach the second "circle" to the second soldered ring.
6. Next, take one of the longer pieces and curve it into a circle shape as in step 3. Open both plain loops and slip them onto the first ring, outside the smaller circle. Close them to secure the piece.
7. Repeat step 6 to form and add the second larger circle to the second piece.
8. Open the earring wires and slip the soldered rings onto them. Close them securely.

Wood Circle Deluxe Earrings

Wood rounds lend a sweet, natural look.

Length: 1⅝ inches

YOU'LL NEED

- Pliers
- 24-gauge wire
- 2 mod circles (mine were drilled front to back)
- Earring wires

1. Cut two 3-inch pieces of wire, and form a double-wrapped loop above each mod circle.
2. Open the earring wires, and slip a mod circle drop into each one. Close the wire loops securely.

Low and Swingy Earrings

These earrings are long, low, and deliberately slightly different from one another. Randomly adorn the lengths of chain with cool beads or charms to create a look that's "match-y"—but unexpected.

TECHNIQUES

- **Plain loops**
  Caribbean
- **Wrapped loops**
  All
- **Briolette/top wrapping**
  Leaves

Caribbean Low and Swingy Earrings

These island-inspired earrings in greens and blues are always fun to wear.

Length: 4 inches

YOU'LL NEED

- Pliers
- Medium-size chain
- 24-gauge wire
- Clear seed beads
- 6 assorted beads in the same color family
- Earring wires

Caribbean Low and Swingy Earrings

1. Cut two 2½-inch pieces of chain and six 2-inch pieces of wire.

2. Form a plain loop at the end of each piece of wire. Place a seed bead, a bead, and another seed bead on each one. Form the first half of a wrapped loop above each one.

3. Randomly place three of the beads along the first piece of chain until you like the configuration. Attach each one to a link of chain, completing the wrap on each one.

4. Repeat step 3 with the other three beads and the second piece of chain.

5. Open both earring wires and slip the first link of one piece of chain into each one. Close them securely.

Leaves Low and Swingy Earrings

Long and lovely, these earrings feature leaves in an asymmetrical pattern.

Length: up to 6 inches (adjustable)

YOU'LL NEED

- Pliers
- Thin chain
- 24-gauge wire
- 2 large (1-inch) leaf charms
- 3 small (⅝-inch) leaf charms
- Chain earring wires
- Jump rings

1. Cut two 3-inch pieces of chain and five 2-inch pieces of wire.

2. Create a wrapped loop briolette-style on each of the large leaf charms. Form the first half of a wrapped loop above the coil on one and slip it onto the last link of chain, completing the wrap. Repeat to join the second leaf to the second piece of chain.

3. Next, form a wrapped loop briolette-style above each of the three small leaf charms. Form the first half of a wrapped loop above each one.

4. Lay one piece of chain out flat and attach a small leaf charm to a link 1 inch above the large leaf charm, completing the wrap to join them. Set this piece aside.

5. Lay out the other piece of chain and measure ½ inch above the large leaf. Attach a small leaf charm there, completing the wrap to join them. Now measure 1 inch above that charm and add the last leaf there, completing that wrap to join them.

6. Attach each chain to an earring wire using a jump ring.

Pop Organic Low and Swingy Earrings

These dramatic earrings, designed by style maven Tricia Royal, mix wood with multicolored accents.

Length: 4½ inches

TIP Try to find beads of different sizes to make these earrings: two large ones and a selection of small and medium-size beads in varying colors and textures. Pick out beads from your stash, and play around until you find a color combination that pleases your eye and your own personal taste.

YOU'LL NEED

- Pliers
- 2 large beads (18–20mm)
- 20-gauge gold wire
- Approximately 20 beads of various colors/sizes/shapes/textures (2–12mm or so)
- Ten to fourteen 2-inch headpins
- 3mm jump rings
- Two 1½-inch pieces of oversize gold chain (Tricia pilfered hers from a vintage necklace)

1. Make a basic dangle with the two large beads—you can add a small bead above and below the large ones if you like.

2. With the remaining beads and headpins, create basic dangles of various lengths. Use two or three beads on some, one or two on others.

3. Divide the dangles up between each of the earrings. Each earring should have one dangle with the large bead and five or six smaller dangles. Play around freely, but try to put approximately the same beads and colors on each of the earrings somewhere so they feel varied but are clearly a pair. Open one jump ring for each dangle.

4. Attach the dangles to the oversize chain with the jump rings. Place most of the dangles on the lowest link of the chain, but for variation and asymmetry, you can add some higher on the earring (especially smaller ones).

5. Open the last two jump rings and use them to connect the earring wires to the earrings you've created.

Starburst Earrings

Like the Starburst Pendant (p. 132), these earrings really pop—they're fun, atomic pieces that work equally well for a date-night soiree or a low-key lunch date. Again, the materials dictate the feel of the earrings—try spiky or glossy, cool colors or warm. The 10-bead version is complex and sturdy, while the six-bead flat style is more delicate—and a lot quicker to make.

TECHNIQUES

- **Plain loops**
  Pearl, Pink and Orange
- **Wrapped loops**
  All

TIP Make sure that your beads aren't too heavy to be successful, wearable earrings—10 beads can really add up weight-wise! You may need to use thinner or lighter versions in glass or plastic, since semiprecious tends to be substantial.

TIP I've created the Pearl Starburst Earrings with chain and the Black Starburst without, but feel free to switch them around.

TIP The Black Starburst Earrings are more delicate than the heavier Pearl Starburst and Pink and Orange Asterisk Earrings, so be gentle with them—they can get misshapen if they're thrown into a handbag or jewelry box. And if your 28-gauge wire gets kinked while you're making the piece, clip the ends down or straighten them with wide flat-nose pliers.

Pearl Starburst Earrings

These 3-D stars are made with delicate oval pearls.

Length: 3½ inches

YOU'LL NEED

- Pliers
- 24-gauge gold wire
- Gold chain (light- or medium-weight)
- Twenty ¼-inch white "pearl" beads
- Earring wires

1. Cut four 3-inch pieces of wire and form a plain loop at one end of each. Also cut a 2-inch piece of chain and set it aside.

2. Add a bead to one piece of wire. Form a loop over the bead—as if you're creating a wrapped loop, bringing the wire around to a 45-degree angle (see the illustration on p. 58) above it—but don't wrap the wire tail at all.

3. Next, add a second white bead to the wire tail. Clip it just above the seed bead, and form a small, tight plain loop to hold it in place. This two-bead piece is a "branch" of the 10-bead asterisk.

4. Make three more branches in the same way.

5. Use your flat-nose pliers to grip the loop in the center of a branch piece and gently angle the two bead spikes downward so they are slightly diagonal. This will help the asterisk spikes sit nicely in the center. Repeat with the other three.

6. Cut a 5-inch piece of wire and form a plain loop at the bottom. This piece will be the "spine" of the asterisk. Place a bead on it.

7. Now you'll start stacking the branches to create your piece. Place one branch on the spine, angled downward. Then place a second one on it, so that the four branch beads are evenly arranged around the spine.

8. Add a third branch, angled slightly up, and then a fourth.

9. Finally, add the last bead to the stack. Shift any stray branches around so that they are in place.

10. Form a *wrapped* loop above the top bead, but don't close it yet—slip the last link of the chain on before wrapping the coil. Coil the wire end firmly so the asterisk is held together well.

11. Tweak any branches that are out of alignment—this piece does have some flexibility. If your first asterisk is a bit skewed, you can clip off the top wrapped loop and start over at step 6 to rebuild it. It may also help if you reinforce the angling from step 5 before stacking your pieces again.

12. Repeat steps 1–11 to make your second earring piece.

13. Open both earring wires and attach the chain-asterisk drops, one on each. Close the wires securely.

Starburst Earrings

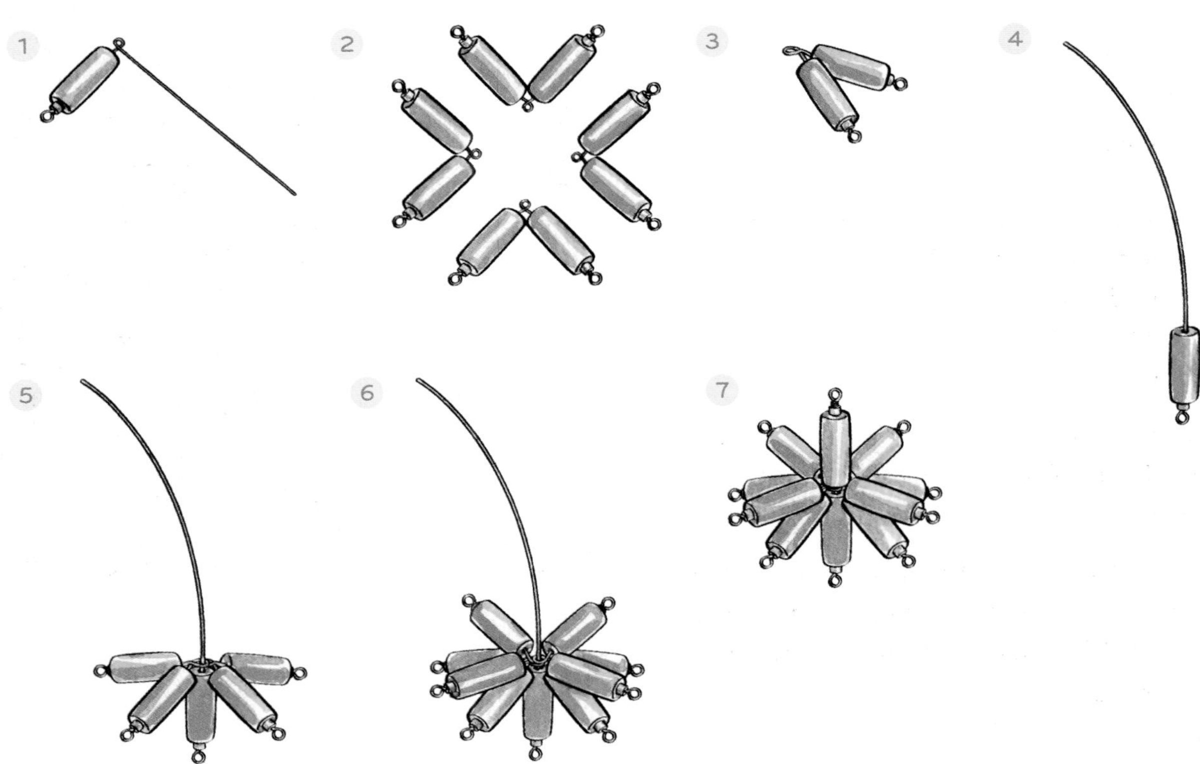

Pink and Orange Asterisk Earrings

These fun, colorful asterisk earrings were designed by craft writer and editor Jennifer Bonnell.

Length: 4 inches

TIP Jen says, "I love the mid-century look of these earrings, and I wanted to use a bold color combo for this pair. But I didn't have any spiky beads in my stash, so I decided to use a mix of smaller glass bead tubes and rounds to create a multicolor spike. I also wanted a super-dangly earring that wouldn't get caught in my hair, so I used eyepins and attached the asterisk with jump rings to make them even swingier than normal. I also find it easier to work with slightly longer pieces of wire, so I used a 6-inch piece of wire to form two branches, rather than cutting several 3-inch pieces."

YOU'LL NEED

- Pliers

- 24-gauge sterling wire
- 20 pink faceted Czech beads
- 20 small light pink glass flower-spacer beads
- 20 orange glass tube beads
- 4 sterling jump rings
- 2 sterling eyepins
- 2 sterling ear wires

1. Cut one 6-inch piece of wire, and form a plain loop on the end. Each 6-inch piece will make two branches.

2. Add a pink bead, a flower spacer, and an orange bead to the wire. Push them snug and form a loop over the bead, bringing the free wire down at a 45-degree angle.

3. Add an orange bead, a flower spacer, and a pink bead to the free end of the wire.

4. Snug up the beads and bend the end of the wire down at a 90-degree angle. Clip the wire, leaving enough behind to form a plain loop. Form a tight plain loop to hold the beads in place. That's one branch done!

5. Repeat steps 1–4 to make seven more branches.

6. Cut a 5-inch piece of wire for the spine, and form a plain loop at one end.

7. Place a pink bead, a flower spacer, and an orange tube bead on the spine.

8. Thread four of your bead branches onto the spine through their center loops, fanning them out slightly so their arms are relatively evenly spaced.

9. Place an orange tube bead, a flower spacer, and a pink bead onto the spine, and snug down the beads tightly to hold the arms of the asterisk in place.

10. Form a wrapped loop at the top of the spine. I added a few additional wraps to tighten the last arm and make sure the asterisk was not too loose or wobbly.

11. Repeat steps 6–10 for the other asterisk.

12. Open a jump ring and slip on the wrapped loop of the asterisk and the eye of the eyepin. Close the jump ring. Repeat for the other asterisk.

13. Hold the earrings up to see how long they dangle. If necessary, clip the eyepins to the same length.

14. Form a plain loop at the end of each eyepin.

15. Open a jump ring, and slip on the plain loop of the eyepin and the earring wire. Close the jump ring. Repeat for the other asterisk.

Black Starburst Earrings

An elegant version of the basic starburst with black glass bugle beads and silver delicas.

Length: 1¼ inches

YOU'LL NEED

- Pliers
- 28-gauge wire
- 12 delicas (or other tiny seed bead)
- Twelve ⅜-inch black bugle beads
- Earring wires

1. Cut an 18-inch piece of wire, and slip a single delica on it, sliding it down to the middle of the wire. Think of the half of the wire extending off to the left as side A and the half extending off to the right as side B.

2. Add a bugle bead to side A, slipping it all the way down to the delica. Thread the end of side B through the bugle bead, away from the delica, and gently pull it taut so that both ends of the wire extend out the same side of the bead, with the delica firmly anchored at the other end. This is your first "spike" of the asterisk and will be the bottom of the finished piece.

Black Starburst Earrings

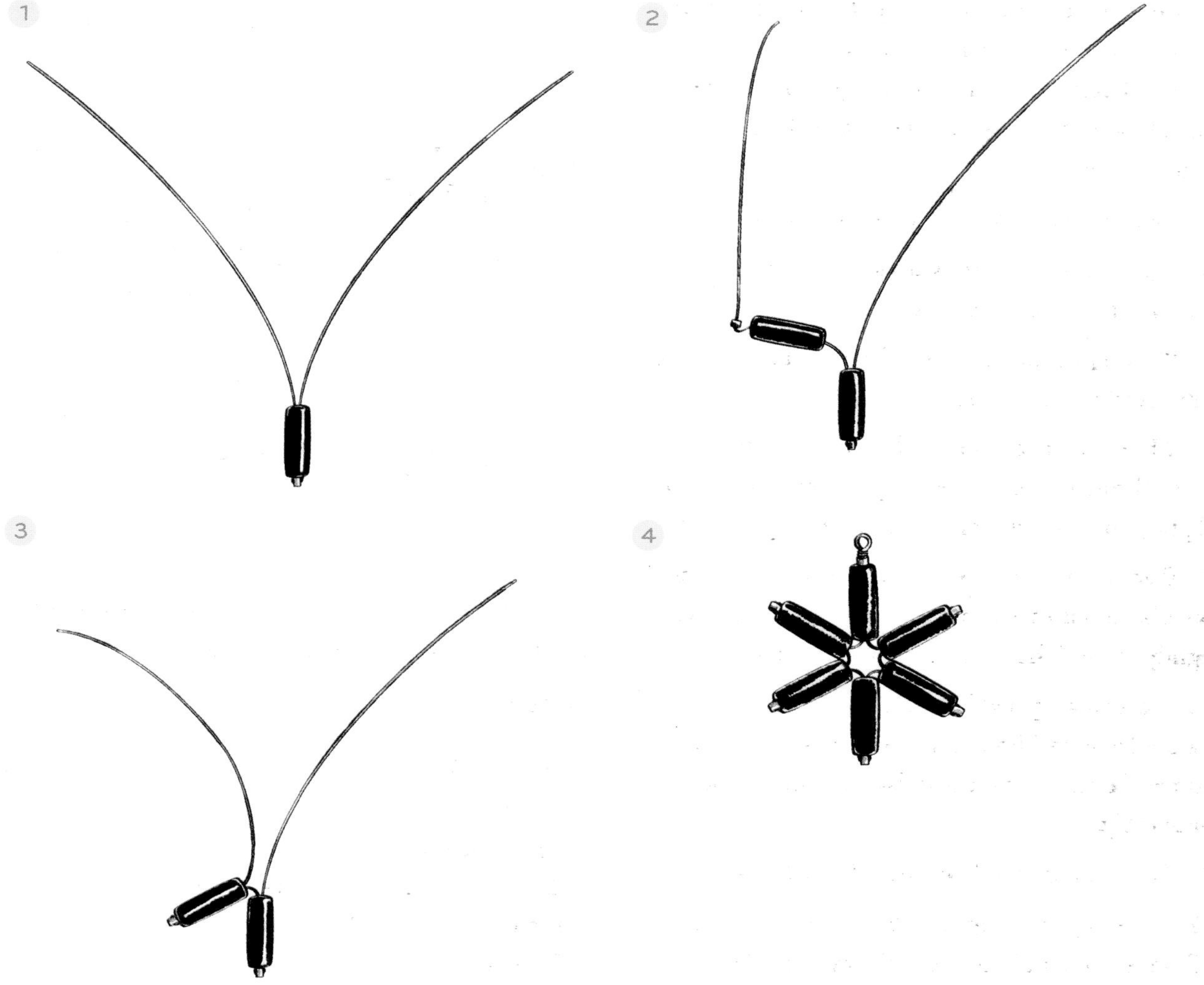

3. Next, you'll build one side of the starburst using side A only. Add a bugle bead and then a delica. Thread the tail of side A back through the bugle bead and gently pull it tight.

4. Repeat step 3 to create a third spike.

5. Now you'll make two spikes on the other side using side B—just repeat steps 3 and 4 to build them.

6. Sides A and B are now ready to unite to create the top spike. Slip a bugle bead onto side A and add a delica. Slip side B through the two beads in the same way so the two wire tails extend above the beads. Gently pull them taut.

7. Gently adjust the spikes so they radiate out evenly from the center. When you like the arrangement, form a wrapped loop using both strands of wire at the top of the piece.

8. Repeat steps 1–7 to create a second starburst piece.

9. Open the earring wire loops, and slip one starburst on each one. Close them securely.

4 Necklaces

One-Strand Necklace

This is an ultra-easy but totally versatile necklace design—just string beads on flexible wire, add a clasp, and seal each end with crimp beads, or create a simple knotted design on silk cord.

TECHNIQUES

- **Basic bead stringing**
  All
- **Crimp beads**
  Smooth and Jagged Leaves and Rounds
- **Knotting**
  Perfectly Pink
- **Bead tips**
  Perfectly Pink

TIP Mix colors or shapes within the super-simple design to add interest and draw the eye. You can make it as fancy and involved or as sleek and spare as you like.

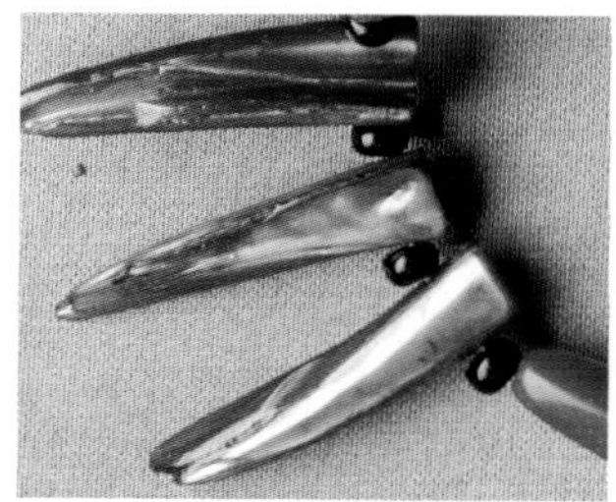

Smooth and Jagged Necklace

The first version uses groups of three jagged mother-of-pearl shell pieces spaced with smooth, elongated resin tubes and glossy black beads.

Length: 16 inches

YOU'LL NEED

- Tape
- Pliers

- 24 inches of Soft Flex beading wire
- Seed beads in size 6/0 (s)
- Six 1-inch resin beads (E)
- 15 mother-of-pearl shell drops (horizontally drilled at the top) (M)
- Clasp of your choice
- 2 sterling silver crimp beads

1. Secure one end of your beading wire with tape at least 5 inches from the end. String 2 inches of the seed beads on to start the necklace design.

2. Add an elongated resin bead, then three mother-of-pearl drops, placing a seed bead between each one (as shown in the photo).

3. Continue the pattern, alternating a resin bead and a group of three drops, until you have five groups of drops and six resin beads on your strand.

4. Add another 2 inches of seed beads. Make sure your necklace is the length you'd like it to be (keeping in mind that your clasp will add a little more length, too).

5. Attach the clasp on each end using crimp beads.

PATTERN: s-E-s-M-s-M-s-M-s-E-s-M-s-M-s-M-s-E-s-M-s-M-s-M-s-E-s-M-s-M-s-M-s-E-s-M-s-M-s-M-s-E-s

Leaves and Rounds Necklace

This piece, designed by my five-year-old nephew Julian Quaresima, is a fun mix of shiny blue rounds and cool textured leaves.

Length: 16 inches

YOU'LL NEED

- Pliers

- 24 inches of Soft Flex wire
- 8/0 green seed beads (s)
- Fourteen ¼-inch blue bugle beads (b)
- 44 green acrylic leaves (L)
- Twenty-one 6mm blue glass rounds (R)
- Hook-and-eye clasp
- 2 crimp beads

FOLLOW the same instructions as for the Smooth and Jagged Necklace, but create this pattern instead:

s-s-b-s-s-b-s-s-b-s-s-b-s-s-b-s-s-b-s-s-b-L-L-R-L-L-b-s-s-b-s-s-b-s-s-b-s-s-b-s-s-b-s-s-b-s-s

Perfectly Pink Necklace

The pink knotted necklace uses an alternating pattern of dark-light-bright shades for a shimmery effect.

Length: 16 inches

YOU'LL NEED

- Knotting tweezers
- Glue
- Pliers

- 1 card of silk beading cord (size 8) in pink
- 2 bead tips
- 12 each of the following colors of 10mm glass beads: hot pink, fuchsia, light pink
- Magnetic clasp

1. Unwind the silk beading cord from its card and stretch it out. Tie a single knot 2 inches from the end farthest from the needle. Add a bead tip to the strand so that the cupping halves face away from the needle and toward the knot, then tie a single knot just above the bead tip, pulling it taut.

2. Slip a hot pink bead onto the cord and position it just above the knot. Now knot above the first bead.

3. Add a fuchsia bead and then a light pink bead in the same way, knotting between each one.

4. Repeat this pattern 11 more times for a total of 36 beads, with a knot between each one. When you add the last bead, make one more knot just above it to hold it in place.

5. Add the second bead tip onto the cord, so the cups are facing away from the beads. Tie a single knot inside the cups.

6. Cut the excess cord from the ends of your necklace, close to the bead-tip knots. Add a drop of glue to each knot to seal it, and then use flat-nose pliers to close the bead tips over the knots.

7. Add one half of the magnetic clasp to one bead tip and curve it closed using round-nose pliers. Repeat on the other side. Let the glue dry completely.

Memoir Necklace

Memory wire is a durable, stiff wire that stays exactly in place, curving around the neck or wrist in a perfect circle. It's easy and quick to work with, and looks great with a repetitive pattern of colorful beads.

TECHNIQUES

- **Memory wire**
  All
- **Gluing**
  All

TIP These necklaces are designed to overlap slightly at the back to create a spare, modern choker feel. They work best with lightweight beads (like wood or smaller glass pieces, for example). But if you want to use heavier beads, cut your piece of memory wire 1 to 2 inches longer so the necklace closes more completely at the back for added security.

Wood and Glass Squares Memoir Necklace

This sleek, spare design mixes wood squares with gold cubes.

Length: 15 inches

YOU'LL NEED

- Cement or instant-drying glue
- Pliers

- 2 round bead ends
- One 15-inch round of memory wire
- Seed beads in a coordinating color (s)
- Twelve 5mm glass cubes (C)
- Eleven ¾-inch wood square beads (W)

1. Glue one bead end onto the end of your memory wire and let dry completely.
2. String your beads on in this pattern: one seed bead, one cube, one seed bead, one wood bead, and repeat 11 times. Add one more seed bead-cube-seed bead to the end.
3. Glue the second bead end to the other end of the wire.

PATTERN: s-C-s-W-s-C-s-W-s-C-s-W-s-C-s-W-s-C-s-W-s-C-s-W-s-C-s-W-s-C-s-W-s-C-s-W-s-C-s-W-s-C-s-W-s-C-s

Lost and Found Necklace

This version has a vintage St. Jude (patron saint of lost causes) medal surrounded by 10 lemon yellow glass rounds, reminiscent of a rosary, with clear beads between. I also used small pieces of clear plastic tubing from a strand of beads to separate the bead clusters from one another.

Length: 15 inches

YOU'LL NEED

- Cement or instant-drying glue
- Pliers

- 2 round bead ends
- One 15-inch round of memory wire
- Seed beads in coordinating color (s)
- 20 pieces of plastic tubing (T)
- 10 glass round beads (G)
- 1 medal or pendant (M)

FOLLOW the same directions as for the Wood and Glass Squares Memoir Necklace with this pattern:

s-s-T-s-s-T-s-s-T-s-s-T-s-s-T-s-s-T-s-s-G-s-s-T-s-s-G-s-s-T-s-s-G-s-s-T-s-s-G-s-s-T-s-s-G-s-s-M-s-s-G-s-s-T-s-s-G-s-s-T-s-s-G-s-s-T-s-s-G-s-s-T-s-s-G-s-s-T-s-s-T-s-s-T-s-s-T-s-s-T-s-s-T-s-s

Flower Charms Memoir Necklace

Illustrator Alexis Hartman designed this spin-off memoir necklace with malachite and clear glass beads.

Length: 15 inches (adjustable)

YOU'LL NEED

- Cement or instant-drying glue
- Pliers

- One 15-inch round of memory wire
- 2 round bead ends
- Small silver beads (s)
- Small gold beads (g)
- 6mm malachite rounds (M)
- 5 flower charms (F)
- 8mm clear glass faceted beads (C)
- Seven 4mm jump rings

NOTE: The flower charms will each be dangling from one jump ring, except for the center charm, which will be suspended on three rings.

FOLLOW the same directions as for the Wood and Glass Squares Memoir Necklace with this pattern:

s-[3 inches of g beads]-s-g-s-g-s-M-g-M-g-F-M-g-M-C-M-F-M-g-M-C-M-g-M-F-M-g-M-C-M-g-M-F-M-g-M-C-M-g-M-F-M-g-M-s-g-s-g-s-[3 inches of g beads]-s

Vintagesque Necklace

This design updates vintage style using sleek, modern spacing. It's a perfect way to redo broken costume jewelry, and since it only uses a handful of "anchor" beads—always an uneven number like 3, 5, or 7—you can often make more than one from a single original piece. Smaller or seed beads bridge the gaps between each larger one.

TECHNIQUES

- **Wire looping**
  All
- **Wrapped loops**
  All

TIP Craft wire is more pliable and less springy than sterling or gold-filled wire, which makes the wire looping easier. You can use precious metal wire if you'd like, but it sometimes resists the looping.

Vintage Amber Necklace

This gorgeous design highlights vintage amber ovals rescued from an old necklace.

Length: 16½ inches

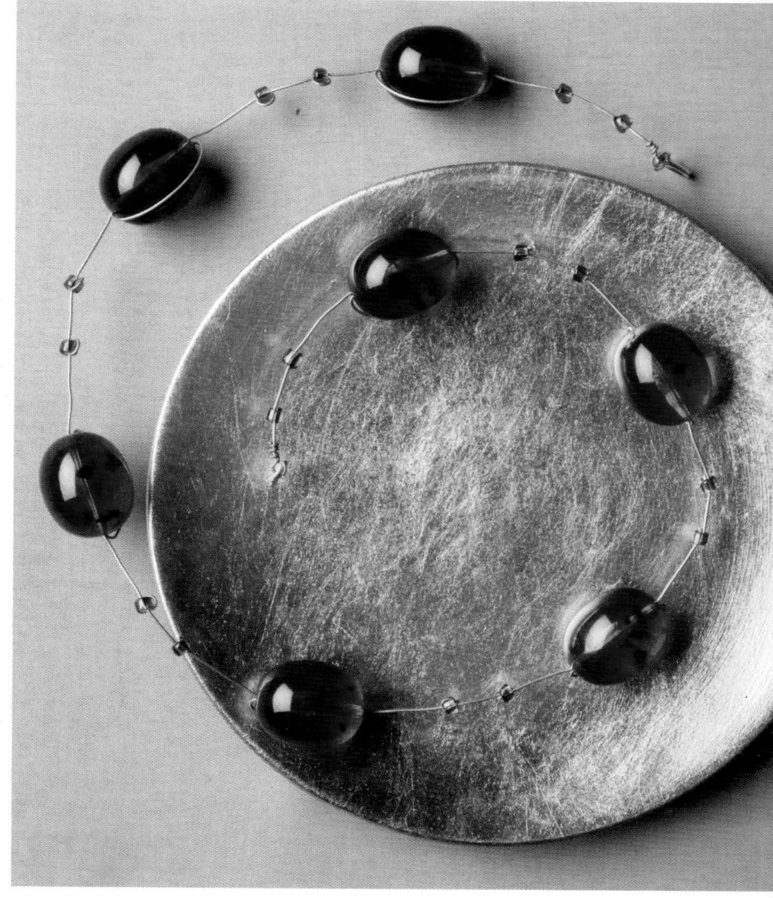

Vintage Amber Necklace

YOU'LL NEED

- Pliers
- Seven ¾- to 1-inch oval beads (O)
- 3 feet of 24-gauge craft wire
- Seed beads in a coordinating color (s)
- Clasp

1. Begin by making the center of the necklace. String an oval bead on the wire, and place it in the middle of the strand. Then take one end of the wire and pass it back through the bead, as shown below.

2. Place a seed bead ½ inch to one side of the oval bead, and loop the wire through the same way to hold it in place. Add another seed bead ¼ inch over and repeat.

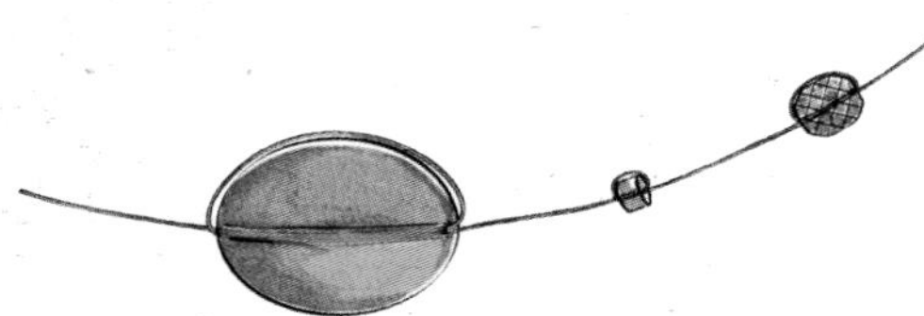

3. Add a second oval bead to the side of the two seed beads in the same way. Continue, alternating an oval bead with two seed beads, until you have four oval beads wired on, and you've ended with two seed beads.

4. Begin adding seed beads and oval beads in the same pattern to the other side of the necklace until you have a total of seven oval beads and both sides end with two seed beads looped on. Check the length of the necklace; add another seed bead to each end if desired.

5. Form the first half of a wrapped loop at one end, about ¼ inch from the last bead. Slip on one half of the clasp before you complete the wrap.

6. Repeat step 5 to add the second half of the clasp.

PATTERN: s-s-O-s-s-O-s-s-O-s-s-<u>O</u>-s-s-O-s-s-O-s-s-O-s-s

Blue Heron Necklace

I designed this blue-and-white necklace for my mother-in-law, Nancy, who loves unusual jewelry. It uses rounds and ovals instead of seed beads as accents for a bolder look.

Length: 16½ inches

YOU'LL NEED

- Pliers
- 3 feet of silver craft wire
- 3 large round anchor beads (I used vintage glass rounds with a splatter design) (A)
- 6 small rounds (R)
- 6 small ovals (O)
- Clasp

FOLLOW the same instructions as for the Vintage Amber Necklace, but substitute this pattern instead, starting with the center anchor bead (<u>A</u>):

O-O-O-R-A-R-R-<u>A</u>-R-R-A-R-O-O-O

Ice Cubes Deluxe Necklace

A versatile piece for everyday or special occasions, this necklace with clear cubes on gold wire is a snap to bead up. This version is made the same way as the others but instead of looping the accent beads, you'll string them on the wire so they move freely between the anchored beads.

Length: 16 inches

YOU'LL NEED

- Pliers
- 3 feet of gold craft wire
- Thirteen 10mm clear glass cubes (C)
- Twenty-eight 6mm clear glass cubes (c)
- Magnetic clasp

FOLLOW the same instructions as for the other necklaces, but create this pattern (remember, don't loop the accent beads!) starting in the center:

c-c-C-c-c-C-c-c-C-c-c-C-c-c-C-c-c-C-c-c-C-c-c-C-c-c-C-c-c-C-c-c-C-c-c-C-c-c-C-c-c

Hardware Store Necklace

These necklaces combine industrial elements from the hardware store for unexpectedly pretty results.

TECHNIQUES

- **Double-wrapped loops**
  Rosette Chain
- **Jump rings**
  S-Necklace
  Circles and Circles
- **S-clasp**
  S-Necklace
  Rosette Chain

TIP Try shopping at neighborhood hardware stores or big superstores for the best selection of materials. As you wander around each, imagine new ways to use the bits and pieces you see—like the S-hooks, mirror rosettes, and O-rings featured here. Most hardware stores offer inexpensive brass- and silver-colored wire in different gauges that can be great for jewelry making—make your own clasps and connectors with heavier weights.

S-Necklace

This simple piece is made from a series of S-hooks and finished with chain.

Length: adjustable

YOU'LL NEED

- Pliers
- 10 large jump rings
- 3 medium-size jump rings
- 12 S-hooks
- 8 inches of medium-weight chain
- 4 inches of 18-gauge wire

1. Open all 10 large jump rings and 2 of the medium rings. Connect 11 of the S-hooks together, each one oriented the same way. This will be the center of the necklace.

2. Cut the chain into two pieces—one 5½ inches long and one 2 inches long. Join one piece of chain to the S-hook at one end of the row you created in step 1, using a medium jump ring. Repeat to join the other piece to the other end of the row of S-hooks.

3. Form the wire into an S-clasp, and slip it onto the shorter end of the chain before finishing it.

4. Join the last S-hook to the longer piece of chain using your last jump ring.

Rosette Chain Necklace

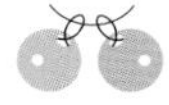 

Designer Jenn Sturiale's handmade chain links and offset acrylic flowers are unexpectedly lovely.

Length: adjustable

TIP Jenn says, "The nice part about this necklace is that the size is infinitely adjustable. You can also make a chain that wraps multiple times around your neck. Different-size washers change the look. I found that split washers size 7mm and under were too heavy of a gauge to work with easily."

YOU'LL NEED

- Pliers
- 11 split washers, size 8mm
- 48 split washers, size 10mm
- One 1½-inch mirror rosette star
- One 1⅛-inch mirror rosette star
- Light utility wire to attach the rosettes to the chain
- Heavy utility wire for the S-clasp

1. Close one large washer so that it's flat.

2. Open one small washer, slip it onto the large washer, then close it. Repeat with three more small washers.

3. Add five more of these patterned link sets (one large washer plus four small washers). Using the light utility wire, connect one side of the 1½-inch rosette to the small-washer end of the chain with a double-wrapped loop.

4. Create another small length of chain consisting of three small washers, one large washer, three small washers. Wire-wrap one end of this chain to the other side of the large rosette.

5. Wire-wrap the other end of this chain to one side of the 1⅛-inch rosette.

6. Create four attached link sets consisting of four small washers plus one large washer, and wire-wrap the end with the small washer to the other side of the small rosette.

7. Snip a length of heavy utility wire, and bend it into shape for the S-clasp. Attach the small side of the clasp to one side of the chain.

Circles and Circles Necklace

Art School Dropout designer Jessee Malone's inspired creation is a delicate arrangement of black O-rings and chain.

Length: 17 inches

YOU'LL NEED

- Pliers
- A variety pack of black O-rings (you'll use a total of 9 in different sizes)
- 6mm or 7mm gunmetal or black jump rings
- 13 inches of lightweight chain
- Two 4mm or 5mm jump rings
- Clasp

1. Arrange the O-rings to form the center design, with the biggest one in the middle. Join three smaller O-rings to each side of the larger circle with jump rings, then join the three smaller ones to one another in the same way.

2. Add one more small circle to each side as shown, joining them in the same way.

3. Cut the chain into two equal-length pieces, and join one half to each side of the circle design, using a jump ring for each one.

4. Use the smaller (4mm or 5mm) jump rings to join the clasp to the ends of the chain.

Three-of-a-Kind Choker

This pretty, versatile choker is as easy to wear as it is to make. This necklace can look equally striking if the three components are identical—as in the Circle Trio—or if the center piece is larger or a different color than the others. Try it super-close fitting or longer and looser.

TECHNIQUES

- **Plain loops**
  Sparkle Martini
- **Wrapped loops**
  Shiny Squares
- **Jump rings**
  All

TIP Try a version with one or five pieces spotlighted in the center, too. You can also choose an unusual chain style, like the ornate copper chain shown, to complement your beads since the design is so spare.

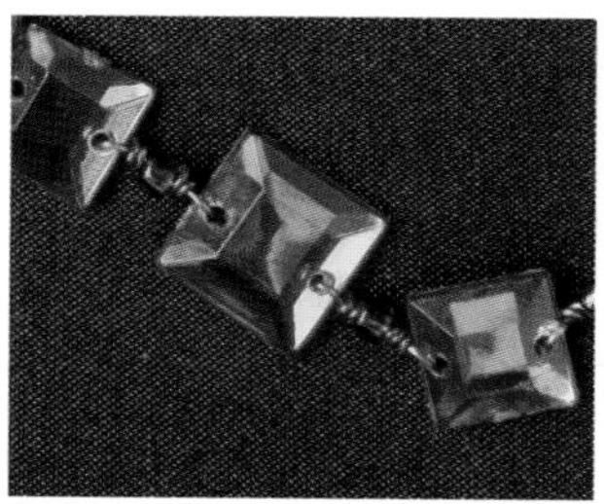

Sparkle Martini Three-of-a-Kind Necklace

It's all about the beads with this simple piece, which spotlights dark red and olive faceted beads on sterling chain.

Length: 17 inches

YOU'LL NEED

- Pliers
- 6 inches of 20-gauge sterling silver wire
- One 14mm faceted bead
- Two 10mm faceted beads
- 16 inches of medium-weight sterling chain
- Clasp
- Two 3mm jump rings

1. Cut three 2-inch pieces of wire, and form a plain loop on either side of the 14mm faceted bead.
2. Join the two 10mm beads on either side of it with plain loops to form the trio centerpiece.
3. Cut the chain into two equal halves, and gently open one of the outer loops to slip one piece of chain onto the bead trio.
4. Attach the second half of the chain to the other side of the bead trio.
5. Attach the clasp to the ends of the chain with jump rings.

Circle Trio Necklace

This spare, striking trio of gold circles on gold-colored chain is easy to wear. Length: 16 inches

YOU'LL NEED

- Pliers
- 14½ inches of thin gold chain
- 4 oval 3mm jump rings
- Three links of oversize circle chain
- Clasp

1. Cut the thin chain into two equal halves and open two of the jump rings. Attach one half of the chain to one of the outside circles using a jump ring. Repeat to attach the second half of the chain to the other side.
2. Use the other two jump rings to attach the clasp to the ends of the chain.

Shiny Squares Three-of-a-Kind Necklace

A more sophisticated take on the basic design, this necklace uses square rhinestones and intricate copper chain.

Length: 15 inches

YOU'LL NEED

- Pliers
- 8 inches of 24-gauge copper craft wire
- 4 seed beads in a coordinating color
- Two 8mm faceted flat rhinestone beads, double-drilled
- One 12mm faceted flat rhinestone bead, double-drilled
- 14 inches of ornate flat copper chain
- Clasp
- Two 3mm jump rings

NOTE: This version is created in the same way as the Sparkle Martini, except that you'll join the rhinestones with wrapped loops.

1. Cut four 2-inch pieces of copper wire. Place one seed bead on each piece, and make the first half of a wrapped loop around each bead.
2. Join one 8mm rhinestone to the 12mm one using one of the wrapped seed beads, and complete the wraps.
3. Join the second 8mm rhinestone to the 12mm one, creating your trio of beads for the center.
4. Repeat steps 3–5 in the Sparkle Martini, using wrapped loops instead of plain ones, to finish the necklace.

Front and Center Necklace

This necklace is built around a cool centerpiece—like a vintage bracelet or a length of circle chain—and finished with simple chain on each side. The middle section can be transformed with scallop detailing below the original piece or left elegantly plain. Like many of the other patterns in the book, this design uses an odd number of links in the center for symmetry.

TECHNIQUES

- **Wrapped loops**
  Bracelet Alchemy
  Victorian Deluxe
- **Briolette wrapping**
  Victorian Deluxe
- **Jump rings**
  All

TIP Save any extra links or components from your original piece for other designs. For example, the orange bracelet I used here had six links, so I took one off to use in a Spaces and Sparkles Pendant (p. 128).

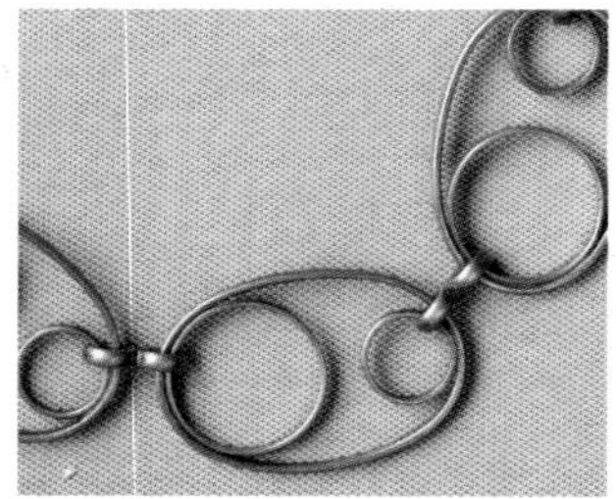

Bracelet Alchemy Necklace

This lovely vintage orange bracelet is reinterpreted with scallops of blue beads.

Length: adjustable up to 17½ inches

YOU'LL NEED

- Pliers
- Vintage link bracelet
- 24-gauge wire
- Seed beads
- Five 10mm vintage beads in a contrasting color
- Medium or large gold chain
- Jump rings
- Clasp

1. Lay your bracelet out flat and take off any extra links until you have an uneven number (3, 5, or 7, for example). In this example, I'm using five links with a total of 6 inches in length.

2. Cut four 3-inch pieces of wire, and form the first half of a wrapped loop on each one, leaving it open. Place a seed bead, a 10mm vintage bead, and another seed bead on each one, and form the first half of a wrapped loop on the other end.

3. Gently curve each bead wrap from a straight line into a scallop shape, and slip the first one onto link number 1 out of 5. Complete the wrap to join them. Then slip the other side of the bead wrap onto link 2, and finish the wrap. You now have one scallop joining links 1 and 2.

4. Repeat the process to add three more scallops below the bracelet, each one connecting two links.

5. Cut the chain into two pieces—one 5 inches long and one 6½ inches long. Join the 5-inch piece of chain to one end of the bracelet using a jump ring or one of the bracelet links. Then join the 6½-inch piece to the other end in the same way.

6. Use a jump ring to attach the clasp to the shorter length of chain.

7. Cut a 3-inch piece of wire, and form a plain loop at one end. Add a seed bead, the last 10mm bead, and another seed bead, and connect it to the end of the longer piece of chain with a wrapped loop. Now your necklace is adjustable—simply clasp it where you like, and let the end with the bead ornament hang below.

Victorian Deluxe Necklace

Sterling circles embellished with black faceted beads alternate between ornate drops and scalloped curves for an elaborate look.

Length: 15½ inches

YOU'LL NEED

- Pliers
- 24-gauge wire
- 3 faceted briolettes
- 3 small cube beads
- 4 inches of oversize circle chain (I used one with seven links)
- Seed beads
- 6 top-drilled drops
- Six 3mm or 4mm jump rings
- 10 inches of thin chain
- Clasp

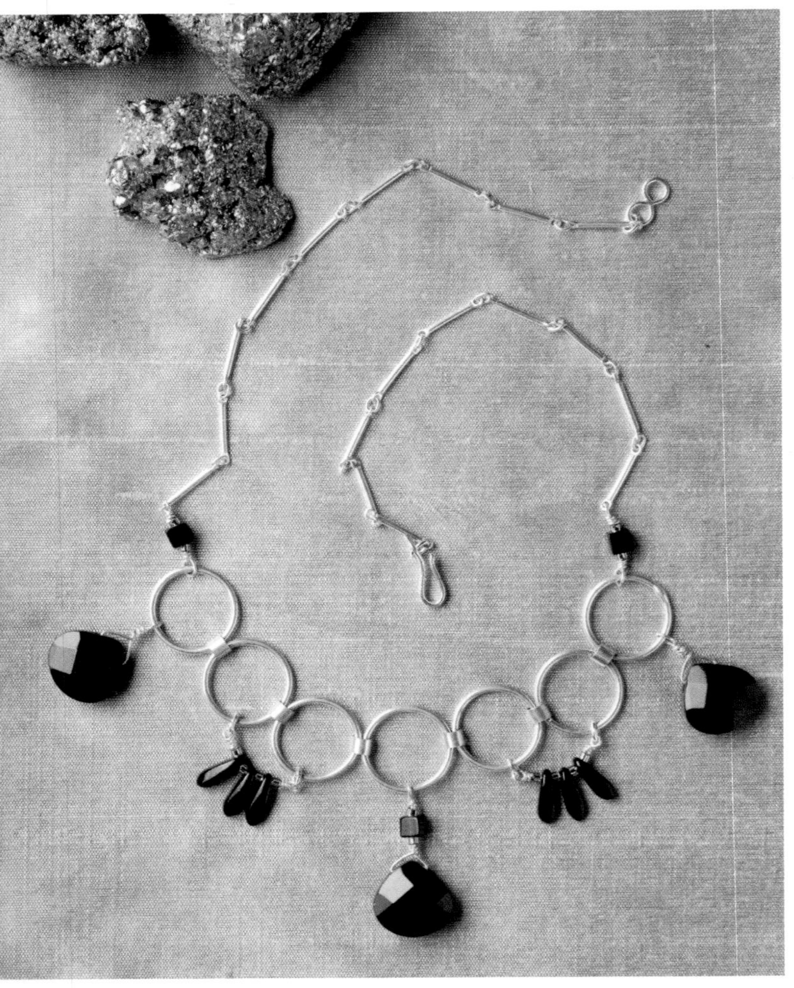

1. Cut seven 4-inch pieces of wire and set all but one aside.

2. Wire-wrap one of the briolettes with the first piece of wire, and complete the first half of the wrap above it, leaving a tail to work with. Place a cube on the wire, and create a wrapped loop above it, slipping it onto the center link of the circle chain before you complete the wrap.

3. Wrap the other two briolettes the same way—without the cube bead, though—and attach them to the two outer loops before completing the wrap.

4. Form a wrapped loop on the fourth piece of wire, and slip on it a seed bead, a drop, seed bead, drop, seed bead, drop, and finally another seed bead. Finish the wrapped loop on the other end, then gently curve the straight line into a scallop shape. Repeat to make another identical piece.

5. Open two of the jump rings, and use them to attach the first scallop to the bottom of the second and third links, connecting them as shown in the photo.

6. Repeat step 5 to attach the second scallop to the fifth and sixth links.

7. Cut the thin chain into two 5-inch halves. Use one of your last two pieces of wire to connect the first piece of chain to the first link of the centerpiece, making wrapped loops above and below a cube bead. Slip the loops onto the chain and centerpiece link before completing the wrap.

8. Repeat step 7 to join the other half of the chain to the other end of the centerpiece.

9. Use your last two jump rings to connect the clasp to the ends of the chain.

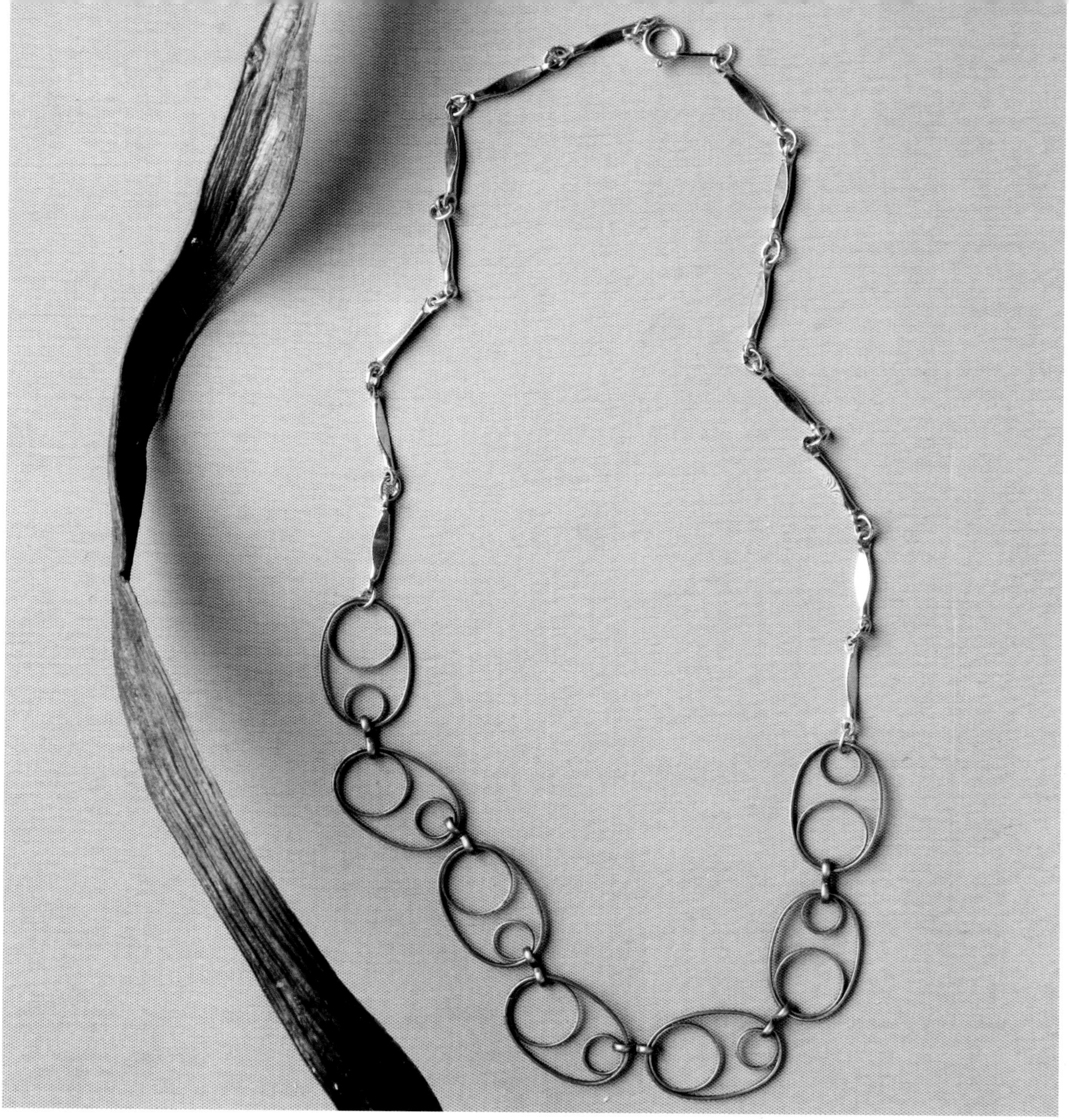

Circles in the Center Necklace

This super-sleek version with circle chain—and no ornamentation—depends on the engaging pattern within the chain itself.

Length: 16 inches

YOU'LL NEED

- Pliers
- 9 inches of thin chain
- Four 3mm oval jump rings
- 6 inches of interesting circle chain (this piece has seven links)
- Clasp

1. Cut the 9-inch piece of chain in half, and use a jump ring to join one piece to the end of your circle chain. Repeat on the other side.
2. Attach a clasp with the remaining two jump rings.

Swingy Necklace

This fun, opera-length necklace can be worn as is or doubled. It doesn't need a clasp (always a plus!), and you can use any combination of colors or materials to make it as bold or as delicate as you'd like.

TECHNIQUES

- **Wrapped loops**
  - Woods and Golds
  - Turquoise Trios
- **Knotting**
  - Swingy Sparkle

TIP Make sure your necklace is at least 24 inches long so it will go over your head easily, and at least 42 inches long if you want to double it. Aside from that, make it as long or as short as you'd like—you can triple a super-long version, or wear it as a belt.

Woods and Golds Necklace

Dramatic gold and brown beads hang on a gold chain.

Length: 54 inches

YOU'LL NEED

- Pliers
- 24-gauge gold-colored wire
- Six 1-inch large rounds (L)
- Six ½-inch medium rounds (M)
- Twelve ½- to ⅝-inch wooden tube beads (T)
- 24 inches of oversize gold-colored circle chain (or chain of your choice), cut into twelve 2-inch pieces (C)
- Small wooden spacer beads (s)

1. Cut twenty-four 4-inch pieces of wire. Form the first half of a wrapped loop around each large, medium, and tube beads, and be sure to add a spacer on the side of each one.

2. Join a trio of beads: First, connect a wooden tube bead to a large round and complete the wrap on each one, then add a wooden tube to the other side in the same way. Don't complete the wraps on the outer ends yet, though.

3. Slip the end link of a piece of chain onto the open loop at one end of the bead trio. Finish the loop to join them. Repeat with the other end. You now have a bead trio with a piece of chain on either side.

4. Join a medium round to one end of the chain in the same way, then add another piece of chain to its other side, completing both loops once the chain is slipped on.

5. Continue joining the necklace in the same alternating pattern until you have six bead trios, six medium rounds, and 12 pieces of chain joining them. Join the last piece of chain to the first trio of beads you created in step 2 to finish the necklace.

PATTERN: C-s-T-s-s-L-s-s-T-s-C-s-M-s-C-s-T-s-s-L-s-s-T-s-C-s-M-s- C-s-T-s-s-L-s-s-T-s-C-s-M-s-C-s-T-s-s-L-s-s-T-s-C-s-M-s-C-s-T-s-s-L-s-s-T-s-C-s-M-s-C-s-T-s-s-L-s-s-T-s-C-s-M-s-(join the two ends here)

Swingy Sparkle Necklace

Glamorous meets easy in this faceted Lucite design on silver-colored elastic.

Length: 36 inches

TIP You can use a cord knotting tool or just grip the elastic with tweezers or needle-nose pliers to knot between each bead. This necklace uses the same pattern of alternating one bead with a trio of beads.

YOU'LL NEED

- Tweezers or cord knotting tool
- Glue
- Fray Check
- 54-inch-long piece of silver-colored cord or elastic
- Twenty-eight ¾-inch faceted Lucite beads (L)

1. Six inches in from the end of the cord, make a single knot. Place a Lucite bead above it as shown, and make another knot directly above the bead to hold it in place.

2. Measure 1 inch from the second knot and make a third knot. Add a second bead, make a knot directly above it, add a third bead, a knot, a fourth bead, and

a final knot. Now you have one single bead and one trio on your cord.

3. Repeat this pattern, always leaving 1 inch between the bead groupings, until you have seven single beads and seven trios on your cord, with two long ends.

4. Make your final knot on the seventh trio using both ends of the cord, and seal it with a drop of glue. Let it dry completely.

5. Cut off both ends of the cord very closely, then add a drop of Fray Check to protect the cord from unraveling. Let that dry completely, too.

PATTERN (L = bead; C = 1 inch of cord; k = knot): L-k-C-k-L-k-L-k-L-k-C-L-k-C-k-L-k-L-k-L-k-C-L-k-C-k-L-k-L-k-L-k-C-L-k-C-k-L-k-L-k-L-k-C-L-k-C-k-L-k-L-k-L-k-C-L-k-C-k-L-k-L-k-L-k-C-L-k-C-k-L-k-L-k-L-k-C-(k—join here by knotting the two cord lengths together)

Turquoise Trios Necklace

More organic than the other two, the Turquoise Trios Necklace also includes a simpler repeating pattern of threes instead of the three-one-three-one style.

Length: 36 inches

YOU'LL NEED

- Pliers
- 24-gauge gold wire
- 20 inches of thin gold chain
- 30 small or medium (I used approximately 6mm) turquoise beads

1. Cut thirty 2½- to 3-inch pieces of wire and ten 2-inch pieces of chain.

2. Wire-wrap one turquoise bead with a wrapped loop on either side. Join a second bead to the first, leaving the outer loop open. Slip one piece of chain on the loop, then close it.

3. Join a third turquoise bead to the other side of the first one, and add another piece of chain to the outer loop before closing it. You'll now have a trio of wrapped beads with pieces of chain on both sides.

4. Continue building the necklace in this way, joining three beads with wrapped loops and pieces of

chain on either side, until you have 10 trios of beads joined by 10 pieces of chain. Join the last trio to the last piece of chain.

Vintage Button Necklace

This series of necklaces uses a fun assortment of vintage buttons—clustered on wire and suspended as drops. Each of these designs works best with buttons that are drilled through rather than on shanks.

TECHNIQUES

- **Wrapped loops**
  Cute as a Button
  Cleopatra
- **Double-wrapped loops**
  Pink Button Drops
  Cute as a Button
- **Crimp beads**
  Pink Button Drops

TIP Find cool vintage buttons at estate sales, thrift stores, or flea markets in tons of sizes and colors. Use assorted shades for a fun, dynamic mix, or try identical ones for a sleeker look.

TIP To weave wire through buttons, slip the wire through the holes of a four-hole button diagonally rather than side to side.

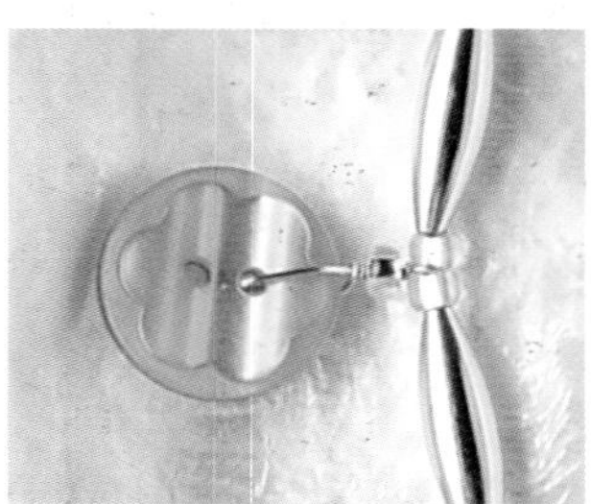

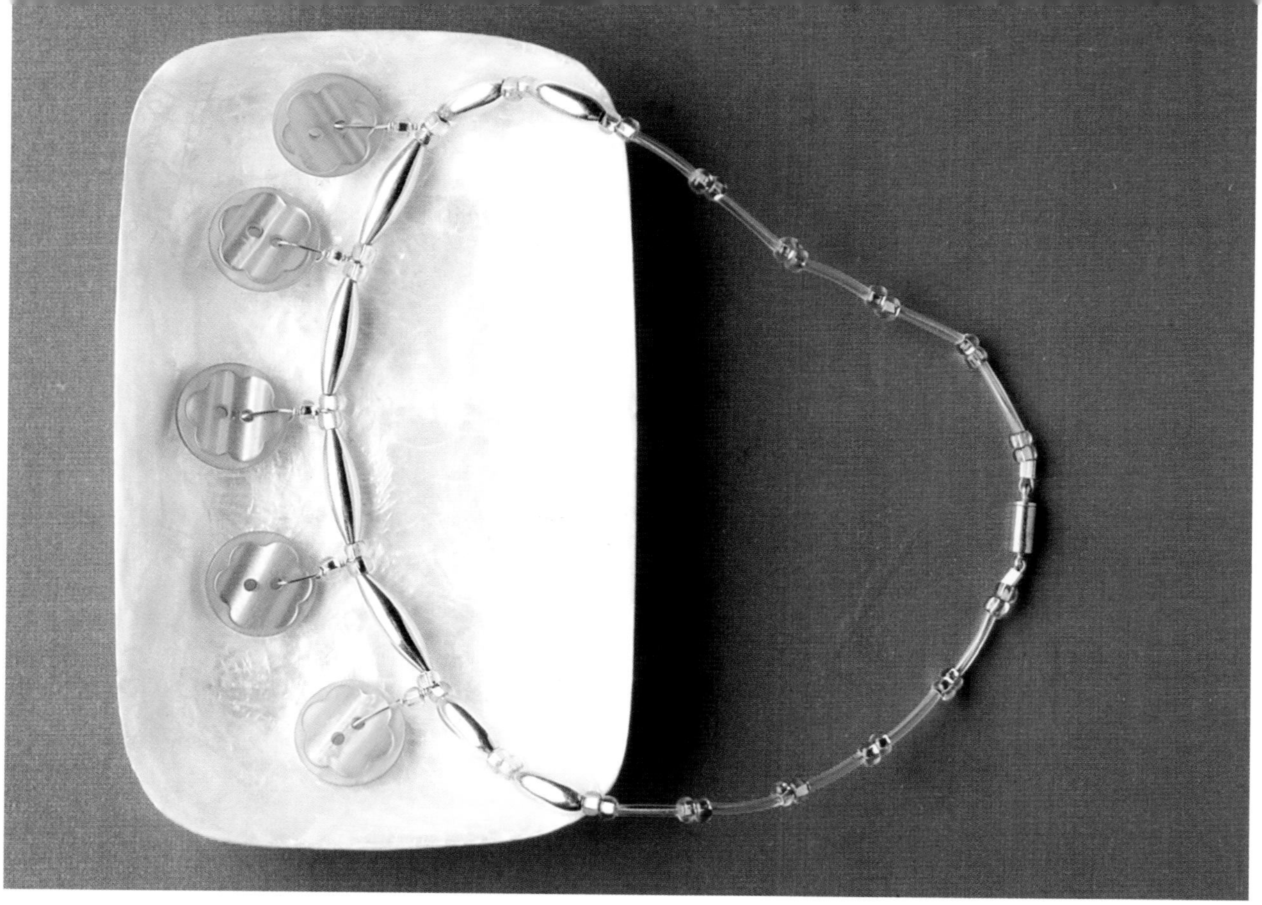

Pink Button Drops Necklace

Five pretty pink vintage buttons dangle from this choker—make a set of matching earrings, too!

Length: 14½ inches

YOU'LL NEED

- Pliers
- Tape
- 24-gauge wire
- 5 vintage buttons (with holes instead of shanks)
- Large seed beads (s)
- 22 inches of Soft Flex wire
- ⅜-inch pieces of plastic tubing (P)
- Four ⅞- to 1-inch-long elongated metal tube beads (LM)
- Four ½-inch-long elongated metal tube beads (SM)
- 2 crimp beads
- Clasp

1. Start by creating the button drops (BD): Cut five 3-inch pieces of 24-gauge wire and form a wrapped loop briolette-style above each button, passing the wire through one of the holes. Place a single seed bead on each one above the coil.

2. Complete a wrapped loop above the seed bead—coiling the wire neatly and leaving a medium-size loop that can easily slip onto the Soft Flex wire—on all five button drops.

3. Next, move on to the bead stringing. Place a doubled piece of tape at one end of the Soft Flex wire, and begin stringing the necklace using the pattern below. String a button drop on, facing front, where the BD symbol is.

4. Use crimp beads to attach each half of the clasp, making sure to run the Soft Flex tail back through the first piece of plastic tubing on each side. Neatly trim the wire and tuck it back into the necklace.

PATTERN: s-s-P-s-s-P-s-s-P-s-s-P-s-s-P-s-s-SM-s-s-SM-s-BD-s-LM-s-BD-s-LM-s-BD-s-LM-s-BD-s-LM-s-BD-s-SM-s-s-SM-s-s-P-s-s-P-s-s-P-s-s-P-s-s-P-s-s

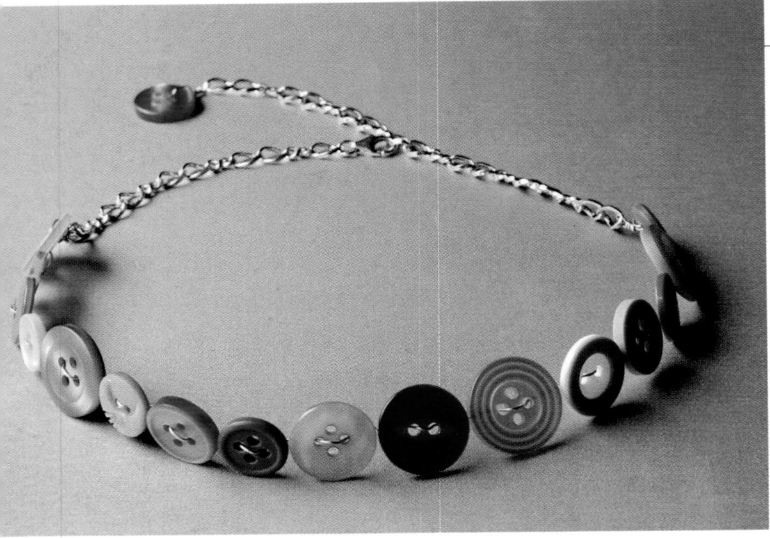

Cute as a Button Necklace

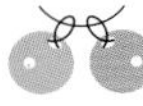 

Not borrowed but blue buttons are neatly suspended on 24-gauge wire. This button necklace sits like a collar, but it's adjustable so it will fit you or a gift recipient perfectly.

YOU'LL NEED

- Pliers
- An assortment of buttons in the same color family (I used 17 blue buttons ranging from ⅜ to ¾ inch across)
- 2½ to 3 feet of 24-gauge gold craft wire
- 9 inches of large gold chain
- Clasp with jump ring

1. Arrange your buttons in a row so you like the mix of colors and sizes together. I made sure mine alternated larger/smaller and darker/lighter. Slip the wire through one of the holes of your first button, and place it about 6 inches from one end of the wire. Feed it through the opposite hole, and pull it taut so that the button "sits" where you've placed it.

2. Add the next button in the same way and secure it in place so it's close to the first one. Add more buttons until you have a section of wired buttons about 9 inches long. Clip the wire ends so they're both about 6 inches long.

3. Feed one of the wire ends back into the outer hole of the last button, looping it through to reinforce it. Form the first half of a wrapped loop with the wire but don't close it. Repeat on the other side.

4. Cut the chain into a 6-inch piece and a 3-inch piece. Join one piece to each side and complete the wrapped loops.

5. Join a clasp to the shorter piece of chain with the jump ring.

6. Now you'll use one last button to accent the chain at the back. Wire-wrap it briolette-style (like the Pink Button Drops) through one of the holes, and join it to the end of the longer piece of chain.

Cleopatra Necklace

Designed by writer and crafter Stacy Elaine Dacheux, this tiered button drop necklace on sparkly, thin yarn is chunky and simple—it's perfect when paired with a nice tank, V-neck, or scoop-neck top.

Length: 15 inches

TIP Stacy says, "It's important to use the same type of four-holed buttons around the size of a quarter for this version. You can pull these buttons off of an old vintage coat, or buy them from your local fabric shop. I like to use all solid colors."

YOU'LL NEED

- Pliers
- Tape
- Large-holed needle that can go through your button holes with ease
- Fray Check or clear nail polish
- 24-gauge wire
- 15 four-holed vintage buttons about the size of a quarter

- Sleek, thin yarn or thicker thread of your choice that will easily slip through the button holes (I used SWTC's Shimmer Yarn in #405 Madison)
- Clasp

1. First, create a two-button drop. To start, cut a piece of wire 4 inches long. Hold the first two buttons tightly side by side between your thumb and index finger. Start threading the wire from the back of the button, up through the holes, down through the top, and then up through the back of the next button. Make sure the wire is tight. Ideally, the button edges should touch one another.

2. Flip it over. On the backside of the attached buttons, take these wire ends and wrap and tuck them around in the middle, keeping the wire tight and reinforcing the bond. Snip away excess wire.

3. Repeat these steps to form a second two-button drop. Set them aside.

4. Use this same process for the three-button drop, except that you use a 6-inch piece of wire and three buttons. Create three three-button drops total. When you are done, there should be five button drops total: two two-drops and three three-drops. You will also have two extra buttons (for the ends).

5. Using a 10-inch piece of wire, begin stringing the top button of each drop to form the necklace according to the pattern at right. All the buttons should be facing front and touching one another so you cannot see any wire. After you have strung all seven buttons across, there should be excess wire on both sides.

6. Create a wrapped loop underneath the end button on each side. Trim the excess wire if necessary.

7. Cut two 8-inch-long pieces of shimmer yarn. Attach the clasp to both pieces of yarn with a simple knot. Attach the other ends of the yarn to the right and left wrapped loop tucked under the button.

8. For the front detail, cut two 2-inch-long pieces of yarn, two 4-inch-long pieces of yarn, and three 6-inch-long pieces of yarn. Match the pieces up, according to length, with the correlating button drops. Tape the necklace to the edge of a table for easy stitching access.

9. Thread the needle and stitch vertically through the button drops. The yarn color should peek out in between the buttonholes of each button. Knot these in the back.

10. Apply Fray Check or clear nail polish to all knots to secure them. Cut excess strays.

PATTERN (B = button; BD = button drops):
B(1)-BD(2)-BD(3)-BD(3)-BD(3)-BD(2)-B(1)

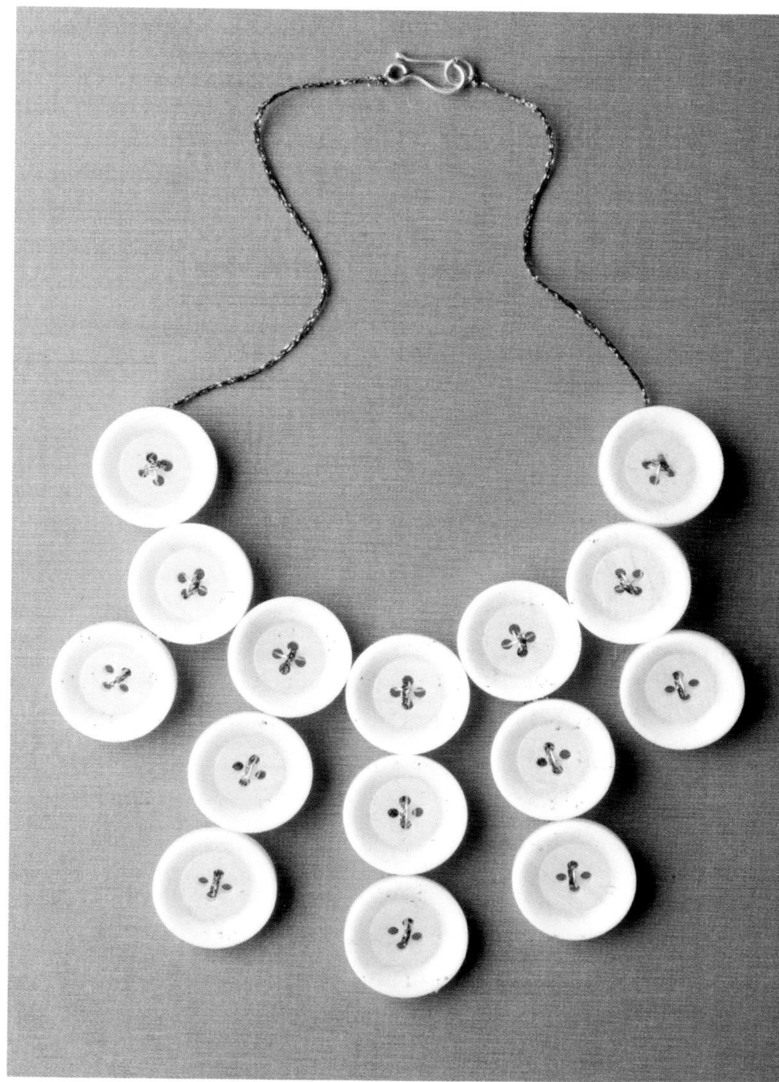

Tiered Necklace

Arrange a repetitive pattern of beads or charms into tiers to create these multi-layered necklaces. The strands complement one another beautifully, and each piece is fully adjustable to wear as a choker or longer, depending on your preference.

TECHNIQUES

- **Bead stringing**
  The Necklace Necklace
- **Crimp beads**
  The Necklace Necklace
- **Plain loops**
  Glossy Carnelian
- **Wrapped loops**
  Glossy Carnelian
- **S-clasp**
  Glossy Carnelian
- **Jump rings**
  Triple-Tiered Filigree

TIP This necklace can be made with virtually any combination of beads, but it works best when there is about 1½ to 2 inches difference in length between the upper and lower tiers. Use a bead tray for easier designing, too.

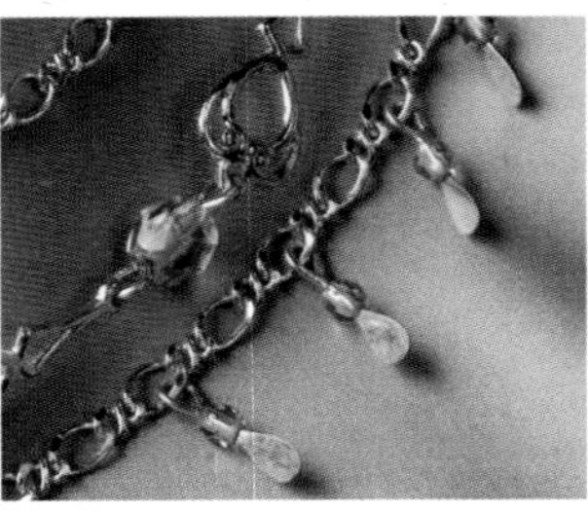

Glossy Carnelian Tiered Necklace

This elegant necklace uses handmade sterling silver links to join smooth carnelian and sparkling glass beads in a subtle pattern.

Length: adjustable

YOU'LL NEED

- Pliers
- 24-gauge wire
- Topaz seed beads
- 11 carnelian ¾-inch oval beads (L)
- Eighteen 10mm faceted topaz glass beads (S)
- Three 12mm faceted topaz glass beads (M)
- Several inches of large chain
- 1 ¼-inch S-clasp
- One 8mm faceted topaz glass bead

1. Cut twenty-one 1½-inch pieces and eleven 2½-inch pieces of wire. You will use the longer wires to form wrapped loops around the carnelian beads and the shorter pieces for the glass beads.

2. Take one longer piece of wire and form a wrapped loop at one end. Add a seed bead, a carnelian oval, and another seed bead. Close it with another wrapped loop. This will be the center bead of the second (longer) tier, shown as L in the pattern.

3. Form a wrapped loop with one of the shorter pieces of wire, and add a seed bead, a 12mm glass bead, and another seed bead. Begin forming the second wrapped loop, but slip it onto the carnelian link before closing it. Finish the wrapped loop.

4. Follow the pattern on p. 94 to add the rest of the beads one by one, working from the center to the right side. When you reach the last link (a 10mm glass bead), leave the outer wrapped loop open.

5. Again working from the center carnelian bead, add the beads on the left side of the design. Leave the outer wrapped loop open on the last link, as you did in step 4. Set this tier aside.

6. Form a wrapped loop at the end of one of the shorter pieces of wire, add a seed bead, a 12mm bead, and another seed bead, then close it with a second wrapped loop. This will be the center bead of the first (shorter) tier, shown as M in the pattern.

7. As in steps 3, 4, and 5, create the rest of the first tier, working outward from the center bead. Leave the outer wrapped loops on the two last links on each end open.

8. Next, measure the two tiers. The first one should be about 14 inches long, and the second about 15½ inches. (If they differ in length from this example, you will simply adjust the length of the chain in the next step.)

9. Cut a 1-inch piece and a 2-inch piece of the large chain. (Note: If you like to wear your necklaces long, cut the chain pieces longer, too—2 and 3 inches, respectively.) Slip one of the two open loops at the ends of the second tier onto the first link of the short

piece of chain and the other onto the first link of the longer piece of chain, but do not close the wrapped loops yet.

10. Slip one each of the open loops at the end of the first tier onto the fourth link of each piece of the chain. Do not close the wrapped loops.

11. Hold the necklace up to see how the tiers hang together. Adjust where they join to the chains if need be, keeping it symmetrical on each side (so if you change one side from the fourth to the sixth link of chain, change the other, too). Once you are pleased with the arrangement, finish all four of the wrapped loops.

12. Join the clasp to the 1-inch piece of chain. (See p. 25 for instructions on making the S-clasp shown.)

13. Cut a 1½-inch piece of wire, and form a plain loop at one end. Place a seed bead, the 8mm bead, and another seed bead on the wire, and begin to form a wrapped loop above the beads. Slip the loop onto the last link of the longer piece of chain, and close the loop.

PATTERN

First (shorter) tier: S-L-S-S-L-S-L-<u>M</u>-L-S-L-S-S-L-S

Second (longer) tier: S-S-S-L-S-S-L-M-<u>L</u>-M-L-S-S-L-S-S-S

The Necklace Necklace

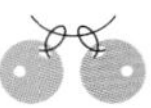

This green glass necklace spotlights a tiny replica of itself in the center circle, echoing not only the design but the circle itself.

Length: adjustable

TIP You can simplify this design by using beads that are all the same size, or close to it, instead of the broad range here. Taking an old piece apart is an easy way to find lots of nice vintage beads in assorted sizes—I used a graduated strand from a vintage costume jewelry necklace for my "pearls." I found my tiny jewelry display at a miniatures shop.

NOTE: In this design, you'll use two seed beads between each larger one on the upper strand but three seed beads on the lower strand.

YOU'LL NEED

- Mod Podge® gloss
- Paintbrush
- Sewing needle
- Glue
- Pliers
- Tape

- 4 feet of Soft Flex wire
- 6 large crimp beads
- 8/0 gunmetal/silver seed beads
- 2 hook-style clasps
- 8 inches of large chain

GLASS BEADS

- Six 10mm faceted ovals (smOV)
- Four 8mm rounds (8G)
- Five 10mm faceted (10G)
- Two 12mm faceted (12G)
- Four 1-inch faceted glass ovals (lgOV)

PEARLS

- Ten 8mm rounds (8P)
- Three 10mm rounds (10P)

- Six 12mm rounds (12P)
- Two 14mm rounds (14P)

CENTERPIECE

- 1 miniature jewelry display
- Silver and green seed beads for tiny necklace
- Metallic silver thread
- One 6mm jump ring
- Small pendant bail
- One 5mm jump ring
- Two 3mm jump rings
- One 1½-inch silver circle

1. First, get the jewelry display ready. Paint it with a coat of gloss Mod Podge and let it dry. Meanwhile, bead the mini-necklace with silver and green seed beads in a symmetrical pattern on the metallic thread (mine was about 2 inches long) with a single 6mm jump ring in the center. Don't tie it yet.

2. When the display is dry, try the necklace on it. Glue the pendant bail on the upper back to turn it into a hanging pendant. When it's set, tie the necklace on the display and knot and secure it at the back with a drop of glue. Smooth the jump ring in front flat, and secure that with a drop of glue too, so the necklace is anchored in two places. Let the glue dry completely and set the display aside for now.

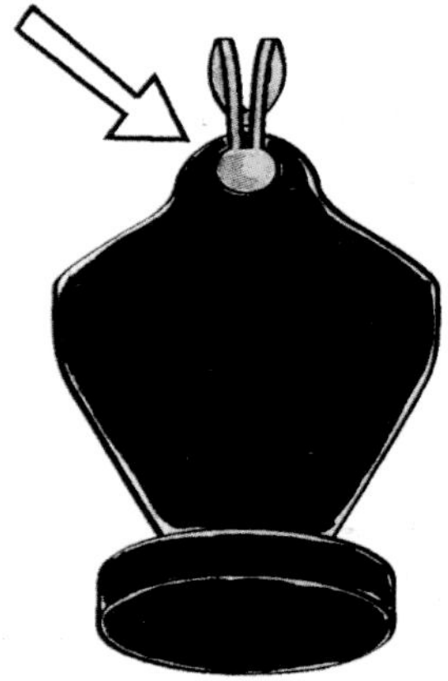

3. Next, create the shorter strand of the necklace. Cut a 20-inch piece of Soft Flex, and tape one end to hold the beads. String the following pattern, leaving the centerpiece out for now (but adding four seed beads in that space so two will be on each side later):

smOV-8P-6G-8P-8G-8P-10G-12P-12G-14P-lgOV-8G-<u>C</u>-8G-lgOV-14P-12G-12P-10G-8P-8G-8P-6G-8P-smOV

4. Tape the other end and set it aside.

5. Cut two 16-inch pieces of Soft Flex to build the lower tier of the necklace. They will each follow the same pattern, so string them identically, from the center outward:

[C]-smOV-12P-12P-lgOV-10G-10P-8G-8P-6G-8P-smOV

6. Tape both ends to hold each of them for now. Set the strands aside.

7. To construct the centerpiece, open the 5mm jump ring and slip it onto the bail loops. Close it securely. Use a 3mm jump ring to connect it to the silver circle's lower hole, so your display is now hanging inside the open circle.

8. Open a 3mm jump ring and attach the centerpiece (through the circle's upper hole) to the center of the upper strand, with two seed beads on each side.

9. Next, join the lower strands to the circle. Add a large crimp bead at the end of one of them (where it's marked [C] on the pattern), and thread the wire around the circle, then back through the crimp bead and first oval bead. Crimp it securely and trim the excess wire. Repeat on the other side. Now your centerpiece is hanging from the upper strand and joined to the lower strands on each side.

10. Add the clasps and chains at the back—one to each strand. For the hook clasps, join them to the left-hand-side strands using crimp beads. Cut the chain into two 4-inch halves, and join each piece to one of the right-hand sides using crimp beads.

11. Wire-wrap the last two beads (one 8mm faceted glass bead and one 10mm pearl) into basic dangles, and attach one to each of the chain pieces as an ornament.

Triple-Tiered Filigree Necklace

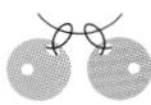

This delicate arrangement of blue glass and gold chain is designed by Adorn *magazine's Linda Permann.*

Length: adjustable

TIP Linda suggests, "Add the dangling charms while the necklace is hanging around something—a dress form, vase, or jewelry display piece."

YOU'LL NEED

- Pliers
- Thirteen 6mm fire-polished glass faceted beads
- 13 eyepins
- 12 drop heart filigree shapes
- 1 yard gold chain
- Four 6mm jump rings
- 1 clasp with three-bar spacer on each side
- 15 paddle-shaped headpins
- Fifteen 3mm fire-polished glass faceted beads

TO MAKE THE CENTER CHAIN

1. Place one 6mm bead on an eyepin, form a plain loop, and connect each loop to the wider side of one drop heart shape. Connect a 6mm bead to the other end of the drop heart shape, followed by another bead.

2. Continue working out from center in this fashion until you have connected six drop heart shapes and six beads on each side of the necklace. Be sure to connect all of the eyepins the same way so that the necklace lies relatively flat. Connect the final eyepin to the middle loop spacer bar on both sides.

3. Cut two lengths of chain: one 12½ inches and one 17½ inches. Use jump rings to connect the

shorter chain to the top loop in the spacer bar on both sides of the closure finding. Connect the larger chain in the same manner to the bottom loop of the spacer bar.

TO FINISH THE BOTTOM CHAIN

4. Make 15 beaded paddle-shaped headpins using 3mm beads. (Note: So that they hang in their best light, hold the paddle shape flat between your fingers or pliers and use a second pair of pliers to bend the wire directly backward, rather than to the side, to form a flat-front plain loop at the end of the pin.)

5. Find the center link of the long chain and attach the beaded pin. Spacing as desired, add seven beaded pins to each side of the chain. (It is easiest to space them by counting links on the chain rather than using a measurement.) Attach all of the pins in the same manner so they hang evenly.

Woven Collar Necklace

These necklace designs use the same simple but eye-catching pattern and directions from the bead-weaving techniques section on pages 25 and 26. You'll create the central design working from one side to the other, following a symmetrical pattern with dangling charms or beads all along the lower edge. These pieces also fit nicely because they're adjustable in length.

TECHNIQUES

- **Bead weaving**
  All
- **Crimp beads**
  All
- **Wrapped loops**
  All
- **Plain loops**
  All

TIP Experiment with different combinations of beads so the top and bottom halves of each diamond-shaped section are about the same length across. In the first necklace, I used the larger cubes above to "balance" the width of the drops below.

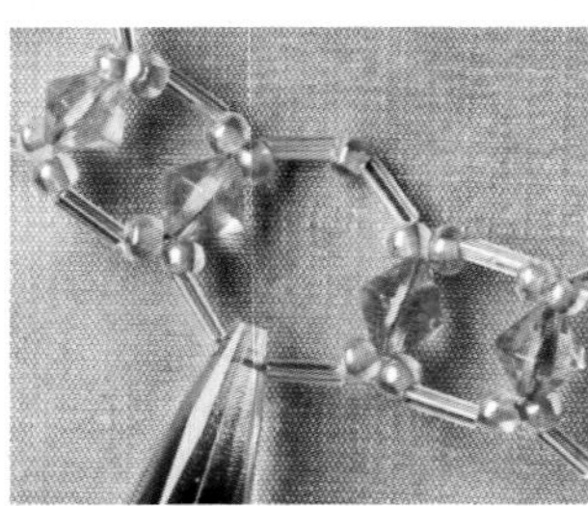

Caribbean Collar Necklace

Blue and green African trade beads dangle from a mix of clear, lime green, and blue glass beads.

Length: adjustable

YOU'LL NEED

- Pliers
- 6 inches of large chain
- 3 feet of Soft Flex wire
- 2 large crimp beads
- Clear 8/0 seed beads (s)
- 18 small green rounds (these will be the connectors) (G)
- Nine ¼-inch blue glass cubes (b)
- 9 African trade beads in a teardrop shape (I used alternating shades of blue and green) (T)
- Sixteen ⅛-inch lime green glass cubes (g)
- Clasp

NOTE: This pattern consists of nine segments and uses a glass drop ornament on all the odd-numbered ones and a small cube on the evens.

1. Cut the chain into 2-inch and 4-inch pieces. Fold the Soft Flex in half and slip the last link of the 2-inch chain onto it. Put a crimp bead over both ends of the wire, slide it all the way down, and crimp it closed. You now have two equal-length pieces of wire to bead on. Think of the current upper one as A and the current lower one as B.

2. Begin your pattern by adding several beads to each strand to form the sides. For this piece, string three seed beads on each strand.

3. Add a green round to A and then slip B through it, coming in the side that A exited. Pull the two tails tight so that the green round is neatly holding the first few beads in place. A will now be lower and B upper since they have crossed inside the large cube.

4. Add two seed beads, a large blue cube, and two seed beads to B (currently the upper strand). Add two seed beads, a teardrop trade bead, and two more seed beads to A (currently the lower strand). Then slip both wires through a green round as you did in step 3. You now have your first segment created.

5. Make the second segment, which will not have a teardrop bead. Add two seed beads, a small lime green cube, and then two more seed beads to each strand. Then slip both wires through a green round as you did in step 3 to connect them.

6. Continue until you have nine teardrop segments strung, with small cube segments in between each one. Add three seed beads to each strand, then add a crimp bead on both strands.

7. Slip the last link of the second piece of chain onto each wire, then bring the wires back through the crimp bead. Slip one piece of wire through each of the beaded strands and pull the tail through so the design is taut and symmetrical. Crimp the bead closed and trim each of the wire tails.

8. Attach a clasp to the shorter piece of chain. Create a basic bead dangle with a small lime green cube and attach that to the longer piece of chain.

PATTERN (remember, this alternates between strands A and B)

Upper: s-s-s-G-s-s-b-s-s-G-s-s-g-s-s-G-s-s-b-s-s-G-s-s-g-s-s-G-s-s-b-s-s-G-s-s-g-s-s-G-s-s-b-s-s-G-s-s-g-s-s-G-s-s-b-s-s-G-s-s-g-s-s-G-s-s-b-s-s-G-s-s-gs-s-G-s-s-b-s-s-G-s-s-g-s-s-G-s-s-b-s-s-G-s-s-g s-s-G-s-s-b-s-s-G-s-s-s

Lower: s-s-s-G-s-s-T-s-s-G-s-s-g-s-s-G-s-s-T-s-s-G-s-s-g-s-s-G-s-s-T-s-s-G-s-s-g-s-s-G-s-s-T-s-s-G-s-s-g-s-s-G-s-s-T-s-s-G-s-s-g-s-s-G-s-s-T-s-s-G-s-s-g-s-s-G-s-s-T-s-s-G-s-s-gs-s-G-s-s-T-s-s-G-s-s-g-s-s-G-s-s-T-s-s-G-s-s-g s-s-G-s-s-T-s-s-G-s-s-s

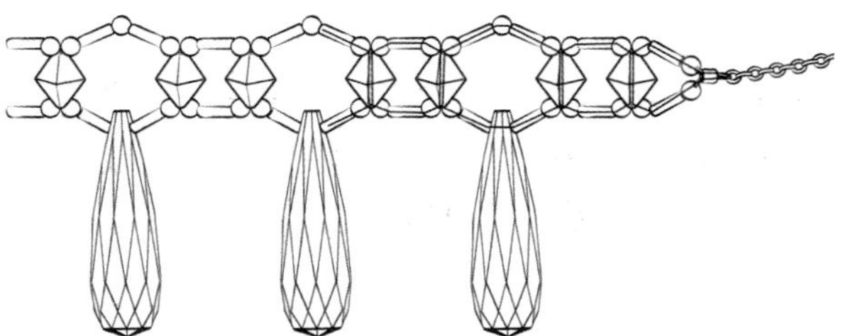

Diamonds and Drops Collar Necklace

These elongated pink drops match their narrow pink chain.

Length: adjustable

YOU'LL NEED

- Pliers
- 8 inches of pink chain
- Clasp
- Five 3mm jump rings
- 2 large soldered rings
- 1 inch of 20-gauge wire
- 13 pink diamond-shaped glass beads (D) (these will be the connectors)
- 3 feet of Soft Flex wire
- 2 large crimp beads
- 8/0 pink seed beads (s)
- ¼-inch pink bugle beads (b)
- 5 pink drops (P)

NOTE: Use the same basic technique and method as for the Caribbean Collar to make this design. This pattern will alternate between a plain segment and a segment with a bead drop, beginning and ending with two plain segments.

1. Cut the chain into two pieces: one 3 inches long and one 5 inches long. Add a hook clasp to the end of the 3-inch piece. Set it aside for now—you'll add it to the end of the necklace.

2. Cut the 5-inch chain into three pieces: one 3 inches long and two 1 inch long. Use jump rings to add the large soldered rings to the chain, connecting the pieces in this order: (end) 1 inch of chain-ring-1 inch of chain-ring-3 inches of chain (necklace).

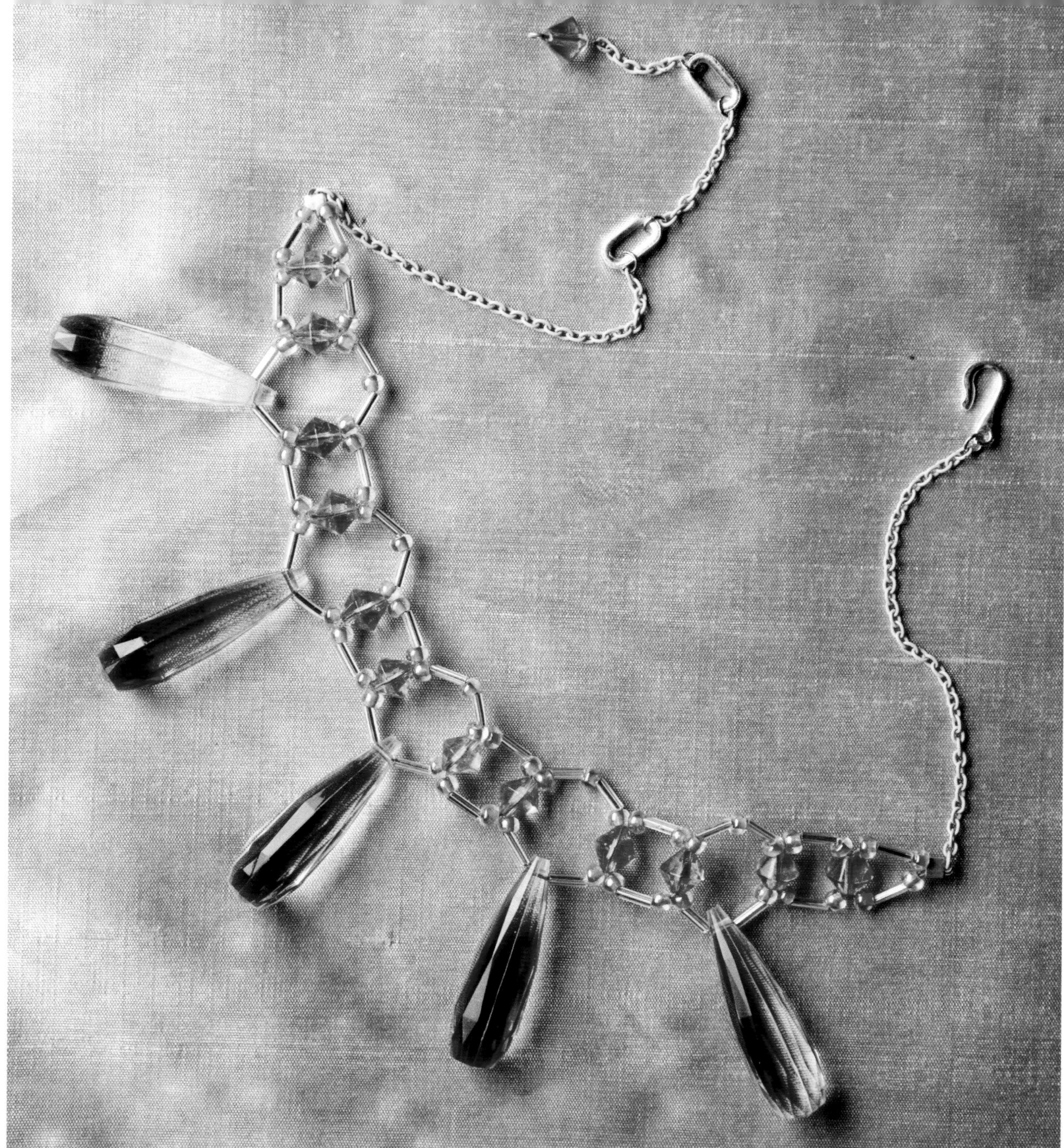

3. Use the wire and a pink diamond bead to make a plain loop bead dangle, and attach it to the last loop of the piece of chain on the 1-inch segment side.

4. Start your necklace with this embellished chain, bringing the Soft Flex through the last loop of the chain on the 3-inch side.

5. Follow the same basic directions given for the Caribbean Collar to finish constructing your necklace.

PATTERN

Upper: s-b-s-D-s-b-s-D-s-b-s-b-s-D-s-b-s-D-s-b-s-b-s-D-s-b-s-D-s-b-s-b-s-D-s-b-s-D-s-b-s-b-s-D-s-b-s-D-s-b-s-b-s-D-s-b-s-D-s-b-s

Lower: s-b-s-D-s-b-s-D-s-b-P-b-s-D-s-b-s-D-s-b-P-b-s-D-s-b-s-D-s-b-P-b-s-D-s-b-s-D-s-b-P-b-s-D-s-b-s-D-s-b-P-b-s-D-s-b-s-D-s-b-s

Stars and Sparkles Collar Necklace

Sophisticated silver stars are highlights in a shiny black design. Length: adjustable

YOU'LL NEED

- Craft glue
- Pliers

- 9 silver star charms (S)
- 9 tiny black flat-backed rhinestones
- Ten 3mm jump rings
- 7 inches of thin chain
- Clasp
- Twenty-five 6mm black crystals (B) (these will be the connectors when underlined as B)
- 3 large soldered rings
- 3 feet of Soft Flex wire
- 2 large crimp beads
- ¼-inch black bugle beads (b)
- Eighteen 3mm black faceted rounds (r)
- 24-gauge wire

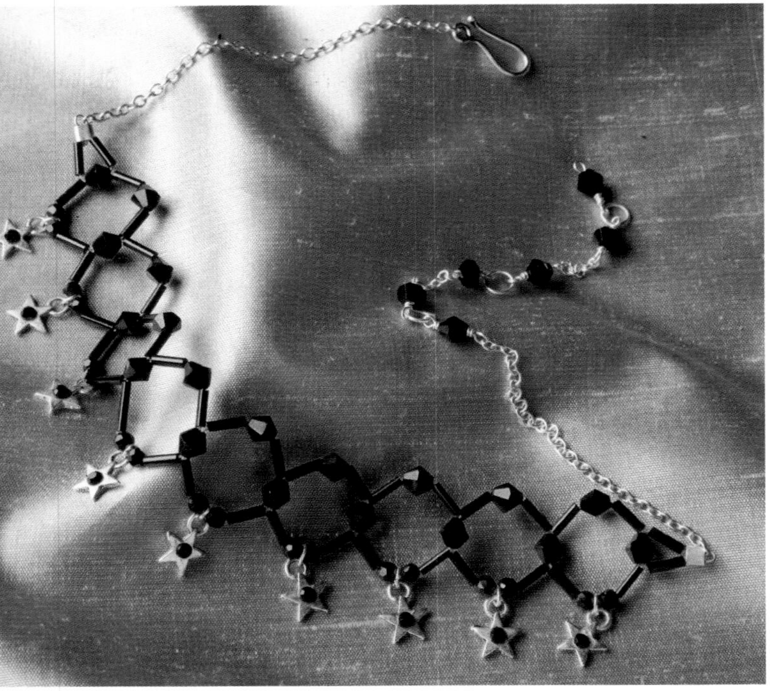

1. Lay the silver star charms out on a work surface, and glue a tiny black rhinestone to each one. Let them dry completely. Put each one on a 3mm jump ring and close the ring—when you bead them into the design, you'll slip the wire through each ring so the stars face front.

2. Cut the chain into two 3-inch pieces and two ½-inch pieces. Add the hook clasp to one 3-inch piece of chain and set it aside for now.

3. Form a basic bead dangle with one 6mm crystal, joining it to a large soldered ring. This will eventually be at the end of the necklace. Make five double-looped bead connectors with 6mm crystals, but don't complete the wraps yet.

4. Lay out the second side of the chain in this order: (end) dangle-soldered ring-bead connector-½ inch of chain-bead connector-soldered ring-bead connector-½ inch of chain-bead connector-soldered ring-bead connector-3 inches of chain (necklace). Complete all the wraps to connect each piece. You will begin the necklace with the clasp end of the chain and finish it with this longer embellished piece of chain, joining it at the 3-inch chain end so the dangle hangs at the outside.

5. Follow the same basic directions given for the Caribbean Collar to finish constructing your necklace (see p. 100).

PATTERN

Upper: b-B-b-B-b-B-b-B-b-B-b-B-b-B-b-B-b-B-b-B-b-B-b-B-b-B-b-B-b-B-b-B-b-B-b-B-b-B-b-B-b-B-b

Lower: b-B-b-r-S-r-b-B-b-r-S-r-b-B-b-r-S-r-b-B-b-r-S-r-b-B-b-r-S-r-b-B-b-r-S-r-b-B-b-r-S-r-b-B-b-r-S-r-b-B-b-r-S-r-b-B-b

Vintage Pin Necklace

This two-stranded necklace is built around a pretty vintage brooch with plenty of sparkle. This is a flexible design—use beads in the sizes and colors of your choice to create your own unique necklace.

TECHNIQUES

- **Plain loops**
  All
- **Wrapped loops**
  All

TIP Find gorgeous vintage brooches at flea markets, thrift stores, or on eBay—or look for family costume jewelry to transform into a modern heirloom. It's fine to use a brooch with a broken pinback for your necklace—just be sure to clip any jagged parts off the back of the piece. You can sand down any rough edges. If the brooch has an intact pin attached, you can leave it on if you like, as I did to make the Perfect Clarity Necklace (p. 106).

TIP Use a clear seed bead on either side of each larger bead in the design.

Vintage Glamour Necklace

Faceted glass and Lucite beads in assorted blues and greens, edged with clear seed beads, echo the tones of the pin, and a matching clip earring is wired into one strand as well. I used a two-stranded clasp from another costume jewelry necklace to finish the piece.

Length: 16 inches

YOU'LL NEED

- Pliers
- Beading board
- Velvet display (optional)

- A vintage brooch about 3 inches across
- A matching clip earring or other costume piece, approximately 1½ inches across (or 2 more beads*)

- A total of 18 beads for the side strands (*or 20 if you don't use a clip earring):

  Four 12mm faceted beads in color #1 (I used light green Lucite)

  One 10mm, two 8mm, and four 6mm faceted beads in color #1 (I used olive green glass)

  Three 8mm faceted beads in color #2 (I used light blue Lucite)

  Four 6mm faceted beads in color #2 (I used sky blue Lucite)
- 24-gauge sterling silver wire
- 8 to 12 inches of medium-weight sterling silver chain
- Clear seed beads
- Two-strand clasp (I used a jeweled vintage clasp)
- Four 3mm sterling silver jump rings

CREATING THE BEADED STRANDS FOR THE TWO TIERS

1. Arrange the brooch and beads on the beading board like the pictured example. If you are using more than one color family (like the blues and greens in the version here), arrange them so they alternate sizes and shades or tones, as shown.

2. Cut eighteen 3-inch pieces of sterling silver wire, which will form the wrapped loops around each bead, and six 4-inch pieces of wire, which will form the structural loops on the brooch and earring.

3. Cut the chain into these lengths: ten ½-inch pieces, two 1¼-inch pieces, and two 1½-inch pieces.

4. Now you'll create the inner strand of the necklace: for the first half, take a ½-inch piece of chain and join it to the first half of a wrapped loop. Add a seed bead, an 8mm bead, and another seed bead to the wire, then close the other end of the wrapped loop. This will be the first bead on the strand—remember, you'll always use a seed bead before and after each of the larger ones.

5. Next, add a 12mm bead, joining it with a wrapped loop, and then a 6mm bead with a wrapped loop, leaving the second half of the last loop open. Join a ½-inch piece of chain to the bead strand, closing the last loop.

6. Add an 8mm bead to the chain with a wrapped loop, leaving the second half open. Now join it to a 1½-inch piece of chain and finish the wrapped loop.

7. Repeat steps 4–6 to create the identical second half of the inner strand. Set these two pieces aside for now.

8. Now you'll create the outer tiers of the necklace, starting with the left half. Take a ½-inch piece of chain and add the next three beads, joining each of them with wrapped loops: a 6mm bead, a 12mm bead, and a 6mm bead—but don't close the last wrapped loop yet. Slip a ½-inch piece of chain onto the open loop and then finish the wrap.

9. Add a 10mm bead and an 8mm bead to the other end of the chain, joining them with wrapped loops, and leave the last one open. Make sure that this bead section is about as long as your clip earring (if you're using one).

10. Add a ½-inch piece of chain, close the loop, then join the other end of the chain to a 6mm bead and add a 1¼-inch piece of chain, joining the pieces with wrapped loops. This will be the left half of the second tier.

11. If you are *not* using a clip earring piece in your design, cut two more 3-inch pieces of wire and repeat steps 8–10 to make the identical right half of the second tier.

12. If you *are* using a clip earring or other vintage piece, repeat steps 8 and 10 (without repeating 9), and set the two pieces of beaded chain aside (which will become the last strang after you wire the earring in).

13. Take the four strands and arrange them on the beading board with the brooch again, so that the beaded ends are closest to the center and the longer chain ends are farthest away, where the clasp will be.

ADDING THE BROOCH (AND EARRING)

14. Turn the brooch over so the wrong side is facing up. Find the four places on the edges where you will join each of the strands to the brooch (as shown). Starting at the upper left "corner" of the brooch, use a 4-inch piece of wire to form the first half of a wrapped loop closely around one element, and leave it open. Repeat for the other three "corners," as shown on p. 104.

15. Eye each of the corners to see how far the join is from the edge. You'll fill that space with clear seed beads so the wire-wrapped beads will show at the edge of the brooch. The corners may need different lengths of beaded wire to make up for any differences if the brooch isn't symmetrical, like mine. Place seed bead(s) on the first wire until they reach the edge of the brooch, and form another wrapped loop above the bead(s), slipping strand 1 onto the loop before you close it.

16. Repeat to attach strands 2, 3, and 4 at each "corner" of the brooch with the completed wrapped loops, making sure that the seed bead sections make the necklace design even on the beading board.

17. If you are using a clip earring element, find two places to wire it to the chain (as you did in step 14 with the brooch). Form a close-fitting wrapped loop at each end. Place a seed bead on the first wire and form another wrapped loop above the bead, slipping the longer piece of strand 4 onto the loop before you close it.

18. Repeat to join the earring to the shorter piece of strand 4.

ADDING THE CLASP

19. Open one of the jump rings and use it to attach strand 1 to the clasp. Repeat with the other three strands and jump rings.

Vintage Glamour Necklace

PATTERN

Inner strand left to right: Clasp-1½-inch chain-8mm-½-inch chain-6mm-12mm-8mm-brooch-8mm-12mm-6mm-½-inch chain-8mm-1½-inch chain-clasp

Outer strand left to right: Clasp-1½-inch chain-6mm-½-inch chain-8mm-10mm-½-inch chain-6mm-12mm-6mm-½-inch chain-brooch-½-inch chain-6mm-12mm-6mm-½-inch chain-clip earring-½-inch chain-6mm-1½-inch chain-clasp

Perfect Clarity Necklace

The crystal starburst connects a sleek neckwire and embellished chain for unexpected and asymmetrical sparkle.

Length: 15 inches

YOU'LL NEED

- Beading board
- Marker
- Pliers
- Velvet display

- One close-fitting neckwire
- A vintage brooch
- 24-gauge wire
- Assorted faceted crystal beads to match the brooch (I used 18, ranging from 6mm to 12mm)
- Medium-weight chain
- Clasp
- Eleven jump rings
- Clear seed beads
- Thin chain
- Three star charms

INNER (NECKWIRE) TIER

1. Set your neckwire on the beading board, and place your brooch on it, off to the right of center: If the circle were a clock face, your brooch would be at

the 5 o'clock position. Mark that spot so you know where to place it when you start building the design.

2. Cut a 16-inch piece of wire and begin wrapping it at the 9 o'clock position of the neckwire, making sure the tail is to the back. Wrap three times and then slip one faceted bead onto the wire until it's all the way at the base of the wire. Loop the tail through again, back to front, to catch the bead. Wrap it securely in place with the wire tail.

3. Add your next bead about ¼ inch farther down the neckwire (wrapping two or three times between them), securing it the same way. Continue adding beads until you have a total of five on the wire.

4. Now you'll add the brooch at the place you marked, wrapping the wire around the first "corner" (as detailed in the Vintage Glamour instructions on pp. 104–105) so it's securely in place. Wrap the wire around the neckwire as you go so the corner is well joined. Next, find a second corner and wrap that in the same way, so the brooch is attached in two places—this will help it hang better.

5. Repeat the same techniques from steps 2 and 3 until you have two more beads on the neckwire. Finish at the 3 o'clock position with three secure wraps, and cut the tail so it's to the back of the wire.

OUTER (CHAIN) TIER

6. Next, you'll cut the medium-weight chain into the lengths you'll need to construct this section: nine 3-link (⅛-inch) pieces, one 1-inch piece, and one 1½-inch piece. You'll also cut eleven 2-inch pieces of wire to wrap the beads.

7. Lay your beads out on the beading board as shown in the lower-tier pattern, left to right.

8. You'll start with the 1-inch piece of chain to create the upper left side of the design. Attach one half of the clasp at one end, using a jump ring. Join the first half of a wrapped loop to the other end. Add a seed bead, a faceted bead, and another seed bead to the wire, then slip a three-link piece of chain on the other wrapped loop before you close it. This will be the first bead on the strand—remember, you'll always use a seed bead before and after each of the larger ones.

9. Continue beading in the same way, alternating a wire-wrapped bead with a short length of chain, until you have seven beads, ending on a bead, and leaving the last loop open. Set this section of the chain aside for now.

10. Using a jump ring, attach the other half of the clasp to one end of the 1½-inch piece of chain. Repeat steps 7 and 8 to alternate attaching four beads and three chain lengths, starting and ending with a bead. Leave the last loop open and set it aside.

ATTACHING THE BROOCH AND ORNAMENTS

11. Look at the back of your brooch and find two "corners" to attach this tier to, one on each side. Cut two 3-inch pieces of wire, and form a wrapped loop around each corner. If need be, you can add seed beads (as in the Vintage Glamour version) to the wire to make up more space, or just wrap it without beads. Finish the second wrap on each corner so there's a loop on the outer edge of the brooch.

12. Arrange the necklace on the beading board or a velvet display, and finish wrapping the loops on the open ends of the chain tiers to the corners so the necklace sits nicely. If you need to add or subtract length, do that now—it's least noticeable in the back, on the plain stretches of chain.

13. Use jump rings to attach a clasp to the back of the chain when the length feels right. My chain measured 16½ inches, including the brooch.

14. Cut a ¼-inch piece, a 2¼-inch piece, and a 3-inch piece of the thinner chain. You'll use these to attach the dangling stars to the brooch and bead links at the front of the necklace, working right to left.

15. Open nine small jump rings and set six aside for now. Take the first three and attach one to each star charm, joining a charm to the end of each piece of chain. Close the jump rings.

16. Take the 2¼-inch piece of chain and use another jump ring to connect the open end to a loop at the bottom right-hand corner of the brooch. Slip another jump ring onto a link about 1 inch down, and use that one to connect it to a loop at the bottom left-hand side of the brooch, letting the chain hang below in a scallop shape. Slip another jump ring onto a link ¼ inch from the star charm, and connect it to the loop on the left of the first bead in the chain so that the star dangles below.

17. Slip a jump ring onto the open end of the 3-inch piece of chain, and connect it to the loop to the right of the second bead in the chain. Add another jump ring to a link about 2 inches down, and connect it to the loop to the right of the third bead in the chain. Let the star charm dangle freely below this connection.

18. Last, use a jump ring to join the ¼-inch chain to the loop to the left of the third bead in the chain. All three star charms will swing freely at different lengths below the beads and brooch.

PATTERN

Neckwire tier (wrapped beads are about ½ inch apart): Five faceted beads-brooch-two faceted beads

Chain tier: Clasp ring-1-inch chain-bead-⅛-inch chain-bead-⅛-inch chain-bead-⅛-inch chain-bead-⅛-inch chain-bead-⅛-inch chain-bead-⅛-inch chain-bead-brooch-bead-⅛-inch chain-bead-⅛-inch chain-bead-⅛-inch chain-bead-1½-inch chain-clasp

Fiery Heart Necklace

I paired wine-red beads from a broken necklace of my grandmother's with bright orange rounds to set off an unusual sparkly brooch.

Length: adjustable

YOU'LL NEED

- Pliers
- Beading board
- 24-gauge gold wire
- Elongated/oval gold chain
- Five deep red oval faceted beads (I used two 14mm, two 12mm, and one 10mm)
- Two 12mm orange angular faceted beads
- Fifteen 4mm bright orange faceted round beads
- Amber seed beads
- A vintage brooch
- Clasp
- One 5mm jump ring

1. Cut fifteen 1½-inch pieces of wire (which you'll use to wrap the 4mm beads) and seven 4-inch pieces of wire (for the larger beads). Also cut 18 single links of chain (if you are using a smaller link chain, cut short pieces that are about ⅛ inch long), two 5-link pieces of chain, and one 12-link piece of chain. Set these aside for now.

2. Arrange your beads on a beading board in the pattern given on the facing page, with the brooch itself at the center. Begin the pattern by creating a basic bead dangle with the 10mm oval bead and attaching it to a 5-link piece of chain. Note: This will be your only bead dangle; every other bead will be a double-wrapped connector. Also keep in mind that the larger beads will each have a seed bead before and after them and the 4mm beads won't.

3. Connect a 4mm bead to the other end of the 5-link chain. Before closing the second loop, connect it to the 12-link piece of chain.

4. Use a 4mm bead connector to link the other end of the 12-link chain with a single link of chain.

5. Follow the pattern given, with a single link of chain between each wrapped bead. Stop at the center where you'll add the pendant, ending on a 4mm bead with a closed loop.

6. Create the second half of the chain, starting with the center and work your way to the end, finishing with a clasp.

PENDANT

7. Arrange the brooch as you'd like it to hang, clipping away any sharp edges on the back.

8. Cut a 4-inch piece of wire, and create a double-wrapped loop-style hanger at the top of the brooch.

9. Open your jump ring and use it to connect the brooch hanger to each of the strands of beaded chain so your necklace hangs smoothly. Close it securely.

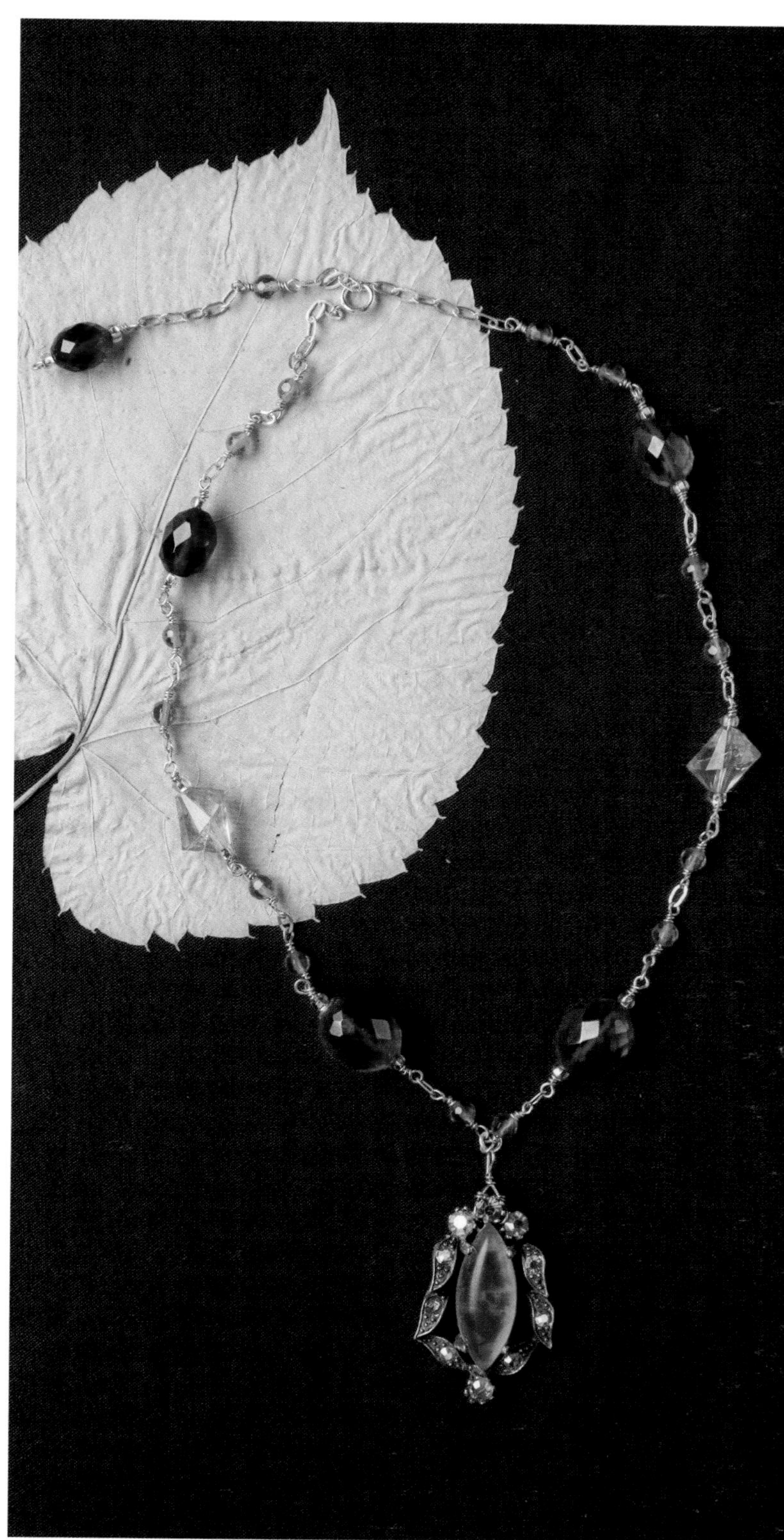

PATTERN: Remember, you'll place one link of chain between each bead—except where the 5-link or 12-link pieces are noted in bold, and at the very center where the pendant hangs.

10mm dangle-**5 links**-4mm-**12 links**-4mm-4mm-12mm-4mm-4mm-12mm angular-4mm-4mm-14mm-4mm-pendant-4mm-14mm-4mm-4mm-12mm angular-4mm-4mm-12mm-4mm-4mm-**5 links**-clasp

5 Pendants

Charming Pendant

This is one of the simplest pendant designs—a charm on a sleek chain or strand. The trick is to choose a piece that's worth spotlighting and to have fun with the details.

TECHNIQUES

- **Wrapped loops**
  All
- **Plain loops**
  Splashy Flower
- **Briolette wrapping**
  Teardrop
  Key to My Heart
- **Jump rings**
  All

TIP You can adapt this design to include all kinds of focal pieces. Drill a small hole in a vintage piece or another unusual trinket, and connect it to a chain for something that's truly one of a kind. If you don't have a drill setup at home, try your local hardware store or metal shop.

Teardrop Charming Pendant

This delicate faceted glass briolette on chain instantly draws the eye to the sparkle—it would be just as striking with a semiprecious piece.

Length: 16 inches

YOU'LL NEED

- Pliers
- Thin chain
- 24-gauge wire
- One horizontally drilled green glass briolette
- Two jump rings
- Clasp

1. Cut two 7-inch pieces of chain and one 4-inch piece of wire.
2. Thread the wire through the briolette, and form the first half of a wrapped loop on each side of it.
3. Slip one side of the wrapped loop onto the first link of the first piece of chain, and complete the wrap to join them. Repeat with the second piece of chain on the other side of the briolette. You may want to curve the wire up slightly (as shown on this piece).
4. Use the jump rings to attach the clasp to the chain.

Splashy Flower Charming Pendant

A bold black and red flower on a chunky chain makes a splashy statement.

Length: adjustable

YOU'LL NEED

- Pliers
- Drill
- A metal flower (I used a vintage pin component)
- 17 inches of medium-size chain
- 2 jump rings (depending on the size of your piece)
- Clasp (I made an S-clasp out of 18-gauge wire)
- 24-gauge wire
- One 12mm faceted bead
- 2 seed beads (optional)

1. Drill holes in two of the flower's petals about ⅛ inch from the edge. I chose the petals at roughly the 10 o'clock and 2 o'clock positions on a clock face.

2. Cut the chain into two pieces, one 10 inches long and one 7 inches long. Open both jump rings and connect one piece of chain to each side of the flower charm.

3. Add the clasp to the end of the shorter piece of chain.

4. Cut a 4-inch piece of wire, and make a plain loop at one end. Slip the 12mm bead onto it (with a seed bead above and below if desired), then form a wrapped loop above it, joining it to the longer piece of chain before completing the wrap.

Key to My Heart Charming Pendant

More than just a key, this pendant conveys a promise.

Length: 19 inches

YOU'LL NEED

- Pliers
- 1 large antique key
- 4 inches of 20-gauge wire
- 18 inches of large industrial chain
- 4 inches of 24-gauge wire
- Clasp (I made a hammered S-clasp out of 18-gauge wire)

1. Create a connector for the key by forming a double-wrapped loop above it with the 20-gauge wire. Connect it to a central link of the chain before closing the upper loop.

2. Add a clasp to one end of the chain.

Modern Drop Pendant

This pendant shares the clean lines and organic materials of the Modern Drop Earrings (p. 40). An asymmetrical embellishment adds interest in the first version, smooth turquoise pairs with soft leather in the second, and sleek mother-of-pearl combines with elegant faceted glass for an eye-catching floret design in the third.

TECHNIQUES

- **Wrapped loops**
  Wood
- **Bead stringing**
  Water Lily
- **Double-wrapped loops**
  Turquoise
- **Crimp clasp**
  Turquoise

TIP Play with scale—pair a delicate or lightweight piece with thin chain or cording, or a larger one with a heavier stringing material for a more masculine feel.

Wood Modern Drop Pendant

This pendant is beautifully organic: a sleek length of wood with two glossy carnelian bits on the side.

Length: 16½ inches

YOU'LL NEED

- Pliers
- Thin chain
- 24-gauge wire
- 2 small glass or semiprecious rounds
- 1 elongated wood drop (horizontally drilled)
- 2 jump rings
- Clasp

1. Cut three pieces of chain: one 4 inches long, one ½ inch long, and one 10 inches long.

2. Cut two 4-inch pieces of wire. Form the first half of a wrapped loop on either side of each round bead.

3. Use the ½-inch piece of chain to join the two wrapped beads, completing the wraps on those sides.

4. Slip the second half of one bead's outer loop onto the last link of the 4-inch piece of chain to join them. Complete the wrap.

5. Next, slip the other bead's outer loop onto the last link of the 10-inch piece of chain, and complete the wrap.

6. Feed the 10-inch piece of chain into the wood drop's drilled hole so it moves freely.

7. Use the jump rings to attach the clasp to the chain.

Turquoise Drop Pendant

This turquoise drop on a leather strand is perfect for him (or her).

Length: 16½ inches or to your liking.

YOU'LL NEED

- Pliers
- 20-gauge wire
- Small or medium-size semiprecious piece, drilled back to front
- Leather cord
- Large coil-style crimp-clasp

1. Cut a 4-inch piece of wire, and form double wrapped loop around the semiprecious piece so it faces forward.

2. Cut the leather cord to the desired length, and slip the wire loop onto it so it moves freely.

3. Place one crimp-clasp half on one end of the cord, and use your flat-nose pliers to crimp it firmly. Repeat with the other half on the opposite end of the cord.

Water Lily Drop Pendant

The creation of designer Tanja Alger, this classically feminine pendant unites mother-of-pearl and glass.

Length: 15½ inches

YOU'LL NEED

- Pliers
- Clear tape
- Soft Flex wire
- 6 silver seed beads
- Delicas in two colors (Tanja used matte black for the base and a sparkly pink to make the center of the necklace pop a little)
- 1 large colored glass bead
- 4 silver rosette spacer beads
- 3 tear-shaped abalone or mother-of-pearl flat beads
- Clasp
- 2 small crimp beads

1. Cut an 18-inch piece of Soft Flex wire, and put a piece of tape on one end. Put on three of the silver seed beads, and then 5¾ inches of delicas in your base color. Follow this with 26 delicas (about 1¼ inches) in your accent color.

2. To form the flower pattern in the center, first add the large glass bead. You'll now essentially be making a loop below and then back through this bead. Start with a single delica in your accent color. (This will hide the wire that's exposed as it bends around in a circle.) Follow this with a silver spacer, then alternate the three tear-shaped beads with the remaining three silver rosettes. Add one more single delica in the accent color, then reinsert the wire into your large glass bead. Pull this tight enough so that the flower shape forms and hangs nicely.

3. Add 26 more accent-color delicas (1¼ inches), followed by 5¾ inches of delicas in your base color and the remaining three silver seed beads.

4. Add a clasp to each end of the wire using crimp beads, and make sure that the wire tails are securely tucked in under the silver beads and the first few delicas.

Ribbon Choker

These pendants are all strung on ribbon for a pretty vintage sensibility—from the ultra-simple stars set off-center on filmy organdy to the splashy flower charm suspended from a narrow, bright satin ribbon and the cluster of assorted aqua trinkets on wide grosgrain.

TECHNIQUES

- **Crimp beads**
  Pink Floral
- **Jump rings**
  Pink Floral
  Lucky Dip
- **Hand-sewing**
  Twin Stars
- **Wrapped loops**
  Lucky Dip

TIP Pair delicate pieces with a lightweight ribbon or larger ones with a sleeker, sturdier one, but make sure your pendant isn't too heavy for the ribbon you've chosen.

TIP If you want to tie your ribbon in a bow, it's easier with a lightweight charm—a heavier one works much better with a metal clasp.

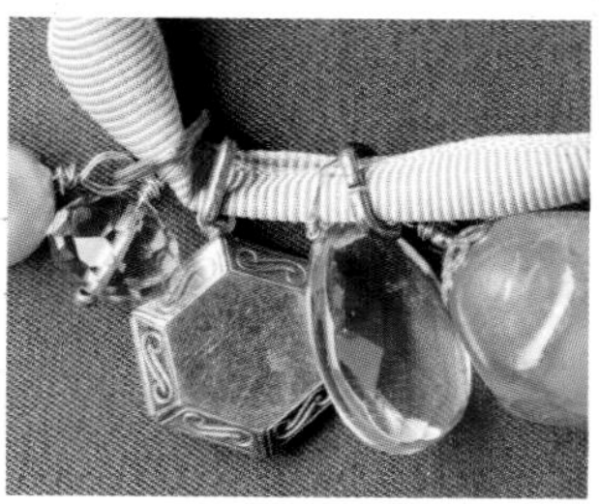

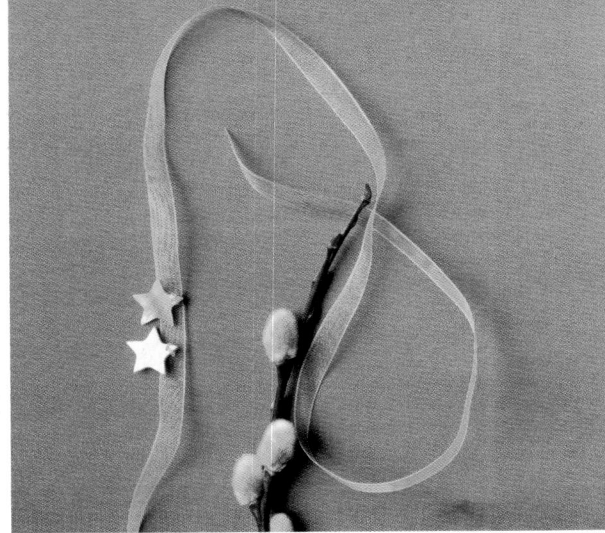

Twin Stars Ribbon Choker

Two mother-of-pearl stars cling to white organdy.

Length: adjustable

YOU'LL NEED
- Scissors
- Fray Check
- 2 straight pins
- Sewing needle and thread
- 36 inches of 3⁄8-inch-wide organdy ribbon
- Two small star charms

1. Trim both ends of the ribbon at a diagonal, and add a drop of Fray Check to protect the edges.

2. Measure the exact center of your ribbon, then mark 1¼ inches to the left of it with a straight pin (A). Measure another ½ inch to the left and mark that with a straight pin as well (B).

3. Thread your needle and begin to attach your first star charm at point A, at the center of the ribbon. Use at least four stitches to secure it, then tie a knot on the back and clip the thread.

4. Sew on the second star at B, close to the top edge so it's a little higher than the first one, in the same way.

5. Put a drop of Fray Check on each knot to seal it.

Pink Floral Ribbon Choker

A pretty metal vintage flower gets new life with a shiny rhinestone and a length of narrow satin ribbon.

Length: 15½ inches

YOU'LL NEED
- Scissors
- Pliers
- 1⁄8-inch-wide satin ribbon
- Vintage charm piece (I added a flat-backed rhinestone to a metal flower with craft glue) on a jump ring or soldered ring
- 2 large crimp beads
- Clasp

1. Cut 20 to 24 inches of ribbon and trim both ends at a steep diagonal. This will make it easier to thread the ribbon through the crimp beads.

2. Slip the vintage charm onto the ribbon. Now slip one crimp bead onto each end of the ribbon, pushing it down 3 to 4 inches.

3. Add the clasp to one side, and then double the ribbon back through the crimp bead, catching the clasp in the folded ribbon and making sure it isn't twisted but that it's lying flat.

4. Repeat step 3 to add the ring to the other side. Make sure the pendant ribbon is the right length.

5. Use flat-nose pliers to securely crimp both beads, then trim the excess ribbon tails with your scissors.

Lucky Dip Ribbon Choker

Fiona Gillespie created this choker with assorted blue and gold vintage charms on extra-wide grosgrain ribbon.

Length: adjustable

YOU'LL NEED

- Scissors
- Pliers
- Fray Check
- Hand-sewing needle

- ⅝-inch-wide grosgrain ribbon
- A few seed beads or crimp beads
- Vintage bead caps (optional)
- 28-gauge gold craft wire
- Assorted glass and plastic vintage beads and/or charms
- Large square base metal jump rings
- Embroidery floss

1. Cut the ribbon to the length you would like your necklace to be, including enough length to make a nice bow if you want.

2. Make the bead charms by threading a seed bead or vintage bead cap onto a piece of wire 6 to 8 inches long. Hold the ends of the wire, and let the seed bead or bead cap fall to the middle. Thread the two ends through a larger vintage bead you are using for your charm. The small bead or bead cap will keep the large bead from slipping off. Let the large bead sit on the small one or bead cap, and use your round-nose pliers to make a loop.

3. Attach the charms, such as the base metal locket Fiona used, and the bead charms to the jump rings.

4. Slide the jump rings onto the ribbon.

5. Trim the ends of the ribbon and apply a bit of Fray Check. Turn the ends under twice, approximately ⅛ inch each time.

6. Using the embroidery floss, sew the ends in place. You can wear the charms all together in a cluster or separate them along the thick ribbon, which will keep them apart if you prefer.

Circle Deluxe Pendant

This is a gorgeous, modern circle defined by its perimeter or its interior negative space. Whether it's semiprecious stone, metal, or shell, a round piece suspended by clean lines is a timeless design to wear casually or for a formal occasion.

TECHNIQUES

- **Double-wrapped loop**
  Jade
- **Knotting**
  Knotted
- **Bead tips**
  Knotted
- **Jump rings**
  Shell

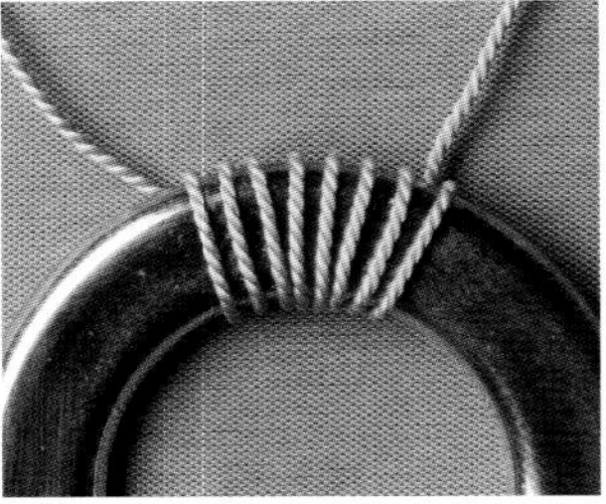

Jade Circle Deluxe Pendant

This smooth, glasslike jade circle reflects the spare neckwire it hangs from.

YOU'LL NEED

- Pliers
- 20-gauge wire
- 1 mod open circle piece
- Neckwire

1. Cut a 5-inch piece of wire and form a double-wrapped loop to connect the top of the circle to the neckwire, leaving the top loop open after forming the first half.

2. Slip the open loop onto the neckwire and complete the wrap, making sure the wire ends are tucked to the back of the coil so they don't show.

Knotted Circle Deluxe Pendant

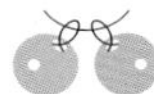  

This open metal circle hangs from a series of knotted loops on pink silk cord.

Length: 16 inches

YOU'LL NEED

- Pliers
- Glue
- 1 package of prethreaded silk beading cord (I used size 8, but just be sure the cord is sturdy enough to support your pendant)
- 2 bead tips
- 1 metal open circle (mine was 1½ inches across)
- Clasp

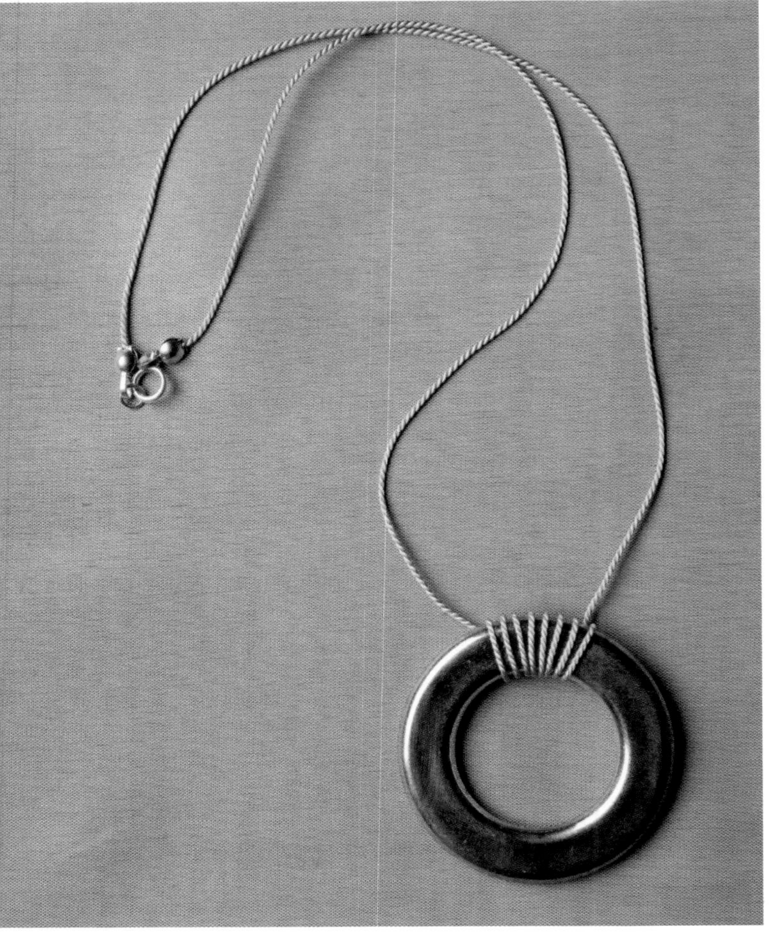

1. Unwrap and stretch your silk cord. To remove any fold marks, dampen it with cool water and let it dry hanging straight overnight.
2. Tie a knot 2 inches from the end of the cord. Slip a bead tip onto the cord.
3. Measure 7½ inches down from the knot, and place the circle charm there. Tie a slip knot around the circle so that the knot sits on the outside edge of the circle. Pull it taut so it clings to the circle.
4. Loop the silk cord around the front of the circle once, and tie another knot parallel to the first one. Continue knotting the same way until you have eight strands knotted onto the top of the circle. Double-knot the last one to secure it.
5. Slip a bead tip onto the cord, and measure 7½ inches above the circle. Tie a knot at that spot.
6. Clip the excess thread just above both knots and secure them with a drop of glue. Close the bead tips over the knots, then add a clasp to the hooks.
7. Gently move your row of knots to the back of the circle pendant so they're completely hidden from the front.

Shell Circle Deluxe Pendant

This is a stunning, classic pendant: an oversize white shell circle on thin, delicate chain.

Length: 18 inches

YOU'LL NEED

- Pliers
- 19 inches of thin chain
- 1 large shell circle piece, drilled (mine was 2½ inches across)
- Clasp
- Two 3mm jump rings

1. Pass both ends of the chain through the hole in the shell, front to back. Slip the ends through the loop before you pull it through. Tighten the slip knot so that the circle hangs securely.

2. Attach the clasp to each end of the chain with the jump rings.

Multi-Drop Pendant

This striking, spare design pairs small accent beads with spiky wires in a variety of configurations—tiny organic shapes hanging in pairs from matte vintage chain, glossy rounds suspended from a shiny neckwire, and elongated white glass pieces.

TECHNIQUES

- **Plain loops**
  Amber
  Color Pop
- **Wrapped loops**
  Color Pop
- **Jump rings**
  Amber
- **Crimp beads**
  Milk Glass

TIP Experimenting with different lengths and materials while retaining the short-long-medium pattern of working in threes is a versatile way to spotlight these multi-drops.

TIP Use a pair of nylon-lined flattening pliers to keep your wires and headpins straight—just slip the pliers over the wire once or twice to align it. Half-hard sterling silver or gold-filled wire will keep its shape much better than craft wire will, too.

TIP Working on your pendants while they're on a 3-D velvet jewelry display is helpful in seeing how they'll drape, rather than if you work on them stretched out on a flat surface.

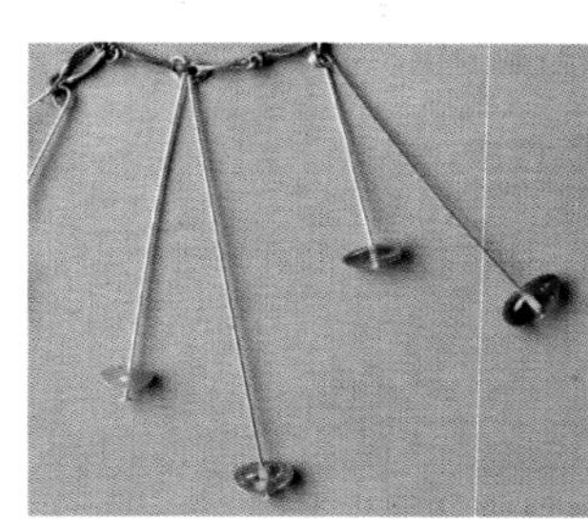
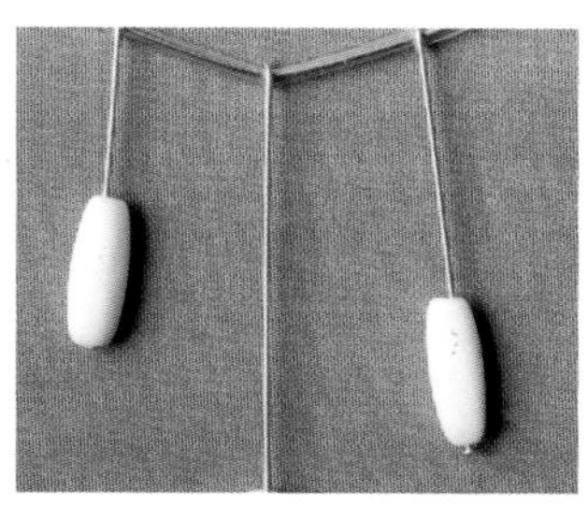

Amber Multi-Drop Pendant

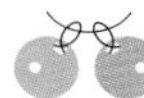   

This unusual pendant includes a flurry of spiky gold wires and amber bits.

Length: 15½ inches

YOU'LL NEED

- Pliers
- Velvet jewelry display neck
- Thin chain with links that will hold two drops each
- Clasp
- Two 3mm jump rings
- Six 24-gauge headpins
- 6 small organically shaped or round beads

1. Cut a 15-inch piece of chain, and add the clasp to the ends using jump rings.

2. Cut the six headpins into the following lengths:

   One ½ inch long (vs)

   Two 1¼ inches long (s)

   Two 1¾ inches long (m)

   One 2 inches long (l)

3. Slip one bead onto each headpin, and form a small plain loop at the top of each pin. Gently open each plain loop.

4. Place the finished chain on the velvet display so you can see how the multi-drops will hang. Choose a link in the center of the chain, and slip the loops of two of the drops in it, (L to R) m and l.

5. Choose a link ¾ inch to the left, and place two of the drops in it, vs and s.

6. Choose a link ¾ inch to the right of the center, and place two of the drops in it, m and s.

7. Once you like the configuration, close each plain loop securely.

PATTERN: vs-s-m-l-m-s

Color Pop Multi-Drop Pendant

These green mother-of-pearl and glass drops are fun and eye-catching.

Length: 16 inches (adjustable)

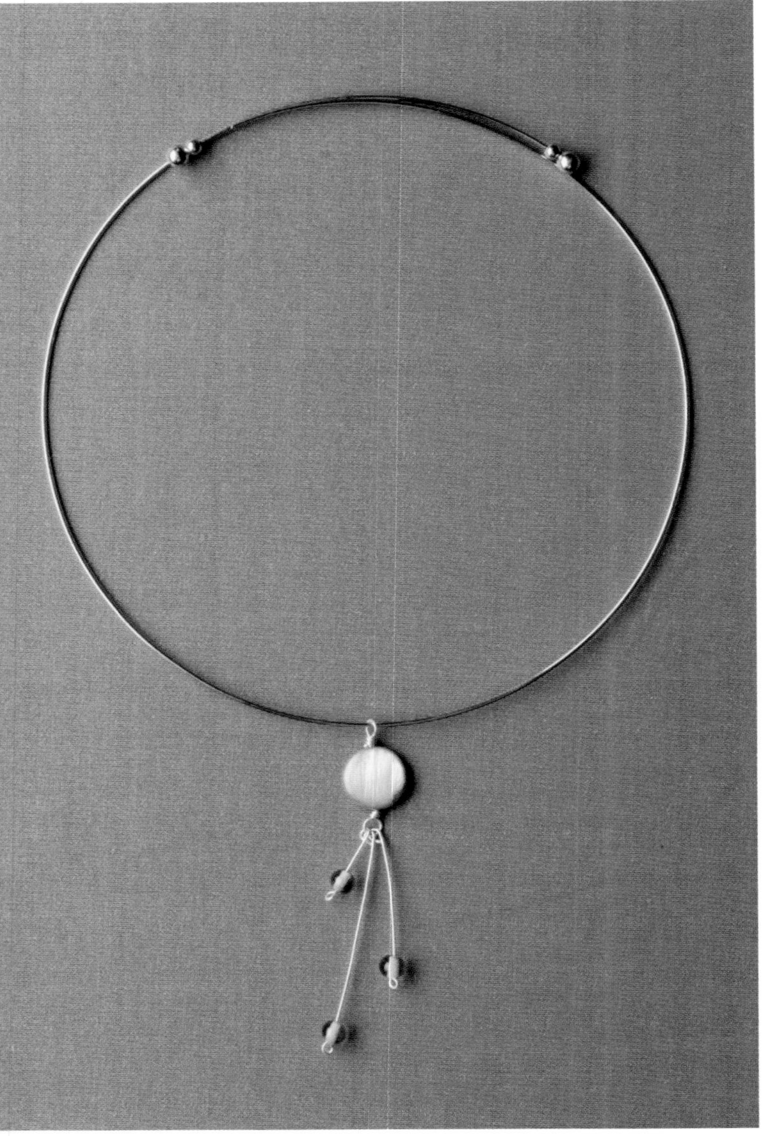

YOU'LL NEED

- Pliers
- 24-gauge wire
- One 8mm mother-of-pearl disk (vertically drilled)
- 3 small glass rounds
- Neckwire

1. Cut your wire into one 3-inch piece, plus the following lengths:

   One ¾ inch long (s)

   One 1¼ inches long (m)

   One 1¾ inches long (l)

2. Form a large wrapped loop at one end of the 3-inch piece, and slip the disk onto the wire. Set aside for now.

3. Form a plain loop at one end of each of the other pieces of wire. Slip one glass bead onto each one. Form a plain loop at the top of each piece and open it out.

4. Place the three drops on the large wrapped loop from step 2 in this order (L to R): s, l, m. Close the plain loops to secure them. (See p. 44 for details.)

5. Form the first half of a wrapped loop above the disk bead, slipping it onto the neckwire before completing the wrap. Make sure the large loop with the multi-drops is facing front.

Milk Glass Multi-Drop Pendant

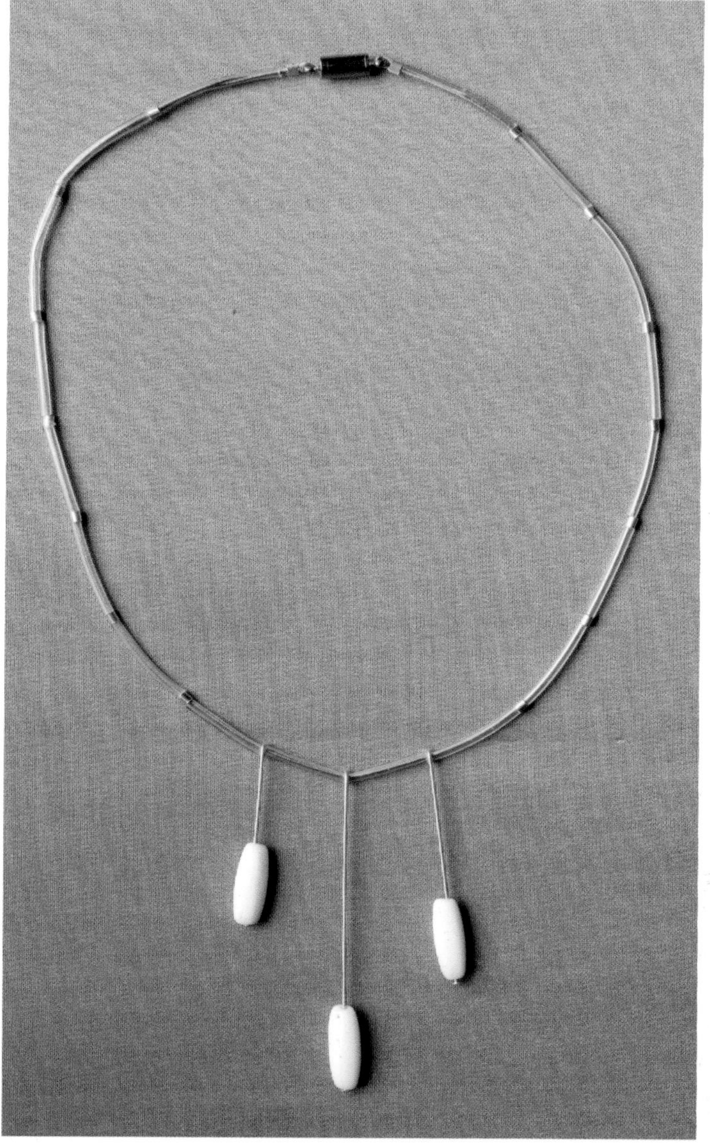

The pendant's pretty white glass drops are suspended from a pattern of crimp beads and plastic tubing for an unexpected look.

Length: 15 inches

YOU'LL NEED

- Pliers
- Three 2½-inch headpins
- 3 elongated beads (I used ⅝-inch white glass pieces)
- 24 inches of Soft Flex wire
- 18 pieces of plastic tubing, each roughly ¾ inch long
- 16 small sterling crimp beads
- Clasp

1. Cut one headpin to 1½ inches long and one to 1⅞ inches long, leaving one uncut. Place one elongated bead on each, and form a flat-front plain loop at the end of each one.

2. Slip the longest drop onto the Soft Flex wire. Add a piece of plastic tubing to each side of it. Next, add the shortest drop to the left side of the center drop and the middle-length drop to the right side.

3. Add another piece of plastic tubing and then a crimp bead to each side. Continue alternating the tubing and crimp beads on both sides until your piece measures the desired length. End with a crimp bead on each side.

4. Add a clasp to each end, and slip the wire back through the crimp bead and the last piece of tubing. Close the outer crimp beads normally, and trim the excess wire.

Spaces and Sparkles Pendant

This pretty, feminine design gets its sparkle from faceted beads that catch the light—Lucite, glass, and semiprecious. Like the Duo Earrings (p. 33), each pendant pairs two swinging components, but in this design the one above is always smaller than the one below.

TECHNIQUES

- **Plain loops**
  Citrine
  Olive
- **Wrapped loops**
  All
- **Briolette-style wrapping**
  Pinks and Peaches
- **Jump rings**
  All

TIP Mix vintage and new pieces in the same color family for an unexpected look, or combine two identical beads (like the citrine) that differ only in size for a more streamlined feel. You can also add a few beads on one side of the pendant chain to accent it.

TIP Wear this pendant as a choker or longer, depending on your preference (and your neckline). You can also vary the length of your sparkling drops from close to dramatically long, like the third version.

Pinks and Peaches Spaces and Sparkles Pendant

This pendant juxtaposes pink and orange Lucite with an orange flower charm, rescued from the Bracelet Alchemy Necklace project (p. 81).

Length: 17 inches

YOU'LL NEED

- Pliers
- Velvet jewelry display neck (optional)

- Thin chain
- Clasp
- Three 3mm jump rings
- 24-gauge wire
- 1 briolette
- 1 vertically drilled accent bead (I used a Lucite flower)
- 1 larger piece (I used a vintage flower bracelet link)

1. Cut a 16½-inch piece of chain, and add a clasp using two of the jump rings. Put your finished chain on the display.

2. Choose a link in the center, and mark it with a piece of scrap wire.

3. Cut a 1½-inch piece of chain, and join your larger piece to its last link, using the third jump ring.

4. Cut two 3-inch pieces of wire and wrap the briolette, completing the wrap. Create the first half of a wrapped loop on the second piece, and slip the open loop into the briolette loop, completing the wrap after they're joined. Slide the accent bead onto the wire.

5. Create the first half of a wrapped loop above the accent bead. Use this loop to join both the chain and dangling larger piece—just slip the center link you marked in step 2 and the last link of the chain connected to the larger piece onto the open loop, then complete the wrap.

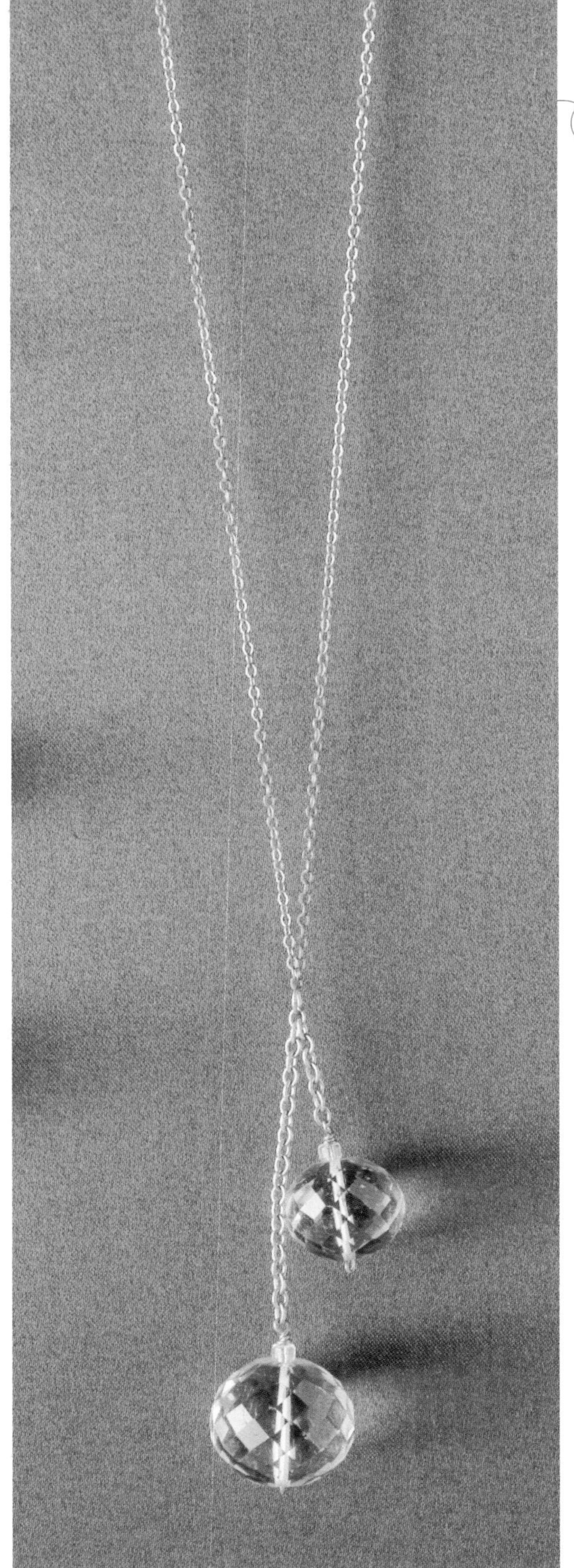

Citrine Spaces and Sparkles Pendant

Another understated variation is this cool, light citrine on matte sterling chain.

Length: 17½ inches

YOU'LL NEED

- Pliers
- Velvet jewelry display neck (optional)

- Thin chain
- Clasp
- Two 3mm jump rings
- Medium-weight chain
- 24-gauge wire
- 2 vertically drilled beads, one slightly larger than the other (I used faceted citrine)
- Seed beads in a complementary color
- One 5mm jump ring

1. Cut a 17-inch piece of thin chain and add a clasp using the 3mm jump rings. Put your finished chain on the display.

2. Choose a link in the center, and mark it with a piece of scrap wire.

3. Cut a 2¼-inch length of medium-weight chain and two 3-inch pieces of wire.

4. Form a plain loop at one end of both pieces of wire, and place first an anchor bead and then a seed bead on each one. Form the first half of a wrapped loop above each bead.

5. Slip the first bead dangle onto one end of the 2¼-inch piece of chain and complete the wrap to join them. Slip the second bead dangle onto the opposite end of the chain and complete that wrap, too.

6. Open the 5mm jump ring. Measure ⅝ inch in from the smaller bead on the chain, and slip the jump ring through a link there. Now thread the jump ring through the center link you marked in step 2, joining the dangles to the necklace, and close the jump ring.

Olive Spaces and Sparkles Pendant

Olive green glass and Lucite shine along a simple chain with a little asymmetry for fun.

Length: 17½ inches

YOU'LL NEED

- Pliers
- Light- or medium-weight chain
- 24-gauge wire
- One 16mm faceted Lucite bead
- One 10mm faceted glass or Lucite bead
- 2 small glass rounds
- Clasp
- 3 jump rings

1. Follow steps 1–5 in the Wood Modern Drop Pendant instructions (p. 115) to create the chain with the two small round beads wired into it, using pieces of chain that are 5 inches, ¾ inch, and 10 inches long.

2. Follow steps 3–6 in the Citrine Spaces and Sparkles Pendant instructions to create the bead dangle with the 10mm and 16mm beads using a 2¼-inch piece of chain. Attach it to the necklace chain, ¼ inch in from the smaller dangle.

Starburst Pendant

This sleek little mid-century-inspired piece is made up of beads radiating out from the center, in both 2-D or 3-D versions. Use glossy semiprecious ovals for a warm look or spiky glass beads to keep it cooler, and wear it out to the next art opening or foreign film penciled in your datebook.

TECHNIQUES

- **Plain loops**
  Carnelian
- **Wrapped loops**
  Carnelian
  Sleek Black
- **Jump rings**
  Carnelian
  Sleek Black

TIP Make sure that your beads are elongated—rounder or fuller ones won't cluster closely enough to make this piece. (You could create a variation of the Sleek Black Starburst Pendant with rounds for a more floral look, though.)

TIP The Carnelian Starburst hangs better at a longer length—not as a close-fitting choker—since the pendant has so much body. The other versions can be shorter if you like and look nice as a close-fitting piece. I also like using modern, streamlined chain or neckwires with this design to match the feel of the pendant.

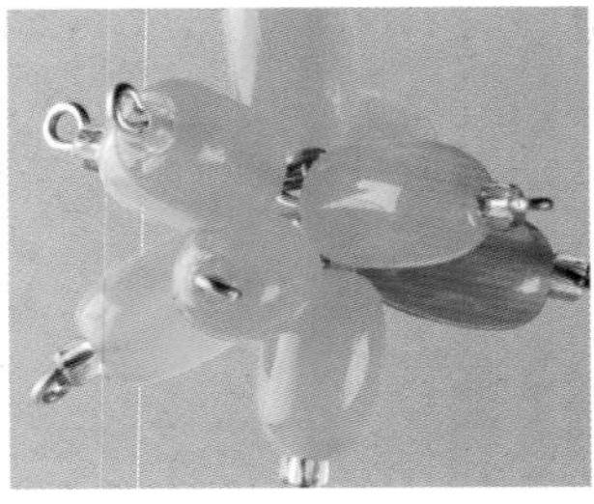

Carnelian Starburst Pendant

This carnelian mid-century-style gem is edged with gold glass seed beads. Please refer to the diagrams for the Pearl Starburst Earrings on p. 58 for help with the pendant construction.

Length: 17 inches long

YOU'LL NEED

- Pliers
- 20-gauge gold wire
- Gold seed beads
- Ten ½-inch carnelian ovals
- Gold-colored chain (medium weight)
- Clasp
- 2 jump rings

1. Cut four 3-inch pieces of wire, and form a plain loop at one end of each.

2. Add a seed bead and then a carnelian bead to one piece of wire. Form a loop over the bead as if you're creating a wrapped loop, bringing the wire around to a 45-degree angle above the two beads.

3. Add a second carnelian bead and a seed bead to the wire tail. Clip it just above the seed bead, and form a small, tight plain loop to hold it in place. This two-bead piece is a "branch" of the 10-bead asterisk. Make three more branches in the same way.

4. Using your flat-nose pliers to grip the loop in the center of a branch piece, gently angle the two bead spikes downward so they are slightly diagonal. This will help the asterisk spikes sit nicely in the center. Repeat with the other three.

5. Cut a 5-inch piece of wire, and form a plain loop at the bottom. This piece will be the "spine" of the asterisk. Place a seed bead and then a carnelian on it.

6. Now you'll start stacking the branches to create your piece. Place one branch on the spine, angled downward. Then place a second one on it, so that the four branch beads are evenly arranged around the spine.

7. Add a third branch, angled slightly up, and then a fourth.

8. Finally, add the last carnelian and a seed bead to the stack. Shift any stray branches around so that they are in place.

9. Form a *wrapped* loop above the top carnelian, making sure the loop is big enough to slip your chain through. Coil the wire end firmly so the asterisk is held together well.

10. Tweak any branches that are out of alignment—this piece does have some flexibility. If your first asterisk is a bit skewed, you can clip off the top wrapped loop and start over at step 6 to rebuild it. It may also help if you reinforce the angling from step 4 before stacking your pieces again.

11. When you love your asterisk, cut a 17-inch (or desired length) piece of chain, and slip the pendant onto it. Attach the clasp to the ends of the chain using jump rings.

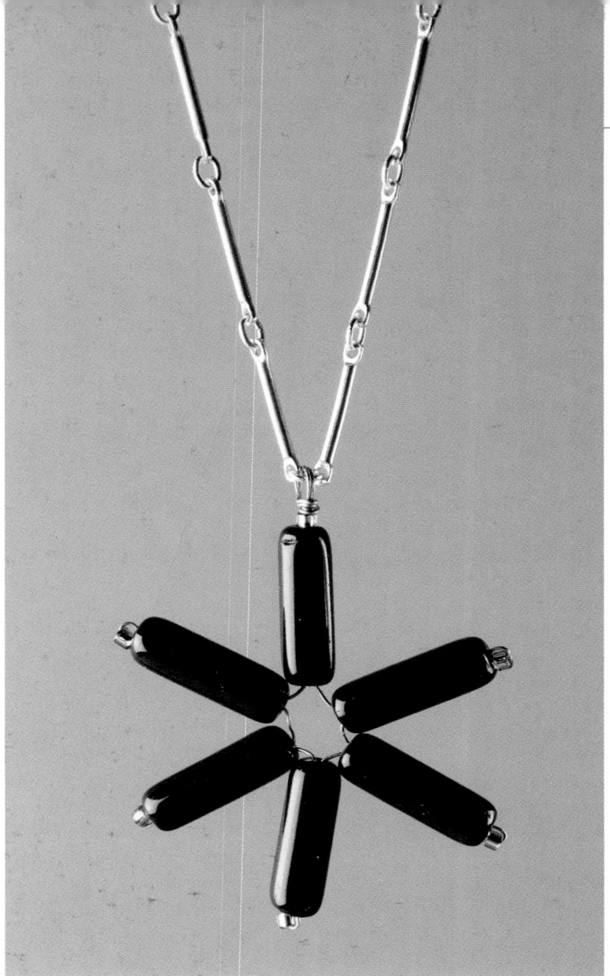

Sleek Black Starburst Pendant

Simpler, but no less beautiful, this pendant brings black cylinder beads and silver delicas together. Please refer to the diagrams for the Black Starburst Earrings on p. 61 for help with the pendant construction.

Length: 16 inches

YOU'LL NEED

- Pliers
- 28-gauge wire
- 6 delicas (or other tiny seed bead)
- 6½-inch black cylinder-shaped glass beads
- 16 inches of chain
- Clasp
- Two 3mm jump rings

1. Cut an 18-inch piece of wire and slip a single delica on it, sliding it down to the middle of the wire. Think of the half of the wire extending to the left as side A and the half extending to the right as side B.

2. Add a cylinder bead to side A, slipping it all the way down to the delica. Thread the end of side B through the cylinder bead, away from the delica, and gently pull it taut so that both ends of the wire extend out the same end of the bead, with the delica firmly anchored at the other end. This is your first "spike" of the asterisk and will be the bottom of the finished piece.

3. Next, build one side of the asterisk, using side A only. Add a cylinder bead and then a delica. Thread the tail of side A back through the cylinder bead and gently pull it tight.

4. Repeat step 3 to create a third spike.

5. Now you'll make two spikes on the other side using side B—just repeat steps 3 and 4 to build them.

6. Sides A and B are ready to unite to create the top spike. Slip a cylinder bead onto side A and add a delica. Now slip side B through the two beads in the same way so the two wire tails extend above the beads. Gently pull them taut.

7. Gently adjust the spikes so they radiate out evenly from the center. When you like the arrangement, form a wrapped loop using both strands of wire at the top of the piece. Make sure the loop is large enough to accommodate the chain you're using.

8. Slip the chain into the loop, then add the clasp to each end using jump rings.

Crystal Flower Starburst Pendant

This lovely creation of twisted wire and crystals is by crafter and writer Diane Gilleland.

Length: adjustable

TIP Diane says, "When working with wire, it's always wise to wear some eye protection. Not only can the ends of your wire be sharp, but they'll also be flopping about a lot as you twist and have been known to scratch."

TIP One thing to keep in mind when twisting small-gauge wire is that if you twist too much, it will break. If you're twisting away and you notice your wire getting thinner as you twist, stop!

TIP The twisted wire branches may look tricky at first, but they're really easy to make. You might want to make some practice ones before you launch into your first pendant.

TIP This pendant rides high on a chain, so it looks best at shorter lengths, like a neckwire, and on delicate or sleek chains. It would also look lovely strung on delicate organza ribbon.

YOU'LL NEED

- Pliers
- 26-gauge sterling silver wire, dead soft
- Eighteen 3mm crystals, six each in three coordinating colors
- Six 6mm bicone beads

1. Cut a piece of wire that measures 36 inches.

2. Thread one of your 3mm crystals onto the wire, and slide it to the center. Hold this so that the wire is forming a vertical line with your bead in the center.

3. Bend the upper half of the wire away from you and down over the back of the bead. Pinch the wire slightly so it's bent snugly over the back of the bead.

4. Next, make a twisted wire branch. You're going to twist the wire so it creates a little stem below the bead. To do this, take the bead in one hand, and with the other hand, hold the ends of your wire so they are slightly apart from each other. Now, twist that bead around and around until you have twisted somewhere from ⅛ to ¼ inch of wire.

5. Take a look at your bead. It now has a "front" and a "back." The back side has a piece of wire wrapped over it. Every bead you add will have a similar front and back. So as you work, try to make sure all these backs face toward the . . . you know, back.

6. Where you stopped twisting your wire, you now have two long, loose ends. Take one of these, and bend it out to the side. You are going to work only with this piece of wire for the moment, so forget about the other one until later.

7. Thread on another 3mm crystal—this time in a different color. Move this bead so it sits about ⅛ to ¼ inch away from the end of your twisted wire.

8. Bend the rest of this end of the wire back down so it wraps around your bead like you did for step 3. Grab the bead and twist it around and around so that the wire twists into another little stem. Stop twisting when you meet up with the first strand you twisted.

9. Next, create a little spacer before adding the third bead. Take the two branches you've just twisted and twist them as a unit, two or three times.

10. Thread on a third 3mm crystal, in a third color. Move this bead so it sits about ⅛ to ¼ inch away from your twisted main stem.

11. Just as you did for the first two beads, bend the wire around the back of the bead, and then twist it until you've twisted the wire up to the first strand.

12. The last step in our twisted branch is to twist a little base in it. So grab the whole branch you've just created, and twist that around three or four times. Congratulations! You've completed your first beaded wire branch.

The Bicone Beads

13. Thread on one bicone bead. Move this bead right up to your twisted branch, then give the non-twisted end of the wire a 90-degree bend to keep your bicone in place while you work on another branch.

14. Make another three-stem bead and wire branch, following steps 2–12 on the facing page. Try to keep it pretty close to the same length as the first one, but don't worry about being precise. Part of the charm of this piece is its slight irregularity. When you get to step 12, and you're twisting up the base of your branch, twist the wire a few extra times so it's tight against your bicone bead.

15. Thread on another bicone bead, and bend the end of the wire at a 90-degree angle to hold it in place.

16. Make another twisted branch.

17. Add another bicone.

18. Make another branch.

19. Stop working with this side of the wire, and move on to the remaining end, which is now much longer than the one you've been using, and likely feeling lonely.

20. Add a bicone, followed by a branch, then a bicone, then a branch.

21. You should now have five bicones and six twisted branches.

22. Add one last bicone. Take the remaining loose ends of wire (both of them) and bring them together so that your bicones form a circle. Twist the loose ends of the wire together carefully so the circle is snugly closed with no gaps.

NOTE: You'll be twisting this wire right behind one of your branches. If you find the branch is in your way, just bend it away. You can bend it back later.

23. Continue twisting the loose ends together until you have about 1 inch of twisted wire.

24. Make a simple wire loop on the back of your pendant. Using pliers, bend this twisted wire into a double circle. Trim away any excess.

25. Bend your pendant gently as needed to make it circular and spread the branches out nicely.

6

Brooches and Barrettes

Sparkle Cocktail Brooch

Wear this sparkly, over-the-top pin on a favorite vintage coat or cocktail dress. It's perfect for the next fancy soiree you're hosting or on a gray winter day when you need a colorful pick-me-up.

TECHNIQUES

- **Wire looping**
  Pink Fizz
- **Painting**
  Alrighty
  Quick Dose
- **Gluing**
  All

Pink Fizz Sparkle Cocktail Brooch

The pink beads on this brooch are wired to a mesh plastic round. Width: 3 inches

YOU'LL NEED

- Scissors
- Pinking shears
- Pliers
- Industrial-strength glue
- 3-inch plastic mesh round
- Felt in a complementary color
- A selection of colorful beads, including several large ones and many smaller ones (I used about 40)
- Seed beads in a complementary color
- 24-gauge craft wire
- 1½-inch pinback

Pink Fizz Sparkle Cocktail Brooch

1. Using the mesh circle as a template, cut out a round piece of felt in the same size. Then use pinking shears to cut out a ¾-inch by 1¼-inch piece of felt. Set both aside for now.

2. Put all your beads on a plate or tray and sort through them. Choose one to be your "anchor" bead—this will be the first bead you use to get your design started. (I used the pink swirl bead pictured.)

3. Cut a 2-foot piece of 24-gauge craft wire. If this length gets unwieldy or kinks while you're working, cut it shorter—you can always bind off when the wire runs out and start again with a new piece.

4. Form a wrapped loop at one end and thread the tail through the mesh circle slightly off center, back to front, leaving the loop at the back. Put your first anchor bead on the wire tail. Now thread the tail back through the circle so that the bead is positioned slightly off exact center, and slip the tail through the loop to catch it. Gently pull it taut.

5. With your first bead in place, pass the wire tail back through a hole in the mesh close to your last "stitch," and choose another bead to add next to your first one. Slip it on the wire, and pull the wire back through to hold it down the same way. Keep adding beads, working in a clockwise pattern around the first one you wired on, and have fun mixing in different shapes, sizes, and shades as you go.

NOTE: If you see a gap or space in the pattern, you can always go back and fill it in with a bead later. Another way to keep the pattern looking full is to mix in two or three seed beads in the narrower spots.

6. Keep working in the clockwise direction, adding new beads as you go. If your wire begins to run out, pull the tail through to the back and gently pull it tight. Then wrap it securely around one mesh grid line three or four times and leave a ½-inch tail, smoothing it flat to the back. Start a new piece as you did in step 4.

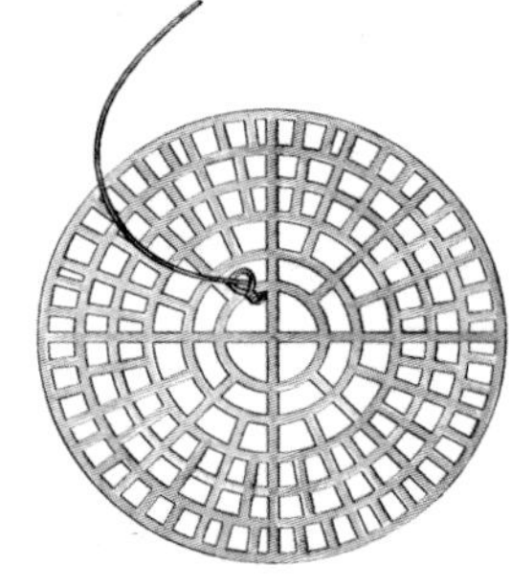

7. As you reach the edges, feel free to add beads that spill over beyond the circle's edges; just wire them on securely so they stay in place. Keep beading until your circle is covered and you're happy with the design. Bind your wire off as described in step 6.

8. Turn your brooch over, beaded side down, and put industrial-strength glue all over the back, distributing evenly. Then press your felt circle down over it, covering the entire back. Let it dry completely, smoothing it down if it bubbles or warps.

9. Choose which side will be the top. Position an open pinback ¾ inch from the top and glue it securely, making sure that the clasp's opening faces downward. Add glue over the pinback's base, and press the felt rectangle horizontally over it. Set to dry.

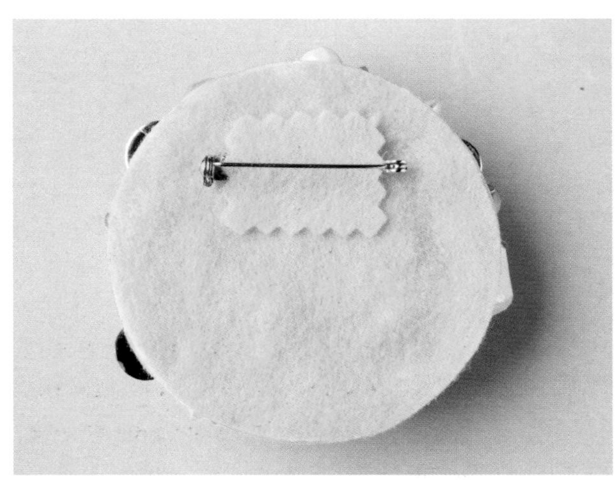

Alrighty Sparkle Cocktail Brooch

Designed by California crafter Cathy Callahan, this gorgeous brooch sparkles with rhinestones. Cathy says, "You can have lots of fun with your design for this one. Here I did a jeweled flower inspired by handbag designer Enid Collins." Width: 3 inches

YOU'LL NEED

- Sketch paper
- Pencil
- Compass
- Sharp scissors
- Gesso
- General-use paintbrushes
- 0 or 00 fine paintbrush (for metallic paint)
- Craft glue
- Hole punch
- Cloth tape measure
- Masking tape
- Six 10x17mm teardrop-shaped acrylic rhinestones
- Six 8mm round acrylic rhinestones
- One 24mm round acrylic rhinestone
- 2 shades of acrylic craft paint (try FolkArt® by Plaid®)
- Metallic gold acrylic craft paint
- Cross-stitch fabric (Aida cloth 22 count) or heavy canvas
- Lightweight chipboard or posterboard
- 2-inch-long pinback
- A few inches of trim
- Clear-coat spray varnish (matte or gloss)

1. Start by making your design. I like to lay out my rhinestones on a sheet of paper and sketch around them (you can use this as your pattern later on).

2. Choose the paint colors. Contrasting or complementing colors for the back of the pin work nicely. (The back of your piece should always look as finished as the front.)

3. Using a compass, trace two 3¼-inch-diameter circles onto some cross-stitch fabric. Then cut out.

4. Just as you would prime a canvas, use gesso to paint one side of each circle. Let dry completely. Then paint each circle with your previously chosen colors. Once completely dry, your circles should be somewhat stiff. Flatten them out if they have curled.

5. On the circle that will be the front of your piece, lightly trace your design in pencil using the pattern you created. Using a fine brush, apply the metallic gold paint. Make sure you cover the pencil lines. Let dry.

6. Using your compass, trace a 3¼-inch-diameter circle onto some lightweight chipboard or posterboard. Cut out. This will later be sandwiched between your two circles.

7. Position a 2-inch-long pinback on the chipboard horizontally and above the center back of your piece so your piece will lie straight and flat when you wear it. The catch should be on the left side. Glue down using craft glue. On your back circle, mark where the pin and catch will be, then make holes using a hole punch.

8. Apply a thin layer of the craft glue to the unpainted side of your back circle. Glue to the chipboard circle, positioning the pin and catch through their respective holes. Make sure the edges line up. Paint over any exposed chipboard.

9. Apply a thin layer of the craft glue to the unpainted side of your front circle. Glue to the chipboard circle, making sure you perfectly line up the edges of the front and back piece, and pinch around the edges to be sure that the edges tack together. Also check that the design on the front piece is facing the way you intend it.

10. Measure the circumference of the brooch, and cut a length of your trim to match. Carefully glue the trim around the front edge of your piece. Put an extra dab of glue where the two ends join to prevent fraying. (It looks better if this join is at the bottom edge.)

11. With masking tape, mask off the pin and catch. Spray the front and back with clear-coat (make sure you do this outside to vent the fumes). You can use gloss or matte depending on your desired effect. One coat should be fine. Let dry completely, then remove the masking tape.

12. Glue down the rhinestones using craft glue. Apply an even layer of glue, making sure to wipe away any excess on the sides once the jewel is in place. Also make sure that you position each jewel evenly inside the metallic shape. Let dry, then enjoy!

Quick Dose of Sparkle Cocktail Brooch

A generous helping of rhinestones glitter-glued onto an old button makes this brooch dazzle.
Width: 2 inches

TIP Use glitter hot glue to add your rhinestones to the brooch so that the glue that peeks through will shimmer along with the stones.

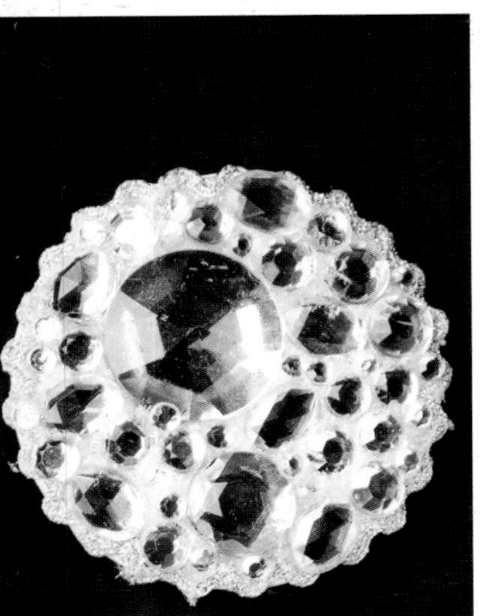

YOU'LL NEED

- White acrylic or enamel paint
- Small paintbrush
- Craft glue
- Hot-glue gun with clear glitter glue sticks
- 1 old 2-inch button with pinback
- 8 to 10 inches of silver baby rickrack
- Assorted clear rhinestones (about 40 in various sizes, including one 26mm and one 16mm round used here)

1. Paint over the front of an old button with white acrylic or enamel paint. One coat is fine. Let it dry completely.

2. Apply a thin line of craft glue all around the edge of the button, and glue down the rickrack, overlapping it neatly. Trim away any excess. Let it dry completely.

3. Decide on the placement of your largest rhinestones. Like the Pink Fizz Sparkle Cocktail Brooch (p. 139), I prefer to set my anchor pieces off center. Use a generous dab of hot glue to set those first large ones in the circle; don't worry about any excess glue running out the sides.

4. Fill in the empty spaces with smaller rhinestones, applying hot glitter glue, then pressing the stones into place. (You can always come back and fill in any gaps with tiny ones if there are spaces.) Keep working to cover the whole surface of the pin, varying the sizes and shapes as you go (I used rounds and ovals) so it's not too repetitive.

5. Continue until the entire surface sparkles with rhinestones. If you need to walk away mid-project, just cover the glue you've dispensed so far with rhinestones so it doesn't harden. Let dry.

Floral Galore Brooch

This set of flowered pins ranges from a gleaming, graphic blossom to a detailed little "garden" perfect for the first day of spring.

TECHNIQUES

- **Gluing**
  - Petals
  - Quick Sparkle Floral
- **Hand-sewing**
  - Flower Garden

Petals Galore Brooch

This mod piece features mother-of-pearl ovals under a vintage button.

Width: 3 inches

TIP Choose a large button for the center so it covers the backing and join where the "petals" meet completely.

Petals Galore Brooch

YOU'LL NEED

- Industrial-strength glue
- Five flat ovals (I used 1½-inch mother-of-pearl pieces)
- One 1-inch cardboard circle
- One 1-inch vintage button, shank style
- Large pinback
- One 1-inch felt circle

1. Arrange your five ovals in petal formation over the cardboard circle in the center. When they are evenly placed, put a generous amount of glue on the cardboard circle and make sure each petal is securely glued down. Add another dab of glue in the center of the circle.

2. Place your button over the center of the "flower," being sure the shank is neatly caught in the glue. Let it dry overnight.

3. Turn the pin over and glue the pinback in place. Once the pinback is set, glue the felt circle over the cardboard to cover the back.

Flower Garden Galore Brooch

Craftster extraordinaire Leah Kramer created this pretty "flower garden." Width: 2 inches

YOU'LL NEED

- Scissors
- Beading needle
- Fabric glue
- 1 sheet of green craft felt
- Multicolored top-drilled flower beads
- Multicolored size 11 seed beads
- Invisible thread

Quick Sparkle Floral Galore Brooch

A sweet complement to the Petals Galore Brooch, this singular metal flower (photo on p. 143) twinkles with a rhinestone center.

Width: 2 inches

YOU'LL NEED

- Hot-glue gun and glitter glue sticks
- Craft glue
- One 1¼-inch button with pinback
- One 2-inch metal flower stamping
- One flat-backed rhinestone

This one is so easy—just put a generous amount of hot glue all over the surface of the button and press the metal flower into it. Then add a dab of craft glue to the center and add a rhinestone there. Let both glues dry completely before wearing it.

- Small piece of cardboard
- Gray 6/0 seed beads (or other beads that look like little rocks)
- Pinback

1. Cut two circles approximately 2 inches in diameter from your felt.

2. Lay one of the circles on your table and play around with arranging the flower beads in different configurations. Be sure not to place them too close to the edge because you'll be making a border of "rocks" around the outer edge. When you've got a good idea of how you want to place the flowers, use the invisible thread and beading needle to stitch them on. To do this, pass the needle through the back of the circle; place the flower bead on the needle; place a seed bead on the needle; pull the needle and thread up and then back down through the center of the flower and through the felt. Tie a knot on the underside using the tail of the thread and the thread that's on the needle.

3. Continue this process as you randomly stitch on the rest of the flowers all over the felt circle. Tie a final knot and cut the thread.

4. Cut a circle of cardboard that's about ½ inch smaller in diameter than the felt. You're going to sandwich this between the two pieces of felt to give the brooch some stiffness. Place your decorated piece of felt on top of the cardboard circle, and place the plain circle of felt on the bottom of the stack.

5. Next, you're going to stitch a border of "rocks" (the gray seed beads) around the outside of the mini flower garden while at the same time sewing the decorated piece of felt to the back layer of felt. The technique used to do this is called backstitching. Here's how you do it:

Pass the needle from the back of the brooch out to the front; place two beads on the needle; then pass the needle back down through, along the edge of the brooch. Pass the needle back through it, going through the last bead you stitched on and continuing in the same direction, then put two more seed beads on the needle. Repeat this all the way around. The idea is that with every step you are adding two new beads and reinforcing the previous bead that you had just stitched on.

6. To finish, add the pinback finding. Cut a strip of green felt that is about 1 inch long and slightly narrower than the pinback. Apply fabric glue to the back of this felt strip and glue down the pinback.

Vintage Button Brooch

A flurry of vintage buttons swirl together on this charming little brooch. You can choose a mix of different sizes and styles, embellish a vintage belt buckle to make your own unique pin, or sport a single oversize button for ultimate simplicity.

TECHNIQUES

- **Wire looping** Lucky Dip
- **Gluing** All
- **Jump rings** Crown Jewels

Lucky Dip Button Brooch

This pretty little pin has assorted vintage buttons in all shades of blue. Width: 2 inches

TIP Gather a wide variety of buttons to layer together for your brooch. It looks especially nice if you mix several larger buttons in with smaller ones in all shapes, styles, and shades, like the Pink Fizz Sparkle Cocktail Brooch (p. 139), for an exuberant, asymmetrical look.

TIP If your button has a shank, pass the wire through it; if it has two holes, come up through one from behind and down through the other hole to the back again. If it has four holes, wire through two of them diagonally.

YOU'LL NEED

- Pliers
- Scissors
- Pinking shears
- Industrial-strength glue
- 3-inch plastic mesh round
- Felt in a complementary color
- A selection of large and small buttons (I used about 20 for mine)
- 24-gauge craft wire
- 1½-inch pinback

1. For this design, cut the mesh round down from 3 inches across to 2 inches. Make a cut at one side and neatly cut towards the center until you are three rings in. Carefully cut around the circle until you have an outer ring and an inner circle. Set the ring aside (you can use it to make the Holiday Ornament on p. 212 if you like), and trim any small, spiky plastic bits off the circle so it's smooth.

2. Using the smaller mesh circle as a template, cut out a round piece of felt in the same size with your scissors. Then use pinking shears to cut out a ¾-inch by 1¼-inch piece of felt. Set both aside.

3. Put all your buttons on a plate or tray and sort through them. Choose one to be your "anchor" button—this will be the first one you use to get your design started. I used the dark blue button with the rhinestone center pictured in the upper right section.

4. Cut a 2-foot piece of 24-gauge craft wire. If this length gets unwieldy or kinks while you're working, cut it shorter—you can always bind off when the wire runs out and start again with a new piece.

5. Form a wrapped loop at one end, and thread the tail through the mesh circle noticeably off center, back to front, leaving the loop at the back. Put your first button on the wire tail. Thread the tail back through the circle so that the bead is positioned slightly off center, and slip the tail through the loop to catch it. Gently pull it taut.

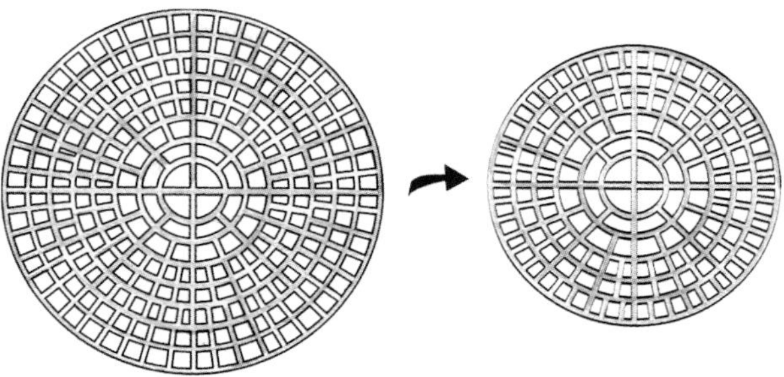

6. With your first button in place, pass the wire tail back through a hole in the mesh close to your last "stitch" and choose another button to add next to your first one. Slip it on the wire and pull the wire back through to hold it down the same way.

7. Keep adding buttons, working in a clockwise pattern around the first one you wired on. Have fun mixing in different shapes, sizes, and shades as you go. This design looks cool if you overlap—you can add smaller or "shorter" buttons under and behind larger ones to create a bouquet effect.

8. If you see a gap or space in the pattern, you can always go back and fill it in with a small button later; just bring your wire across the back to that spot and add it in.

9. Keep working clockwise, adding beads as you go. If your wire begins to run out, just pull the tail through to the back and gently pull it tight. Then wrap it securely around one mesh grid line three or four times and leave a ½-inch tail, smoothing it flat to the back. Start a new piece as you did in step 5.

10. As you reach the edges, feel free to add buttons that spill over beyond the circle's edges; just wire them on securely so they stay in place. Keep beading until your circle is covered with buttons or you're happy with the design.

11. Bind your wire off the same way as described in step 9.

12. Turn your brooch embellished side down and spread industrial-strength glue evenly over the back. Press your felt circle down over it, covering the

entire back. Let it dry completely, smoothing it down if it bubbles or warps.

13. Choose which side will be the top. Position an open pinback ½ inch down from the top and glue down securely—making sure that the clasp's opening faces downward. Add glue over the pinback's base, and press the felt rectangle horizontally over it. Let dry completely.

Quick Vintage Button Brooch pictured on p. 146

A must-have brooch, this features a simple hot pink button on an old button back.

Width: 1½ inches

YOU'LL NEED

- Small paintbrush
- Industrial-strength glue
- 1-inch button with pinback
- White enamel or acrylic paint (or the color of your choice to coordinate with your button)
- 1½-inch plastic four-hole button

1. If your 1-inch button is brightly colored, add one coat of white paint over the surface so the colors won't peek through the button holes. Let it dry completely.

2. Apply glue all over the surface of the painted button, and press the four-hole button onto it so it's centered over the pinback button. Let dry completely.

3. If any glue comes up through the button's holes, clean out with a toothpick—it's easiest if you let it set a little (about 20 minutes), then carefully poke it out.

Crown Jewels Button Brooch pictured on page 146

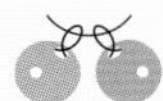  

Laura Stokes of Charcoal Designs designed this fetching crown brooch. Width: 2 inches

TIP It's better to drill the hole first in case your buckle cracks. Soft plastics are less likely to crack or break than harder, more brittle ones. Also, you can use a hand drill or drill press, or take your buckle to a hardware store to have it drilled. Or skip the embellishment charm to keep it simple.

YOU'LL NEED

- Pliers
- Drill
- Industrial-strength glue
- Vintage belt buckle
- Vintage crown charm
- Jump rings
- Crown metal stamping (I used a brass filigree piece)
- Assorted buttons
- 20-gauge wire
- Pinback

1. Drill a hole at one corner of the belt buckle—this will be the bottom of your brooch. Add a vintage crown charm with a jump ring.

2. Glue a crown filigree piece over the main part of the buckle. Let dry and then wire-wrap or glue buttons over it.

3. Glue the pinback to the back of the buckle, near the top.

Glitter Barrette

These embellished hair clips pack a lot of sparkle into such a little design! Coordinate them with a Sparkle Brooch, Floral Galore Brooch, or a Vintage Button Bracelet or Necklace for an extra-cute set.

TECHNIQUES

- **Gluing** All
- **Hand-stitching** Felt Rosette

TIP Don't make your barrette too heavy or gravity will take its toll on your hairstyle!

Buttons and Sparkles Glitter Barrette

These sparkly little hairpins are a quick, fun present to make.

Width: 1¼ inches

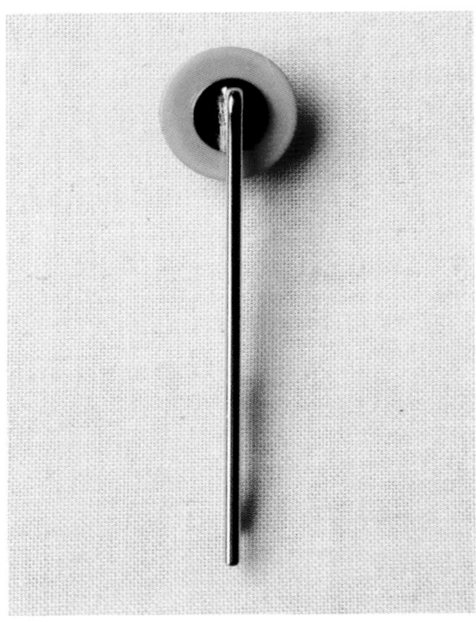

YOU'LL NEED

- Craft glue
- Industrial-strength glue
- Button of your choice, one for each bobby pin (I used a ⅝-inch pink and ⅜-inch red button for mine)
- Rhinestones (one for each button)
- Bobby pin with flat circle

1. Use a drop of craft glue to join the rhinestone to the button, covering the holes in the center. Let it dry completely.

2. Dab a little industrial-strength glue on the round base of the bobby pin. Firmly press the back of the button onto the base, centering it, and let it dry completely. You may want to let it dry with the button facing down or propped against something else so it stays in place.

Felt Rosette Glitter Barrette

   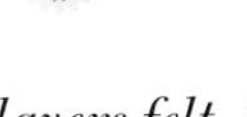

This pretty hair clip layers felt, buttons, and rhinestones.

Width: 1¼ inches

YOU'LL NEED

- Pinking shears
- Sewing needle
- Craft glue
- Two small pieces of felt in different colors (I used bright and dark green)
- Thread in a coordinating color
- 1 large button (I used a 1¼-inch white one)
- Hair clip
- 1 small button (I used a ⅜-inch one in a flower shape)
- 1 medium-size rhinestone (I used green)
- 8 small rhinestones (I used clear)

1. Cut a 2-inch circle out of one color of felt and a 1½-inch circle out of the other. Layer them together, the smaller one on top, and baste them together with a few stitches.

2. Sew the large button over the two circles, securing it with at least three stitches. Flip the piece over and hold the hair clip to it, centering it in the circle. Stitch first one side, then the other to the felt pieces using three or four stitches for each side.

3. Add a little craft glue to each side of the clip where you stitched to reinforce it, making sure you don't glue the clip shut. Let it dry completely.

4. Flip the clip right side up and glue the small button onto the larger one, exactly in the center. Glue the medium-size rhinestone to the small button.

5. Next, add the eight tiny rhinestones in a circle around the small button. Use a drop of craft glue to secure each one. Starting at the top, glue one rhinestone on in each of the 12, 3, 6, and 9 positions, as if it were a clock face. Then fill in the design with one rhinestone in between each of the first four, working symmetrically.

6. Let dry completely.

Quick Glamour Glitter Barrette

A vintage rhinestone flower glued on an oversize clippie is just the thing for an upswept look.

Width: 3 inches

YOU'LL NEED

- Hot-glue gun with glitter glue sticks
- Oversize hair clip
- Vintage or new rhinestone flower (I used one 1¼ inches across)

Apply a generous dab of hot glue to the widest end of the hair clip. Press the flower into the glue to set it in place. Let dry completely before wearing.

Vamp Hair Comb

This stunning comb keeps your hair back with eye-catching style. Look for cool, striking pieces to use as ornaments for your hair combs: vintage metal leaves, feathers, or even playing cards. Since the comb itself is bigger than a single hair clip/barrette, it can support heavier or more elaborate designs, like the vintage brooch piece that pairs with the whisper-light feathers in the '20s Berlin Vamp Hair Comb.

TECHNIQUES

- **Wrapped loops** All
- **Hand sewing** '20s Berlin
- **Wire looping** All

TIP Try making a matching set with smaller combs, or embellish a huge one to anchor an updo for a glamorous night out.

Bronze Leaves Vamp Hair Comb

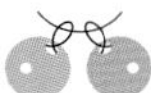 

Make a sultry Vamp Hair Comb with wired-on bronze leaves and copper beads—very 1920s–'30s style.

Length: 5 inches

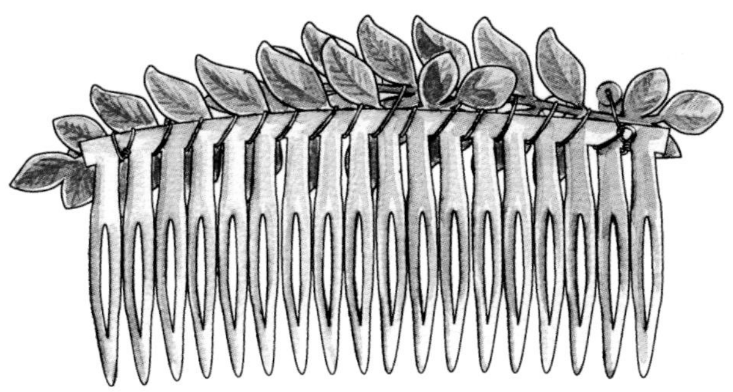

YOU'LL NEED

- Pliers
- Quick-dry glue
- 20-gauge copper wire
- 6/0 seed beads in the color of your choice
- Hair comb
- Vintage leaf stampings

1. Cut a 16-inch piece of wire and form a wrapped loop at one end. Put three seed beads on it.

2. Slip the wrapped loop between the first and second teeth of the comb, on the back/inside, and run the wire tail through it. Don't pull it taut yet—leave a big, open loop on the front.

3. Arrange your piece or pieces on the comb—if you're using more than one, you may want to overlap them slightly. When you're happy with the arrangement, pull the wire tight, catching the vintage piece in place and making sure that the beads are on the front of the wrap.

4. Add three more seed beads, and wrap the wire again between the second and third teeth.

5. Continue wrapping the wire until you reach the end of the comb. Wrap one final time, then carefully coil your wire tail around the wrap on the inside of the comb, making sure there are no rough edges poking out. You don't need to wrap between each and every one of the comb's teeth—wrap where it fits with the pattern.

6. If necessary, add a drop of glue under the design at each end to secure the edges of the leaf pieces.

Player Vamp Hair Comb

Designed by Christy Petterson of a bardis, *this unique hair ornament is made from playing cards wired to a store-bought comb.*

Height: 6 inches

TIP These playing-card hair combs are great because they're durable and have awesome designs on them. The look of the comb can be changed by selecting cards with different graphics and by varying the number of shapes that you include.

YOU'LL NEED

- Scissors
- Hole punch (a star shape or small circle)
- Pliers
- 3–5 playing cards
- 28-gauge brass wire
- Hair comb
- 16–20 seed beads of contrasting color

1. Select some playing cards and cut out different organic shapes freehand. Make some shapes tall and some round, and experiment with different pairings.

2. Punch a hole at the bottom of each shape.

3. Put the shapes in groups of two or three. Vary the height.

4. Slip wire through the hole in a card and between the first and second teeth of the comb. Continue wrapping wire around the comb and through the hole, pulling the wire taut.

5. After you've wrapped the wire a couple of times, add two or three beads. Wrap again and add a few more beads. Wrap a couple more times, pull it all

taut, and click the end of each piece of wire so that it ends on the back side. Flatten the end pieces and make sure they aren't poking out.

6. Continue adding shapes to the comb all the way across or until you like how it looks.

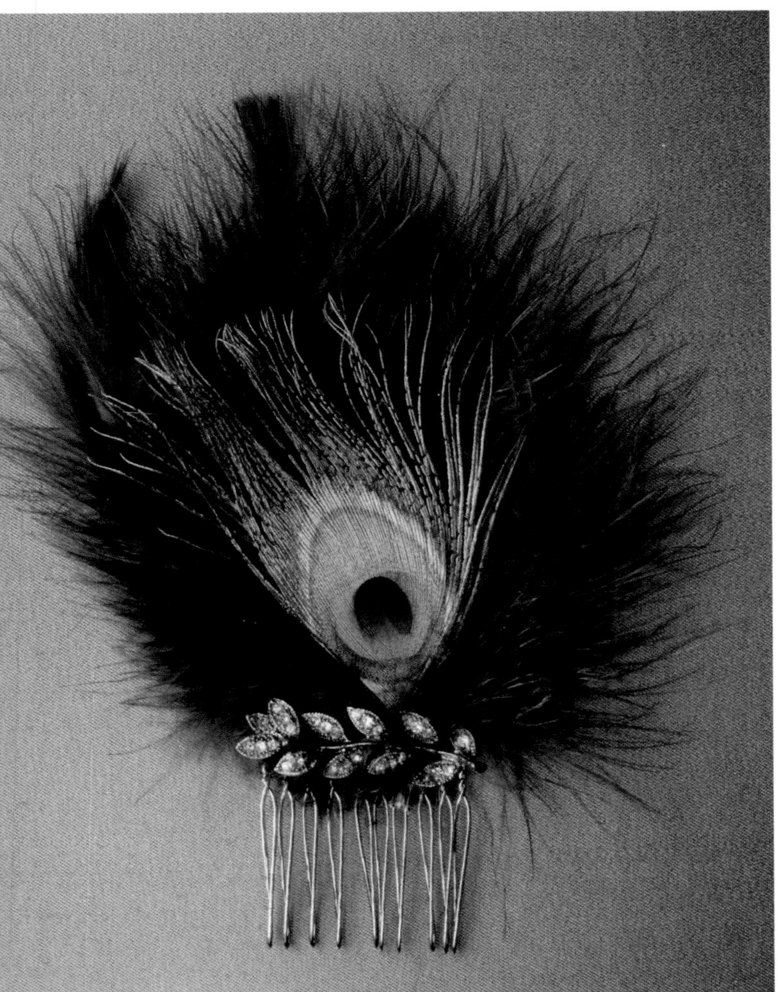

'20s Berlin Vamp Hair Comb

This enticing mix of feathers and jewels, designed by stylist Nicola Corl, is a vintage-inspired stunner.

Height: 3½ to 6 inches

YOU'LL NEED

- Pliers
- Sewing needle
- Metal hair comb
- Vintage brooch piece approximately the same width as the comb
- 20-gauge wire
- Assorted feathers up to 2 inches long
- Thread in a coordinating color

1. Attach a vintage brooch to the hair comb by wire-wrapping (follow the directions for the Bronze Leaves Vamp Hair Comb on p. 152). You could also glue or solder it, depending on weight.

2. Wind feathers through the back, top to bottom, pulling them to the correct lengths, then hand-sew to hold securely in place. Snip off any excess that pokes out the bottom.

Sparkle Band

Embellish a plain headband with glam sparkly beads or rhinestones, or knot it with hemp and bone beads for a more relaxed feel. Either way, you'll be the only girl at the party wearing one!

TIP Adapt your design to the width of your headband. Don't pile tons of beads on a narrow one—wiring single pieces on will work best.

Midnight Sparkle Band

Pull your hair back with glossy black Lucite beads wired right onto a narrow band.

YOU'LL NEED

- Pliers
- Glue

- Narrow metal headband
- Assorted black Lucite faceted rounds (I used three 18mm, four 12mm, and eight 10mm)
- Black Lucite crystals (I used six 6mm and fourteen 3mm)
- 24-gauge black craft wire

1. Place the headband on a table or work surface (a grooved bead tray would work well, too), and arrange the beads around it, following the pattern on p. 156—though you may want to adapt it to be

TECHNIQUES

- **Wire looping**
  Midnight
- **Gluing**
  Quick Glamour
- **Knotting**
  Hemp

longer or shorter if you like. My beaded section measured 10 inches, and I started wire-wrapping about 2 inches from the end of the band on each side.

2. Wrap the craft wire around the band four times to begin beading. Loop each bead on with a tight wrap, then wrap again between each bead to secure them all.

NOTE: You'll wrap once between each small crystal on the sides and twice between each larger round on the top since they're heavier.

3. At the end, wrap four times to secure the bead, then add a drop of glue to the beginning and end. Let it dry completely before wearing.

PATTERN:

NOTE: The numbers refer to bead size in mm.

3-3-3-3-3-6-3-6-3-6-10-12-10-12-10-18-10-18-10-18-10-12-10-12-10-6-3-6-3-6-3-3-3-3-3

Quick Glamour Sparkle Band

Fit for a princess, this headband is covered with glitter-glued rhinestones and edged with silver rickrack.

TIP I embellished a silver-colored headband with clear, sparkly rhinestones. If your band is a dark or bright color, you can paint it with acrylic or enamel paint so it doesn't show underneath your stones and glue.

TIP There is no set pattern to the rhinestone placement—I added the three largest stones at the crown of the band and filled in around them. Have fun making up your own design—use other colors or shapes if you like.

TIP Keep different sizes of rhinestones close at hand and easy to grab since you'll need to add stones quickly before the glue dries.

YOU'LL NEED

- Craft glue
- Hot-glue gun with glitter glue sticks
- One silver headband, 2 inches across at widest point
- 1 yard silver baby rickrack
- Assorted rhinestones (I used three 24mm rounds, two 18mm rounds, two 14mm rounds, and one 20mm star, as well as assorted rounds, ovals, and marquise shapes in smaller sizes, for a total of about 200 stones, mostly small)

1. On the headband, use craft glue to add rickrack all around the edge as in the Quick Dose of Sparkle Cocktail Brooch (p. 142), curving the band at the ends and overlapping neatly at one end. Let dry completely.

2. Working from one end, apply a layer of glitter hot glue to the surface, then fill in the area with small rounds, ovals, and marquise shapes. I added my first larger round about 2 inches into the design. You can always go back and add tiny rhinestones to fill in gaps. Mixing up the sizes and shapes usually makes for a more visually interesting piece.

3. Continue gluing rhinestones around the band, mixing in larger stones where you'd like to accent them. I added a star slightly off center for fun. You could also add these larger stones first and then fill in all around them.

4. When you've covered the whole band, go back and add tiny rounds anywhere that's blank or uneven. Let dry completely before wearing.

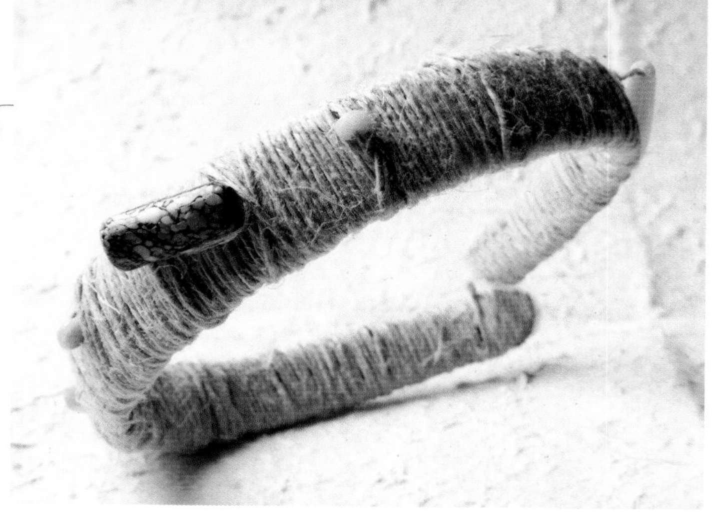

Hemp Sparkle Band

This completely unique design from crafter and writer Kelly Wiglesworth uses a mix of hemp and bone beads.

YOU'LL NEED

- Scissors
- One headband
- 1 spool thin hemp cord
- Bone beads
- One colorful glass bead for center

1. Take two strands of hemp and tie knots on the end of the band to begin. Wrap them tightly around the band, tying on more rope as needed.

2. Use bone beads to ornament the sides and a ceramic color-splash bead for the center. After wrapping several inches up the side of the band, string the bead on one of the strands of hemp and secure it in the center of the band by wrapping the other strand of hemp around the bead. For the longer bone beads, just wrap one strand of hemp continuously around the headband to create a backdrop for the bead and string the bone bead on the other strand, then continue wrapping the band with both strands of hemp when they meet up again.

3. Finish by securely knotting at the other end so the wraps are taut.

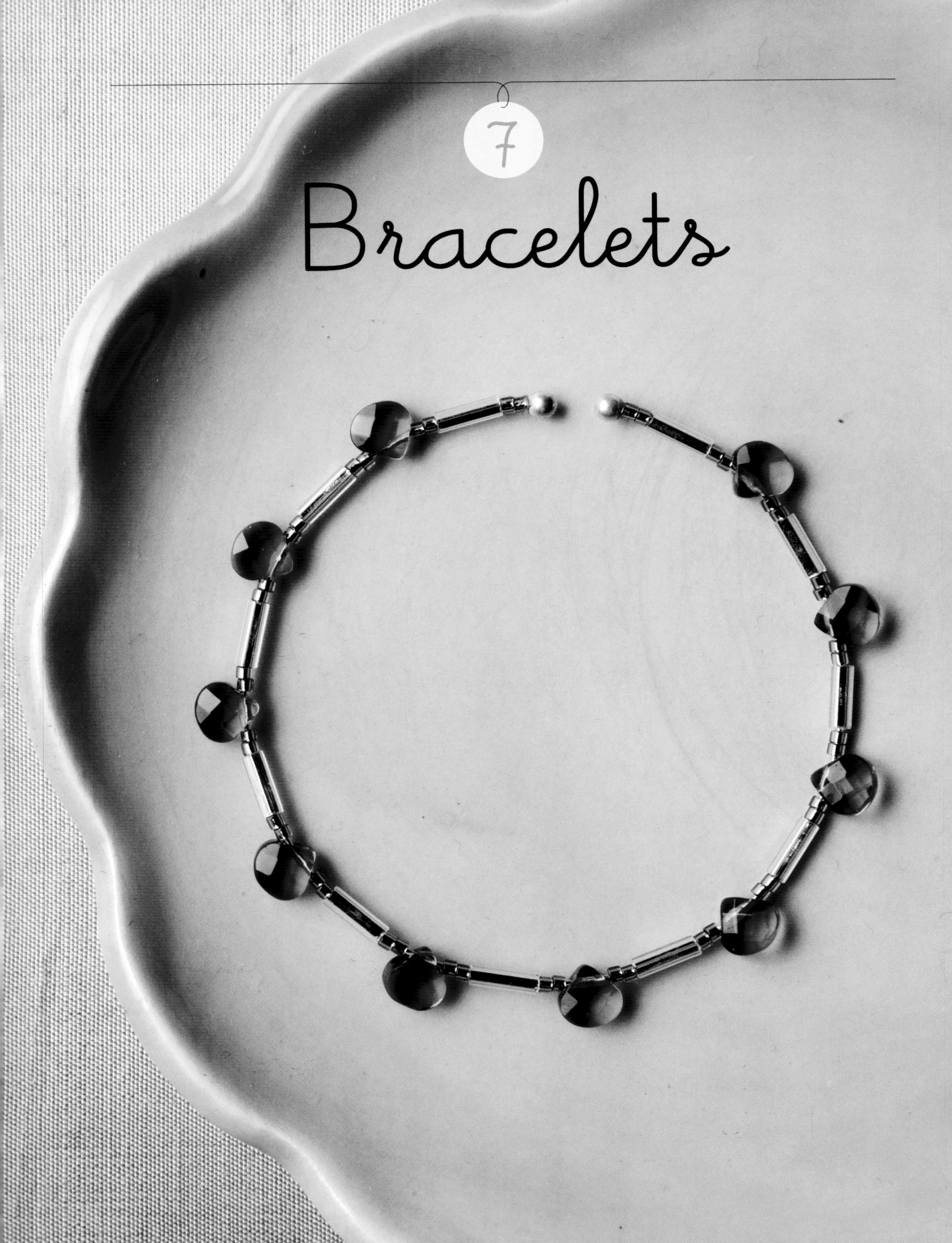

7

Bracelets

One-Strand Bracelet

These one-strand bracelets are so easy to make that you'll find yourself dreaming up new combinations every time you stop by the bead store or take an old necklace apart. They make a fun gift, too—customize them to be as elegant, as cute, or as sleek as you like.

TECHNIQUES

- **Bead stringing**
- **Crimp beads**
  Row of Ovals
- **Knotting**
  Bronze Knotted
- **Gluing**
  Candy Shop

Row of Ovals One-Strand Bracelet

This colorful, simple piece combines multihued ovals with blue and lime green cubes.

Length: 7½ inches

TIP Try to keep your bracelet design balanced. Using beads similar in size or weight will ensure it's not always falling to one side as you wear it. If you use identical beads, you'll create a sleeker piece, even if they're bright and eye-catching, too.

Row of Ovals One-Strand Bracelet

YOU'LL NEED

- Tape
- Pliers

- Soft Flex wire
- Seven 16mm oval beads (O)
- 4 small glass cube beads (SC)
- 4 larger glass cube beads (LC)
- Seed beads (s)
- 2 crimp beads
- Clasp

1. Cut a 15-inch piece of wire and double a piece of tape 4 inches from one end.

2. String beads in this pattern: s-SC-s-O-s-LC-s-O-s-SC-s-O-s-LC-s-O-s-SC-s-O-s-LC-s-O-s-SC-s-O-s-LC-s.

3. Add one crimp bead and thread the wire through the clasp then back through the crimp bead. Slip the wire tail inside the first four beads and pull it taut. Securely flatten the crimp bead with your flat-nose pliers.

4. Remove the tape from the other end of the wire and add a crimp bead. Attach the other half of the clasp following step 3.

5. Trim both wire tails closely.

Candy Shoppe One-Strand Bracelet

Jenny Ryan of Sew Darn Cute designed this elastic bracelet in sweet, candy-like colors.

Length: 6 to 7 inches (adjustable)

TIP Elastic cord comes in all sorts of bright colors—experiment using clear beads here and there to allow the colored elastic to show through. Doubling up your elastic cord will make your bracelet extra-strong. This bracelet is a great way to use up random beads from your collection.

YOU'LL NEED

- Beading needle
- Glue

- Thin elastic cord (0.6 works great)
- Assorted beads: glass, plastic, vintage and/or new

Bronze Knotted One-Strand Bracelet

These faceted bronze beads are neatly knotted on silk. Length: 7 inches

YOU'LL NEED

- Pliers
- Knotting tweezers
- Glue
- 1 package of prethreaded silk beading cord (size 8) in brown
- 15 bronze 10mm glass beads
- 2 bead tips
- Magnetic clasp

Follow the instructions for the knotted Perfectly Pink Necklace (p. 65), using only one color of beads instead of three. You'll create and finish the bracelet in the same way, but stop when you've knotted 15 beads (or the bracelet has reached the length of your choice).

1. Cut a 24-inch length of elastic cord and thread it through the eye of a beading needle. Tie the ends into a knot, leaving a tail.

2. String a random assortment of beads, alternating colors and sizes as you go (as few as 20 beads or as many as 35, depending on their sizes). Stop adding beads when your bracelet reaches 6 to 7 inches long (according to the size of your wrist). End with one of your larger beads.

3. Tighten the elastic until taut, and tie a small knot between the first and last beads. Put a tiny drop of glue on it to seal it and let dry.

4. Trim the elastic ends closely, and if desired, use the tip of the beading needle to poke the knot inside one of the larger beads.

Memoir Bracelet

Memoir bracelets, which are strung on memory wire, retain their circular shape perfectly. Try a combination of large beads with tiny seed beads, a mix of delicate pieces, or even an assortment of charms for a modern "charm bangle."

TECHNIQUES

- **Memory wire**
- **Briolette-style wrapping and/or jump rings**
  Charm Bangle

TIP Like the Memoir Necklace (p. 67), make sure your beads aren't too heavy for this style. If you use larger, more substantial beads, try cutting your memory wire rounds about 1 to 2 inches longer so the two ends overlap for added stability.

Lucky Blue Memoir Bracelet

This bracelet features blue oval beads with a lucky eye bead.

Length: 7 inches (adjustable)

YOU'LL NEED

- Glue
- Pliers

- One 7-inch round of memory wire
- 2 round bead ends
- Eleven 10mm glass oval beads (G)
- Seed beads in a coordinating color (s)
- 1 small lucky charm on a jump or soldered ring (C)

1. Glue one tip onto the end of your memory wire and let dry completely.

2. String your beads on in this pattern: G-s-C-s-G-s-s-G-s-s-G-s-s-G-s-s-G-s-s-G-s-s-G-s-s-G-s-s-G-s-s-G. Continue until you have 11 oval beads on the wire. You'll start and end with an oval bead.

3. Carefully glue the second bead end onto the tail. Let it dry completely.

Delicate Briolettes Memoir Bracelet

This bracelet mixes translucent amethyst glass briolettes with tiny silver beads. Length: 7 inches (adjustable)

YOU'LL NEED

- Pliers
- Glue

- 10 small briolettes (BR)
- 12 bugle beads (B)
- Delica seed beads (s)
- 7 inches of memory wire
- 2 bead ends

Follow the instructions for the Lucky Blue Memoir Bracelet (at left) using this pattern:

s-s-B-s-s-BR-s-s-B-s-s-BR (repeat 10 more times).

Charm Bangle Memoir Bracelet

This modern combination is striking and easy to wear.

Length: 7 inches (adjustable)

YOU'LL NEED

- Pliers
- Glue

- 9 charms (C)
- Jump rings and/or 24-gauge wire
- Eight 5/8-inch pieces of plastic tubing (P)
- Two 1/8-inch pieces of plastic tubing (SP)
- 7-inch round of memory wire
- 2 bead ends

Make this bracelet the same way as the Lucky Blue, but the charms will be neatly separated by pieces of tubing. Form briolette-style drops (or use jump rings) to suspend each charm, and simply slide each one on through its loop. Follow this pattern: SP-C-P-C-P-C-P-C-P-C-P-C-P-C-P-C-P-C-SP.

Hardware Store Bracelet

These simple bracelets use hardware store materials for a fun, unexpected, and inexpensive design. They're all flexible ideas—use different combinations of "charms" or embellishments to make yours ultra-personalized.

TECHNIQUES

- **Jump rings**
  So So
- **Double-wrapped loops**
  So So
  Key to My Heart
- **Hook clasp**
  Key to My Heart

TIP You can find a great variety of colors and sizes of ball chain at hardware stores. Look for interesting link chains, too—they're usually in brass or silver. Both types are available by the foot pretty inexpensively. Be sure to get the heaviest chains cut to the lengths you need at the store, instead of ruining your own wire cutters.

So So Hardware Store Bracelet

A super-stylish piece, this bracelet features washers and S-hooks on silver-colored ball chain.

Length: 7 inches

YOU'LL NEED

- Pliers
- 20-gauge wire
- 7 inches of ball chain and clasp
- 4 S-hooks
- 5 washers
- 4 jump rings

1. Cut five 4-inch pieces of wire and make the first half of a double-wrapped loop around each washer.

2. Lay your ball chain out in a straight line, and arrange your S-hooks and washers, alternating them. Space them out evenly—for my bracelet, I added one every fourth link.

3. Beginning on the left side, put one washer charm on after the fifth link in to complete the top half of the loop.

4. Open all four jump rings and set all but one aside. Slip one ring onto an S-hook and place it next to the first washer.

5. Continue adding washers and S-hooks to the ball chain, alternating so they are evenly spaced four links apart until you reach the other end.

Key to My Heart Hardware Store Bracelet

An industrial brass chain paired with a single key is striking in its simplicity.

Length: 8½ inches

YOU'LL NEED

- Pliers
- 20-gauge craft wire
- An antique or new key
- 8 inches of heavy brass chain
- 16-gauge brass wire

1. Using 20-gauge wire, form a double-wrapped loop to connect your key to the chain—I added my key three links from one end.

2. Make a modified hook clasp with the 16-gauge wire. Be sure that the hook itself is flush with the bracelet. Add the clasp to the opposite end of the chain.

Gone Fishin' Hardware Bracelet

AlternaCrafts *author Jessica Vitkus says, "One day I drifted into the bait and tackle section and found these intriguing little guys called snap swivels, which come in different metals, sizes, and colors. I like the idea of using something like sports gear to make something delicate. Add beads and link the swivels together into jewelry in less than an hour."*

TIP Play with scale by trying different swivel sizes and metals, different beads, or even charms.

YOU'LL NEED

- Pliers (optional)
- 6–8 size 10 snap swivels (from the fishing tackle section or store)
- Several dozen glass seed beads (make sure you have extras)

1. Take your first snap swivel and open it with your fingers or pliers. This involves unhooking the bowed side from the straight side.

2. String several seed beads onto the snap swivel in one of two ways. You can pour a few beads into the palm of your hand and poke them with the open wire end. Or you can hold one bead between your thumb and forefinger and place it on the open end of the snap swivel.

NOTE: Not every seed bead will fit around the swivel's hook, so you will have to fish (sorry!) for the skinnier ones. This is why you need extras.

3. When you are happy with the beads on your first swivel, take the next snap swivel and hook it on so the two swivels lie head-to-tail as shown.

4. Shut the first snap swivel with your fingers or pliers.

5. Repeat steps 1 to 4 on the second swivel.

6. Continue until you are happy with the size. Link the head of the last swivel to the tail of the first.

BONUS: To make the larger-scale bracelet, use six snap swivels in size 130 pound. I beaded them with brass, silver, and copper *hishi* from Ethiopia.

The Charming Bracelet

The traditional charm bracelet gets a fresh new interpretation in glossy gold, a flurry of blues, and an A–Z of colors and shapes. Put your own spin on it in the combination you like best!

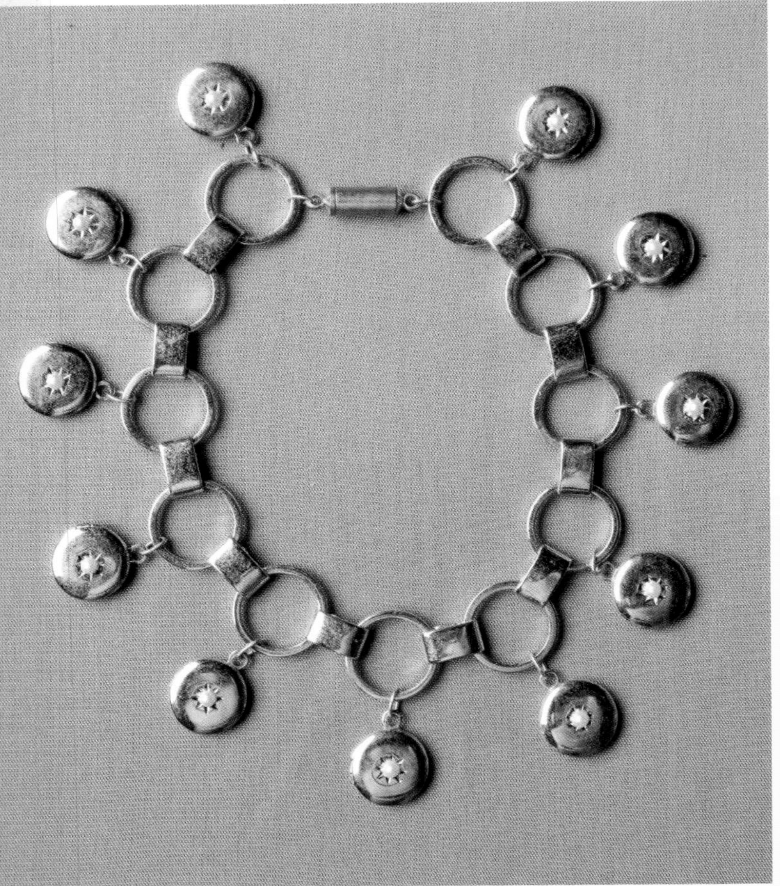

TECHNIQUES

- **Jump rings**
  Little Lockets
  Bric-a-Brac
- **Wrapped loops**
  Tangled Up in Blues
  Bric-a-Brac

TIP Try using all kinds of things to make charm bracelets—beads, lockets, charms, found bits and pieces. Also, to save time, open all your jump rings before you start attaching each piece.

Little Lockets Charming Bracelet

A collection of gold lockets hang from a round gold chain.

Length: 7 inches

Tangled Up in Blues Charming Bracelet

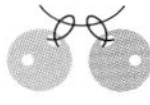

This happily jumbled collection includes blue vintage and new pieces on chain.

Length: 7 inches

YOU'LL NEED

- Pliers
- 24-gauge wire
- Assortment of 30 beads in the same color family—different shades and shapes
- Headpins
- Medium-size chain
- 2 jump rings
- Clasp

1. Cut one 3-inch piece of wire for each briolette-style wrap you will make. Form briolette wraps above any teardrop-shaped bead (I used five), and form the first half of a wrapped loop above each one.

2. Take one headpin and add a seed bead, one anchor bead, and another seed bead. Form the first half of a wrapped loop above the beads and set it aside. Repeat until all your beads are on wire.

3. Cut a 6½-inch piece of chain and lay it out flat. Choose one bead at random, slip it onto the first link, and complete the wrap.

4. Continue adding beads, one per link, in a random mix until you reach the other end of the chain.

5. Use jump rings to attach your clasp.

YOU'LL NEED

- Pliers
- Oversize circle chain
- 13 Jump rings
- 11 small vintage lockets
- Magnetic clasp

1. Cut your chain to 6½ inches long. Open up 11 jump rings and set all but one aside.

2. Place the first ring on the first link of chain and add a locket, making sure it's facing up. Close the ring securely.

3. Add a locket to each link of chain until you reach the other end.

4. Use a jump ring to attach the clasp at each end of the chain.

Bric-a-Brac Charming Bracelet

Designed by Jennifer Perkins of Naughty Secretary Club, this colorful bracelet is one of those baubles that is all about organized chaos. When absolutely nothing "matches," suddenly that's the very element that ties everything together.

Length: 7 inches

TIP This is a great project for using leftovers in your stash—and might just inspire you to start keeping a drawer for all the little lost bits you only have one of.

YOU'LL NEED

- Pliers
- Industrial-strength glue
- 11 random cabochons, buttons, or other various flat-back goodies
- Ready-made link bracelet with flat disks for gluing or soldering
- Headpins
- Small jump rings
- Random stash of mismatched beads (20 used here)

1. Arrange your 11 flat-back pieces in a pattern that appeals to you.

2. Once you have created your design, glue the pieces onto the pads of the bracelet with a big glob. Let the glue dry, following the manufacturer's recommendation on how long this will take.

3. While the glue is drying, start making your beads into charms using headpins and basic wrapped loops. Remember that this bracelet is about being random, so try to choose all different beads. If those beads can be multicolored, that's better yet.

4. Once the glue is dry, you can add your bead charms to the bracelet. In between each glue pad is a circle link—this is where you attach the charms. Using small jump rings, affix all the bead charms to the loops, two on each loop but one on either side—top and bottom, if you will. Do not put charms on the last two links of the bracelet, since that would make it tricky to get your new bracelet on your wrist.

Vintage Button Bracelet

Dip into your button box to make this cute, simple bracelet—whether you use heirloom pieces from your great-aunt or a handful you picked up at an estate sale, your wrist will be adorned with plenty of style.

TECHNIQUES

- **Hand-stitching**
  Red Sparkles
  Vintage Bakelite
- **Gluing**
  Red Sparkles
- **Wire wrapping**
  Cute as a Button

TIP If you're stitching your buttons onto elastic, your bracelet will be much stretchier if you knot each button as you go instead of keeping the thread intact. If you want to sew them on with one continuous strand, just make your bracelet a little longer so it slips on over your hand easily without breaking the thread (as I did my first time out).

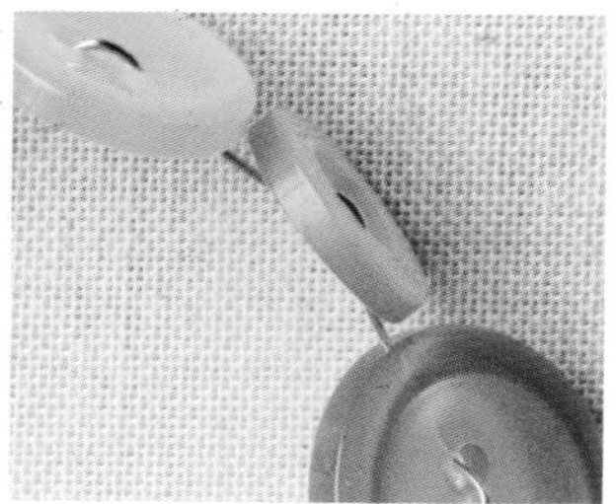

Red Sparkles Vintage Button Bracelet

This bracelet is a flashy mix of red buttons and rhinestones.

Length: 7½ inches

YOU'LL NEED

- Sewing needle
- Marker in the color of your buttons (optional)
- Fray Check
- Craft glue
- Buttons of your choice (I used 16⅜-inch red flowered buttons)
- 1 foot of ⅛-inch elastic
- Thread in a coordinating color
- Small rhinestones (one for each button)

1. Thread your needle and tie a double knot at one end. If you want to disguise the white of your elastic, you can color it in with marker to match the buttons.

2. Hold your first button in place over the elastic (about 1 inch in from one end) and stitch it on, reinforcing it three times. Once your first button is in place, you can either knot the thread and cut it off, or simply bring your needle up through the elastic to stitch on the second button.

3. Arrange the second button so that it's touching but not overlapping the first one and stitch it on the same way. Add the next buttons the same way until your bracelet is about 1 inch from being finished. Try it on for fit.

4. Finish the bracelet by stitching the last two buttons through both thicknesses of elastic: trim the elastic ends to the right length, keeping in mind they will overlap exactly, and put a drop of Fray Check on each end. Make a few quick basting stitches to hold the double layer in place, then stitch on the last two buttons. Tie a strong knot at the end of the sewing and add a drop of Fray Check to seal it.

5. Use a drop of craft glue to add a rhinestone to each button, covering the stitches in the buttonholes. Let it dry for several hours or until the glue is set.

Vintage Bakelite Button Bracelet

Designed by writer-craftivista Betsy Greer, this piece is made with oversized Bakelite buttons on elastic covered with yarn—so it's adjustable and stretchy.

TIP Throw out the rules that colors can clash. Before you start stitching, dump all your buttons on the floor and play around with shades that "shouldn't" work, seeing what pops when you least expect it. For big, chunky buttons, use wider and sturdier elastic.

YOU'LL NEED

- Scissors
- Sturdy sewing needle
- Fray Check
- ¼-inch-wide elastic
- 6 or 7 chunky vintage buttons in various colors
- Thread in a complementary color to the buttons
- 2 feet of wool yarn

1. Using your wrist as a guide, wrap the elastic around your wrist, leaving an extra 2 inches at either end, and cut.

2. Once you've determined how your buttons are going to be placed on the bracelet, lay them out on the floor or table in front of you. The number of buttons needed depends on the size of the buttons and your wrist—you can gauge how many you will need by the length of elastic.

3. Select a color of thread that best complements (or contrasts) the buttons you've chosen. Cut a piece of thread roughly a foot long, then thread it through the needle. Tie the two ends together.

4. Holding the elastic taut, sew the button onto the elastic, making sure it's evenly placed on the elastic. For a more classic look, when using buttons with four holes, make an X. Sew the button to the elastic, reinforcing it two more times, and cut the thread.

5. Repeat steps 3 and 4 until the elastic wraps around your wrist with room for just another button. Overlap the two ends of the elastic and sew the last button in place. Remember that the bracelet will have to go over your hand.

6. Dab Fray Check on the cut edges of the elastic.

7. Tie wool yarn onto the elastic, under a button, and knot it. Wrap it around the spaces in between the buttons, taut enough that it won't slide, until the elastic is entirely covered. Knot again at the end.

Cute as a Button Bracelet

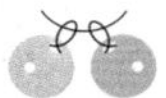   

These pink buttons on wire have a classic and beautiful look.

Length: 6¾ inches

YOU'LL NEED

- Pliers
- An assortment of buttons in the same color family (I used 11 pink buttons ranging from ⅜ to ¾ inch across)
- 18 inches of 24-gauge gold craft wire
- Clasp

1. Arrange your buttons in a row so you like the mix of colors and sizes. (I alternated larger with smaller and darker with lighter.) Slip the wire through one of the holes of your first button, and place it about 6 inches from one end of the wire. Next, feed it through the opposite hole and pull it taut so that the button "sits" where you've placed it.

2. Add the next button in the same way, and secure it so it's close to the first one. Add more buttons until you have a section of wired buttons about 6 inches long. Clip the wire ends so they're each 5 to 6 inches long.

3. Feed one of the wire ends back into the outer hole of the last button, looping it through to reinforce it. Form the first half of a wrapped loop with the wire but don't close it. Repeat on the other side.

4. Slip half of a magnetic clasp onto each open loop, then complete the wrap to close them.

Woven Bracelet

These bracelets take a simple woven pattern in very different directions—try including your favorite beads as the centers so they really stand out. Flip back to the beadweaving techniques on pp. 25 and 26 for reference as you go.

TECHNIQUES

- **Bead weaving**
  All

TIP Use long, vertical beads as your "ladder rungs" for a wide cuff style or narrow/wider beads for a cool, streamlined version. This is such a versatile design once you have the basic pattern down—have fun with it!

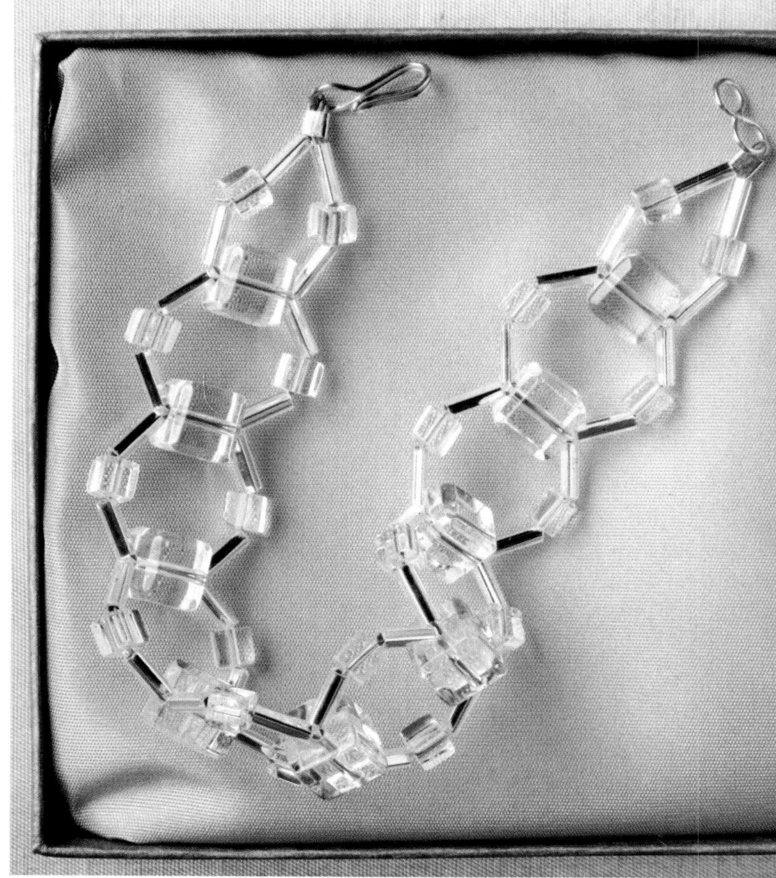

Ice Cube Deluxe Woven Bracelet

These clear glass cubes are woven together to form an elegant statement.

Length: 7 inches

Ice Cube Deluxe Woven Bracelet

YOU'LL NEED

- Pliers
- Tape

- Soft Flex wire
- Clasp or chain
- 2 large crimp beads
- Glass bugle beads, ¼ inch long (b)
- 20 small glass cubes, about 4mm (g)
- 9 large glass cubes, about 8 mm (these will be the connectors) (G)

1. Cut a 3-foot piece of beading wire and slip the clasp (or the last link in a piece of chain, to make it adjustable necklace-style) onto it. Add a large crimp bead over both wire tails, and slip it all the way down the wire so it is just over the clasp or chain. Crimp it closed. You now have two 1½- foot wire tails extending out of the crimp bead to work with.

2. Think of the tail that is currently upper as A and the other as B. Begin your pattern by adding several beads to each strand to form the sides. For this piece, string a bugle, a small cube, and another bugle on each strand.

3. Next, add a large cube to A and then slip B through it, coming in the side that A exited. Pull the two tails tight so that the large cube is neatly holding the first few beads in place. A will now be lower and B upper since they have crossed inside the large cube.

4. Add a bugle, a small cube, and another bugle on each strand, then slip both wires through a large cube as you did in steps 2 and 3.

5. Continue until you have nine large cubes strung. Add a bugle/small cube/bugle to each strand, then add a crimp bead over both strands.

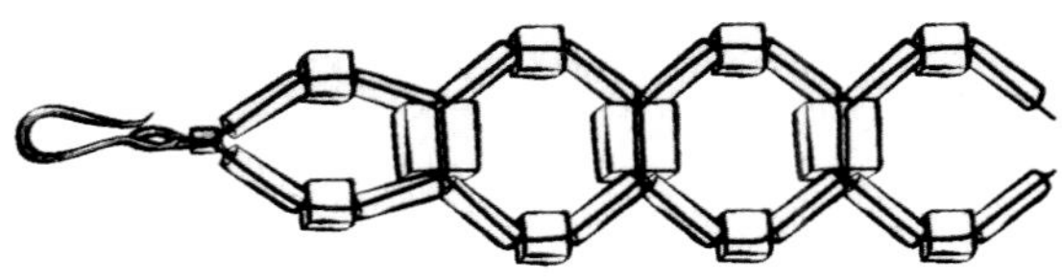

6. Slip the other half of your clasp (or the last link of a second piece of chain) onto each wire, and bring the wires back through the crimp bead. Slip one piece of wire through each of the beaded strands, and pull the tail through so the design is taut and symmetrical. Crimp the bead closed, then trim each of the wire tails.

PATTERN: identical upper and lower (both strands pass through G each time):

b-g-b-G-b-g-b-G-b-g-b-G-b-g-b-G-b-g-b-G-b-g-b-G-b-g-b-G-b-g-b-G-b-g-b-G-b-g-b

Perfectly Pink Woven Bracelet

This sparkly-pearly bracelet has a sweet vintage feel.

Length: 7 inches

YOU'LL NEED

- Pliers
- Tape

- 3 feet of Soft Flex wire
- 2 large crimp beads
- 9 large pink pearl rounds, approximately 10mm (these will be the connectors) (P)
- 40 pink faceted Lucite rounds, approximately 8mm (p)

FOLLOW the same technique for Ice Cube Deluxe using this pattern: identical upper and lower (both strands pass through P each time):

p-p-P-p-p-P-p-p-P-p-p-P-p-p-P-p-p-P-p-p-P-p-p-P-p-p-P-p-p

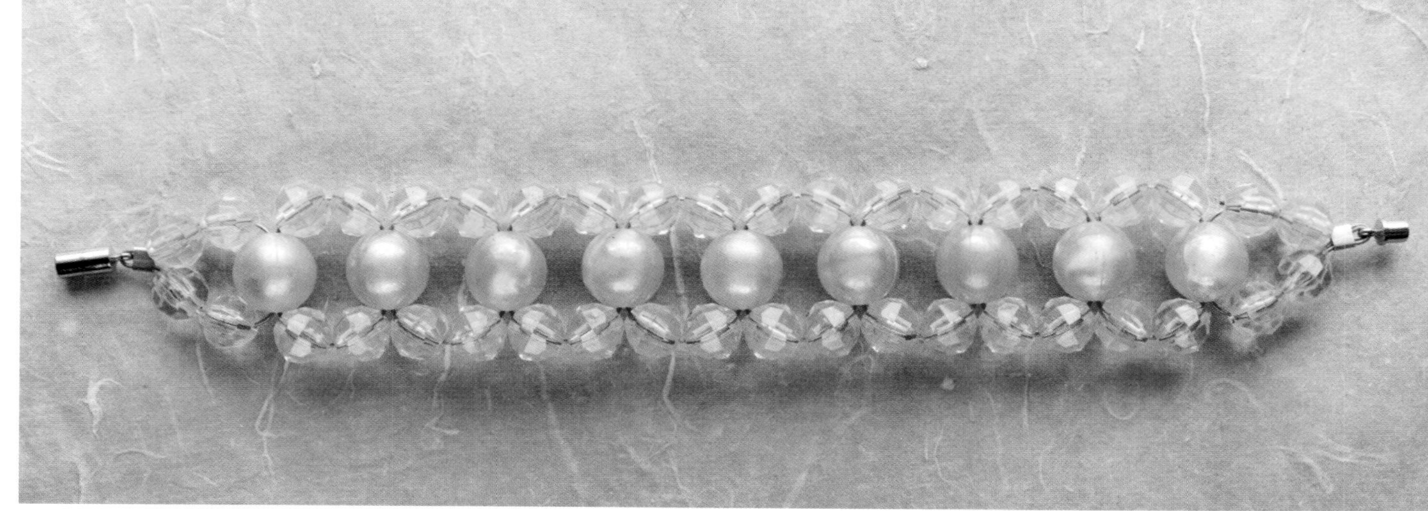

Glossy Black Woven Bracelet

This version is sleek and eye-catching.

Length: 7 inches

YOU'LL NEED

- Pliers
- Tape
- 3 feet of Soft Flex wire
- 2 large crimp beads
- 7 large black ovals (mine were about 20mm long; these will be the connectors) (B)
- Thirty-two 6mm black rounds (b)
- Black seed beads

Follow the Ice Cube Deluxe technique using this pattern: identical upper and lower (both strands pass through B each time):

NOTE: Each black round (b) has a seed bead on each side of it.

b-b-B-b-b-B-b-b-B-b-b-B-b-b-B-b-b-B-b-b-B-b-b

8 Embellishments

Sparkle It! Ribbon Trim

Use ribbon to dress up everything from your date book to your keychain,and whip up a few greeting cards while you're at it!

TECHNIQUES

- **Gluing**
  - Blossom Book
  - Star Ribbon Greeting Card
- **Hand-stitching**
  - Bits and Baubles Keychain

TIP Find unusual ribbons by the spool instead of by the foot at fabric stores—it's cheaper that way, too.

TIP If you're gluing ribbon to a flat surface (like a card or book cover), you can trace a straight line with a pencil and ruler, then apply a thin line of glue along the mark—an easy way to keep your ribbon straight and neat.

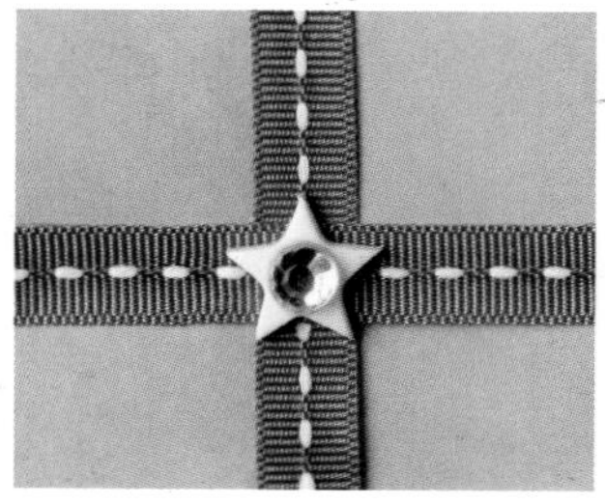

Blossom Book

Make a plain book pretty with a rhinestone "blossom."

Height: 5½ inches

YOU'LL NEED

- Craft glue
- Scissors
- Plain-front notebook (I used a 3½-inch by 5½-inch Moleskine® book)
- Six inches of ⅛-inch satin ribbon
- One 24mm round rhinestone
- Two 10mm marquise rhinestones

1. Choose where you want to position your flower design on the notebook, and apply a thin line of glue where the ribbon will go. Press the ribbon down, making sure that it extends under where the "flower" will be and that there's an extra tail of ribbon below the edge of the cover, too. Once the glue has set for about 15 minutes, gently tuck the ribbon end inside the book cover. On my book, I glued on a 3½-inch length of ribbon.

2. Glue on the large rhinestone so it covers the upper raw edge of the ribbon, then glue the marquise rhinestones (the "leaves") in place on each side of this "stem," 1 inch below the flower.

3. Once the glue is dry, clip the ribbon tail to approximately 1 inch long. Glue it in place on the inside book cover and let it dry completely.

Bits and Baubles Keychain

Jessica Wilson of Jek-A-Go-Go created these dazzling little ribbon-and-felt rosette keychains. As she says, "You don't need much to make this nifty project, and the possibilities are endless!"

Length: 6 inches

YOU'LL NEED

- Sewing needle and thread
- Scissors
- Sewing machine (optional)
- Pinking shears
- Vintage button
- Wool felt scraps (2 colors)
- ¼-inch-wide grosgrain ribbon
- Key ring
- Flat-backed rhinestones

1. Using your needle and thread, sew the button onto the center of a piece of felt in color 1, about 2½ inches square.

2. Cut the felt around the button into a circle about ½ inch from the edge of the button. Cut another piece of felt in color 2 about 1 inch larger than your button's piece. Keep it square.

3. Cut the ribbon to 8 inches, and fold it in half. Make a quick running stitch near the fold about ⅛ inch down. This will be where you thread the key ring through the ribbon.

4. Place the ribbon, open edge down, onto the larger piece of felt. Place the round piece of felt with the button on top of the ribbon, leaving 3 inches of the ribbon poking out. Now you'll stitch the round piece to the square piece to anchor the ribbon between the two layers.

5. Stitch a running stitch by hand or machine all the way around the button using a contrasting color for the thread. If using a machine, you may want to hand-turn your needle since the circumference of stitching is small. Once you are done, trim the threads and cut your outer square into a circle using the pinking shears. Be careful not to cut the ribbon.

6. Add your key ring and any jewels or extras.

Star Ribbon Greeting Card

Adorn plain paper with ribbon and a little star for a quick and easy card.

Size: 5½ by 4¼ inches

YOU'LL NEED

- Scissors
- Paper cutter (optional but recommended)
- Ruler
- Pencil
- Craft glue
- Fray Check

- One 8½- by 11-inch piece of blue cardstock
- 16 inches of ⅜-inch-wide brown-and-white grosgrain ribbon
- One flat star charm or button
- One small rhinestone

1. Cut your paper in half so you have two 5½- by 8½-inch pieces. Fold one piece neatly in half so you have a 5½-inch-wide by 4¼-inch-tall card. (Save the other half for your next card project.)

2. Cut two pieces of ribbon, one 6 inches long and one 10 inches long. Mark a horizontal guideline 1 inch above the bottom edge of the front of the card, and then a vertical guideline 1¼ inches from the left side of the card on both the front and back of the card. Apply a line of glue along the vertical line, front and back, and gently press the 10-inch piece of ribbon over it, making sure that there is a short ribbon tail extending past the paper on both edges.

3. Repeat with the shorter ribbon and the horizontal guideline. Let the glue dry completely.

4. Use your scissors to trim the ribbon edges so they're flush with the paper. Add a drop of Fray Check to seal the ends.

5. Use a dab of glue to add first the star and then the rhinestone where the ribbon crosses. Let the glue and Fray Check dry and your card is ready to send!

Sparkle It! Household

Sure, you can make yourself magnets, candleholder ornaments, and a set of wineglass charms for your next drinks party...but why not make an extra set so that next time you're going to someone's house for dinner, you can bring a fun host(ess) gift along? It's easy to make all kinds of fun, personalized household ornaments—try colors or styles that blend with your décor or really pop.

Sparkling Magnets

Mix up colors, sizes, and shapes for fun, or make a sleek matching set—it's up to you!

Width: ½ to 1 inch

TIP These magnets are a true instant-gratification project—a set takes minutes to make and just a few hours to set. Use a flat metal surface so your magnets remain stable while they dry.

YOU'LL NEED

- Silicone glue
- Six ½-inch round magnets
- Six rhinestones (I used a range of sizes, from 10mm to 24mm)

1. Place your magnets on a magnetic surface, and apply a generous dab of glue to each one.
2. Press a rhinestone onto each. Let them dry for three to four hours before using.

Instant Shrine Candleholder Ornament

Encircle a plain glass votive holder with a ring of pretty beads. Use any double-drilled beads you like—solid colors, patterns, or religious designs. Translucent beads will look especially nice as a candle burns.

Size: variable (mine measures about 8 inches around)

YOU'LL NEED

- Scissors
- Cement or instant-drying glue or Fray Check
- Plain glass candleholder
- Elastic cord that passes through all your beads easily, with a beading needle if needed
- Double-drilled beads (mine were resin squares decorated with glittery Virgin Marys, ½ inch across; I used 12)
- 22 small wooden beads (I used half orange and half pink, alternating them)

1. Measure the circumference of your candleholder, and cut two pieces of elastic that are at least 4 inches longer than that length. Lay them out on a flat surface parallel with each other.

2. Slip one double-drilled bead onto both strands, one high and one low. Add a small bead on each strand, on both sides of the larger bead.

3. Continue adding large beads, alternating them with small beads as you go.

4. When your beaded section is long enough to go around the candleholder, tie a double knot in each piece of elastic, pulling it taut so it will hug the glass. Seal each knot with a drop of glue or Fray Check, and snip the elastic tails flush with the knot.

Name-Dropper Wineglass Charms

These cute wineglass charms by designers Emilie and Jessica Zanger need no introduction. Try any variation in colored and alphabet beads you like, from Greek gods and goddesses to rock stars, and your guests can choose their identity for the evening.

Length: 3½ inches

YOU'LL NEED (FOR FIVE CHARMS)

- Wire cutter
- Round-nose pliers
- Flat-nose pliers
- 20-gauge craft wire
- 20 headpins
- Variety of decorative beads with holes large enough to accommodate the wire and headpins
- Black-and-white plastic letter beads

1. Cut a 4-inch length of wire using the wire cutter, and shape it into circle. You can use a cylindrical object that's 1 inch or slightly larger in diameter (such as a glue stick) to make this part easier. You'll wind up with about ¼ to ½ inch of wire overlapping at each end. Use the round-nose pliers to bend one of these ends back on itself, forming a V shape at the end of the wire. If you want the loop that goes around the base of the wineglass to be beaded, now is the time to string the beads.

NOTE: Do not use large beads that will make the loop too snug around the base of the wineglass, and don't string the beads too tightly together. You want to be able to slide them around a bit. Use the round-nose pliers to bend the other end of the loop back and at an angle perpendicular to the other end. You'll now have two little hooks that can be linked together to close the circle.

2. String one small accent bead onto a headpin, then string the black and white plastic letter beads onto the headpin to spell out the name. Be sure to go in reverse order if you want the name to read top to bottom. String another small accent bead onto the end of the headpin so that the name is "book-ended" by two beads.

3. String a second headpin with decorative beads in whatever color and pattern motif you desire.

4. Form a plain loop above the top loop on each headpin.

5. Now that your components are all made, you just have to assemble the charm. Decide where on the base of the charm (the loop) you want to add the hanging headpins. Then take the flat-nose pliers and slightly bend the open end of the eyes you just created to the side to allow the wire to slide through. Spread apart the beads on the loop where you want to add the headpins, and slide the wire of the loop through the eyes of the headpins. Use the pliers to close the eyes again. Voilà, you're done!

6. Repeat steps 1–5 as many times as you want to create enough charms for every guest on the list.

Sparkle It! Accessories

Embellish a plain pair of hoops or bangle by wiring on sleek or spiky beads for an easy style update, or make yourself an instant new sparkler by adding a rhinestone to a metal ring blank. Adding flair to a basic piece can be much quicker than starting from scratch, too.

TECHNIQUES

- **Wrapped loops**
  All
- **Wire looping**
  All

Get Wired Bangle

This combination echoes the Wood Modern Drop Pendant's sleek feel (p. 114).

Width: 3½ inches

TIP Be gentle with your wire. The extra-long pieces can get kinked and "work-hardened" as you go. If your wire is getting brittle, just stop, unwind it, and start over again with a fresh new piece.

Sparkler Cocktail Ring

Make this piece in a few minutes and wear it out the next day (or night)—it's an easy pick-me-up. Match it to your Sparkle Cocktail Brooch (p. 139) or Sparkle Band (p. 155) for coordinated glamour.

YOU'LL NEED

- Cement glue
- Ring blank with flat surface
- Rhinestone of your choice, bigger than the ring's top

1. Apply a dab of glue to your ring's flat surface and press the rhinestone into it, centering it over the top.
2. Let it dry overnight before wearing it. Leave it ring side up to dry so that the stone stays in place.

YOU'LL NEED

- Pliers
- 24-gauge wire
- One wooden bangle bracelet
- Small carnelian rounds (I used 16)

1. Cut a 5-foot piece of wire and form a wrapped loop at one end.
2. Hold the wrapped loop on the inside of the bangle, and bring your wire tail all the way around the outside, slipping the wire through the loop to hold it. Pull it taut so it's held firmly in place on the inside of the bangle, like the Vamp Hair Comb on p. 153.
3. Begin wrapping the wire around the bracelet, holding the completed loops as you go. Every second wrap, add a small carnelian bead, using the tightness of the wrap to hold it in place.

NOTE: If you are using a two-sided bangle like the one pictured, orient the beads so they alternate sides. If you're using a flat or rounded bangle, place the beads along the same path, or alternate angling them toward one side or the other.

4. Continue wrapping the wire evenly around the bangle until you reach your starting point.
5. Form a wrapped loop around your last full wrap, making the wrap as tight and neat as you can. Clip the wire tail so it's tucked in.

Wired Hoop Earrings

Designed by artist Bethe Mack, these gold hoop earrings are embellished with a cool assortment of pearls and cylinders—change how many beads you add on at a time for visual interest. There's no exact pattern to follow, so have fun with the design!

Length: 2½ inches

YOU'LL NEED

- Pliers
- Cement or instant-drying glue
- 28-gauge craft wire
- One pair of plain hoops
- ¼-inch-long silver bugle beads
- ¼-inch-long pearl beads

1. Cut an 18-inch piece of craft wire, and wrap it around the top of the hoop four times to begin the embellishment. Add any two beads to the strand of wire and slide them to the very end, then bring the wire around the hoop three times to hold them in place. Adjust the beads so they are at a cool angle, not lying flat to the hoop.

2. Repeat with two to four more beads of your choice, creating the wired angles as you go. Longer segments, like the ones with four beads, will spiral around the hoop instead of spiking outward. Continue beading and wrapping the same way all around the hoop, wrapping three times between each grouping.

3. When you reach the end, wrap four times, then secure the beginning and end of the wraps with a drop of glue.

4. Repeat to form your second earring.

Sparkle It! Wearables

It's easy to personalize a plain garment—just think up a pattern and embellish your piece with a fun new design. Here are some suggestions for adding a little punch to your wardrobe, but the possibilities are endless!

TECHNIQUES

- **Hand-stitching**
  All

TIP If you are stitching your beads on with polyester sewing thread (especially nice when you want to match your garment's unusual color exactly), be sure to use the beeswax-and-iron trick on p. 27 to strengthen it.

TIP If you are sewing beads on, use at least three stitches for each one so they stay on securely. You'll also want to hand-wash or dry-clean your garment after you embellish it instead of machine-washing.

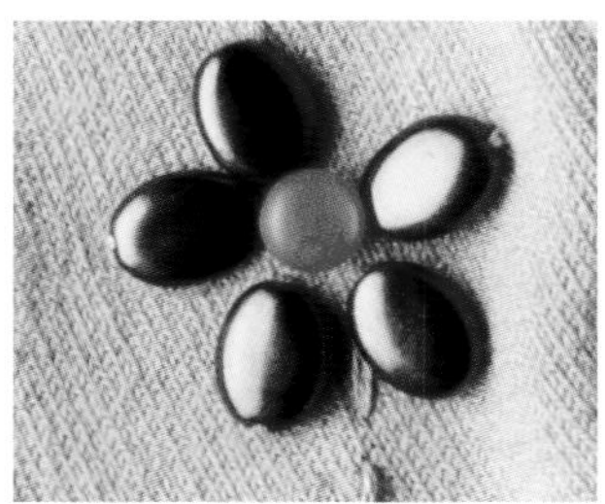

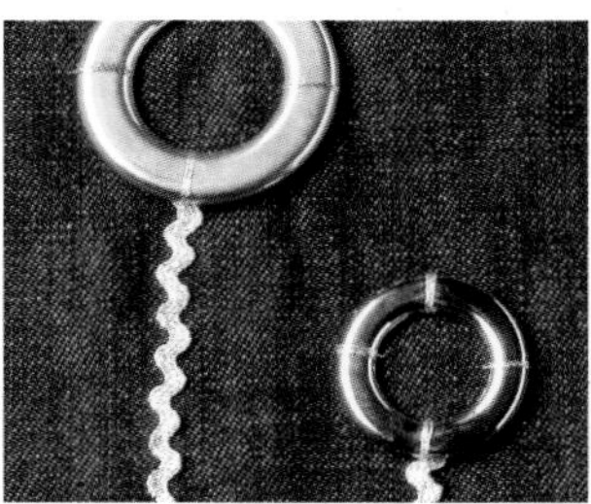

Blooms and Vines Sweater

This plain V-neck was just crying out for some pretty pink and brown flower action! I love asymmetry in designs like these, so I added two flowers on the upper left side with simple running-stitch vines in between each one.

Design length: 6 inches

YOU'LL NEED

- Straight pins
- Scissors

- Sweater of your choice
- Needle and thread to match your sweater
- Two ¼-inch pink buttons
- 10 brown glass oval beads
- Sage green embroidery thread

1. Put on your sweater and use straight pins to mark where you'd like the centers of your upper flowers to be. Hand-stitch the buttons on securely in those two places. Once they're in place, arrange five beads around each one to represent the petals.

2. Starting with the top bead (petal) on the uppermost flower, stitch it on securely. Continue around the flower clockwise, stitching on each petal in turn. When you get to the final one, knot it securely.

3. Stitch the petals around the second flower in the same way.

4. Cut a piece of six-strand embroidery thread about 36 inches long. Take two of those strands and thread your needle with them. Double it so you are stitching with four strands of thread, then tie a knot at the end.

5. Starting at the top above the first flower you created, sew a curving vine (as shown) using a simple running stitch. On every third stitch, make a backstitch instead to hold the seam nicely. Continue with the line between the two flowers and below the second one. Knot securely at the end of the vine.

Tattoo T

Author and creative maven Megan Nicolay created this striking pattern, reminiscent of a geometric-meets-floral tattoo—the secret is embroidered washers arranged and stitched on, transforming a plain T-shirt into a customized classic.

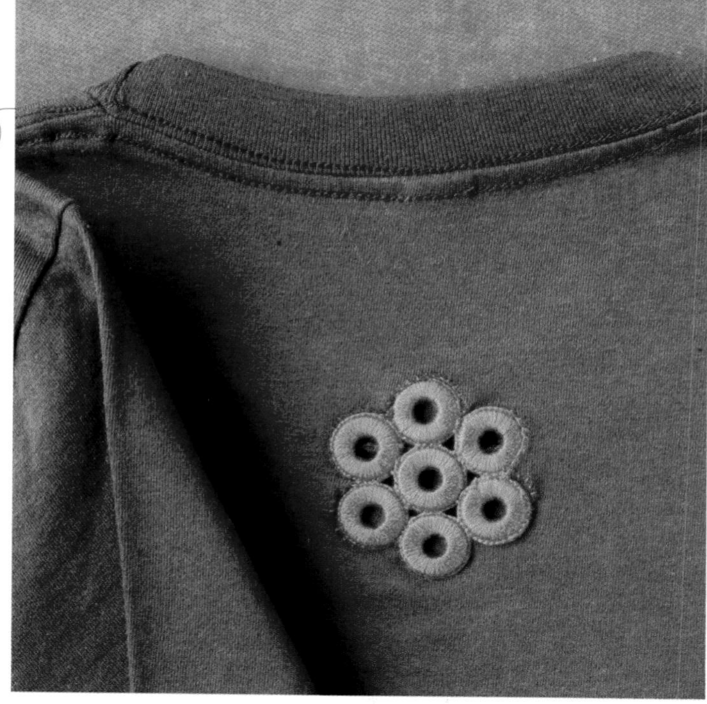

TIP Raid the attic closet for an old T-shirt and the basement for the toolbox. To avoid rust issues when washing, use stainless steel (can be a little pricier) or galvanized (less shiny) washers. Or, for a lighter weight, use plastic washers from your plumber (easier washing, too).

YOU'LL NEED

- Embroidery needle
- Scissors
- Pencil or non-permanent pen
- Embroidery thread (contrasting color to T-shirt)
- 7 washers (¼-inch stainless steel, galvanized, or plastic)
- 1 fitted T-shirt

1. Thread a needle, then run it through the center of one washer, leaving a 3-inch tail. Make a simple knot. Run the needle around the edge and through the center. Before pulling the thread tight, run your needle through the loop of thread your stitch created. Pull it tight. Repeat the stitch (a modified blanket stitch) until the entire washer is covered in thread.

2. To finish, tie the two ends in a knot, run the excess thread under the stitches you made, and trim off the ends.

3. Repeat steps 1 and 2 until all seven washers are covered.

4. Split a length of embroidery thread, so you have only three strands. Thread it onto your needle, and use a whipstitch to sew the edges of two of the washers together. Run your needle through the raised seam around the outer edge of one, and attach it to the raised seam of the other. Make small stitches about ⅛ to ¼ inch along the shared edge.

5. Add a third washer, connecting it to the first two at two points, creating a sort of triangle.

6. Continue adding washers to create a flower-like shape (one washer in the center, with six surrounding it).

7. Turn your T-shirt inside out. Lay the flower on the back of the T-shirt near the neckband, centering it. Trace around it with a pencil or non-permanent pen, and carefully cut out the shape about ⅛ inch *inside* the traced line.

8. Separate one strand of the embroidery thread and thread it onto your needle. Use a blanket stitch to go around the inside of the flower cutout. Tie off your ends.

9. Lay the washer flower over the cutout in the T-shirt, and line up the edges. Use three strands of embroidery thread on your needle to stitch a point of the cutout in between two of the "petals."

10. Next, stitch the opposite point between the opposite petals. Continue stitching until all six points are attached to the flower. Optional: Stitch the entire circumference of the flower to the T-shirt.

11. Turn the T-shirt right side out and try on your temporary tattoo!

VARIATION: Shoulder tattoos: Using 14 washers, prepare and stitch them together in the same way, making two flowers rather than one. Make your tracings and cutouts on each sleeve of the T-shirt before attaching the tattoos to the shoulders for a little peek-a-boo.

Circles Deluxe Skirt

This navy denim skirt gets a fast metallic pick-me-up from two stitched-on circle "flowers" with rickrack stems. Mix silver and gold if you like, or stick with just one color.

Design height: 8 inches

YOU'LL NEED

- Scissors
- Sewing needle and thread
- Pins
- 1 foot of baby rickrack in silver
- Plain skirt
- Two metallic circles (I used a 1½-inch gold one and a 1-inch silver one)

1. Cut two pieces of rickrack for the stems—one 6½ inches long and one 4½ inches long. Lay them out where you'd like them on your skirt—I arranged mine 6½ inches and 8 inches from the right side, as shown. Make sure about ½ inch extends beyond the hem of the skirt, and pin each piece down when you like the placement. Place the circles at the top of each piece to see what the design will look like.

2. Hand-stitch the rickrack to the skirt, knotting at the end of each seam. Tuck the ends under the skirt hem, and secure those pieces with a few stitches to hold them.

3. Next, place the larger circle on its stem. Sew it in place with three stitches at 12, 3, 6, and 9 on the clock face.

4. Repeat to add the smaller circle.

VARIATION: Add "leaves" of felt or doubled pieces of rickrack.

Sparkle It! Winter

Stay stylish and cozy in these winter pieces. Add some of your favorite bright or contrast colors as embellishments on your darker cold-weather stuff.

TECHNIQUES

- **Hand-stitching** All
- **Felting** Turquoise Tree Top
- **Gluing** Valentine's Day Mittens

Atomic Asterisk Coat

I added a little starburst-style decoration to the lapel of my grandmother's 1950s black wool coat—kind of like a perma-brooch! I think she would have loved the idea, since she was so crafty.

YOU'LL NEED

- Straight pins
- Sewing needle
- Scissors

- Coat of your choice
- Thread to match your coat
- 7 round beads in a contrasting color
- 6 elongated beads in a contrasting color (I used ⅝-inch-long white glass beads)

Atomic Asterisk Coat

1. Try on the coat and choose where you want your asterisk to go. I decided on the outer edge of one lapel, so it really popped visually. Place a straight pin where your center will be.

2. Using a doubled and knotted thread, stitch on your center round bead securely. Arrange your six elongated beads around it as shown in the photo. Stitch the top one on first, and continue stitching on beads in a clockwise pattern, making sure they are all symmetrically angled out from the center.

3. When all six beads are in place, add the six round beads, one between each pair of long beads (as shown). Stitch them on the same way as the others.

4. Once you've stitched the sixth one, tie a double knot to hold it in place, just as you would with a conventional hand-sewing project.

Valentine's Day Mittens

These little hearts really cheer me up on a cold afternoon of running errands around town.

YOU'LL NEED

- Sewing needle and thread
- Glue
- Four heart buttons or beads (flat-backed)
- Plain mittens
- Four pink rhinestones

1. Arrange the hearts wherever you'd like them on your mittens, and hand-sew them on with at least four stitches each, knotting securely.

2. Place a drop of glue on the center of each heart and add the rhinestones. Let the glue dry overnight before wearing them.

Turquoise Tree Top

This adorable recycled-sweater hat is designed by knitgrrl Shannon Okey. She says, "I love shaping felt into new things—the leaves on this hat are nothing but cutouts from the rest of the sweater, beaded and attached to the top like a forest full of beads!"

Design width: 10 inches

TIP The average child's head is 18 inches, a woman's is 20, and a man's is 22 inches around. See yarnstandards.com for this and other measurements, especially if you're making this as a surprise for someone and she gets suspicious when you wrap a tape measure around her head! If you don't already have a sweater on hand that you'd like to use, scour the thrift shops for one with a super-long ribbed cowl neck, like the one I used here. The neck piece is guaranteed to fit over your head, and the ribbing is a bonus design feature.

YOU'LL NEED

- Round salad plate or other template
- Sharp scissors or rotary cutter
- Straight pins
- Sewing needle and/or yarn needle
- Wool sweater (at least 50% wool, preferably more)
- Thread to match your sweater
- Decorative yarn (optional)
- Variety of seed beads in coordinating and contrasting colors

1. Felt your sweater by running it through the washer on hot wash, cold rinse with a little detergent, then dry it in the dryer. (Yes, you ARE trying to shrink it. Don't try this with other sweaters you want to wear.)

2. Cut off the turtleneck, or if you don't have a sweater with a turtleneck piece, cut the bottom off. The piece should be 6 to 8 inches tall. If you're using a sweater bottom, measure it around your head and cut to fit.

3. With the piece inside out, seam the side of the sweater bottom to make it the appropriate size (if needed).

4. Using a round salad plate or other template, cut a circle for the hat top out of another sweater section. A rotary cutter makes this easy.

5. Pin the round top into place on the cut side of your hat, with the hat itself inside out. You may need to trim off excess fabric to make it fit, depending on your hat size and salad plate size.

6. When the top fits the bottom portion well, stitch it into place with thread and/or contrasting yarn (I used both, and you can see the metallic yarn peaking through at the brim).

7. Cut leaf shapes out of remaining sweater pieces. Do as many as you'd like—cover the entire top if you want.

8. Using sewing thread and seed beads, make leaf veins, outline the leaves, and otherwise embellish each leaf.

9. Sew the leaves onto the hat crown in groupings. For best effect, stitch the top and bottom of the leaves so they arc from the top of the hat. Felt is sculptural, so have fun with it!

Handbag Charm

Why not dress up a plain handbag with a pretty charm? These simple pieces are easy to make in any color or style, and they're an instant wardrobe update if you put them on and take them off as you change bags.

TECHNIQUES

- **Wrapped loops**
  Spaces and Sparkles
  Squared-Off and Stylish
- **Briolette-style wrapping**
  Spaces and Sparkles
- **Jump rings**
  Handbags Are a Girl's Best Friend
  Squared-Off and Stylish

TIP Make coordinating pieces to match your earrings or pendants (like the Spaces and Sparkles charm).

Spaces and Sparkles Handbag Charm

This simple, pretty peach and pink dangle is complemented with sky-blue ribbon.

Length: 1¾ inches

Handbags Are a Girl's Best Friend Charm

Designer Torie Nguyen of Totinette created this intricate silver purse and filigree charm, which adds a dash of prettiness to any bag.

Length: 3½ inches

YOU'LL NEED

- Pliers
- 3 links of large chain
- ½ inch of smaller silver chain
- 3 inches of smaller silver chain (can be the same as the ½-inch or different)
- 8 jump rings (sizes will vary depending on the size of your beads, charm, and filigree piece)
- 1 round silver filigree piece (from a bead store or taken from an existing piece of jewelry)
- 1 handbag charm (or charm of your choice)
- 1 large lobster clasp
- 1 lightweight headpin
- 1 rhinestone bead
- 1 crystal bead with holes at top and bottom (mine is from an old chandelier)

1. Determine the center link of the 3-inch piece of silver chain. Place this link on a jump ring along with one end of the ½-inch chain. Attach the jump ring to the bottom of the filigree piece.

2. Attach one end of the 3-inch chain (that is dangling from the filigree piece) to the left side of the piece using a jump ring (if the piece were a clock, it would be at 9 o'clock). Repeat with the other end of the chain on the right side (at 3 o'clock).

3. Use a jump ring to attach the handbag charm to the other end of the ½-inch chain.

4. Attach one end of the three-link large chain to the top of the filigree piece with a jump ring.

5. Use a jump ring to attach the lobster clasp to the other end of this chain.

6. Use a headpin to attach the rhinestone bead to the bottom of the crystal bead using a wrapped loop.

7. Place a jump ring through the hole at the top of the crystal bead. Using another jump ring, attach this jump ring to the jump ring at the top of the filigree piece.

8. Clip the charm on your favorite handbag and sparkle!

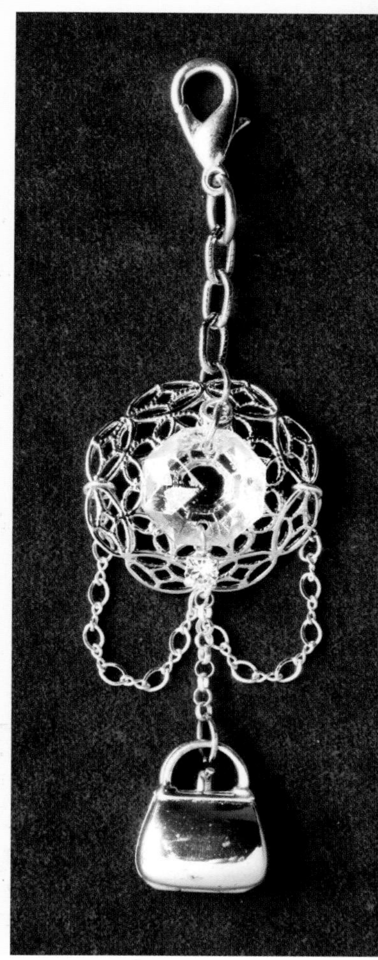

YOU'LL NEED

- Pliers
- 24-gauge wire
- One briolette
- One vertically drilled accent bead (I used a Lucite flower)
- ⅛-inch-wide satin ribbon

1. Follow steps 4 and 5 in the Spaces and Sparkles Pendant instructions on p. 129 to make the two-bead drop, but complete the wrap without joining it to anything else.

2. Cut an 8-inch piece of ribbon and slip the charm onto it by the loop. Tie it to a purse strap in a bow, and trim each end at a diagonal.

Squared-Off and Stylish Handbag Charm

Clip on one stand-alone piece like this black agate bead for a simple but striking addition to your purse.

Length: 4 inches

YOU'LL NEED

- Pliers
- 20-gauge wire
- One 1½-inch black agate piece
- 1 inch of oversize chain
- 1 large jump ring
- 1 large clip

1. Cut a 4-inch piece of wire, and turn the agate piece into a basic dangle, joining it to the last link in the chain before you complete the top wrap.

2. Open the jump ring and connect the chain to the clip, closing it securely.

3. Clip it on your favorite black bag as a sleek ornament.

Good-Luck Charm

Make your own luck with this project! These charms are super-customizable—you can use any of your own lucky bits in any combination.

TECHNIQUES

- **Wrapped loops**
  My Lucky Day
  Suerte Love Charm
- **Jump rings**
  All
- **Hand-sewing**
  Tassel Talisman

TIP Be inventive—use any base to start with, from a tassel to a piece of chain or a metal stamping, and ornament it as you like.

My Lucky Day Charm

I made this charm with lots of personalized favorites—including my lucky number/birthday, astrological sign, and birthstone—along with old standards like the horseshoe and wishbone.

Length: 4 inches

YOU'LL NEED

- Pliers
- Glue
- Charms and embellishments of your choice (I used eight total, both vintage and new)
- 1 metal stamping or filigree to serve as the base
- 1 small jump ring for each charm (I used 3mm)
- Small cabochons or rhinestones to add sparkle (optional; I used a green rhinestone and a small garnet)
- 24-gauge wire, if any of your charms need a connector
- Two 5mm jump rings
- 1 inch of chain
- Large clasp or clip

My Lucky Day Charm

1. Arrange your charms around your base. I first glued down the horseshoe over the center and then designed around it.

2. Open jump rings and attach your charms to the main body of the piece.

3. Glue down any sparkles (like the horseshoe's green rhinestone and the garnet). Let the piece dry thoroughly.

4. Use the two 5mm jump rings to link the top of the charm to one end of the piece of chain and the clasp or clip to the other.

Suerte Love Charm

Crafty Chica Kathy Cano Murillo says, "Love is complex and multi-layered. So is this wild and whimsical charm that has everything you need to get lucky in the romance department: lots of hearts, milagros *(Mexican miracle charms), and a few other surprises, too. Show it off by wearing it as a necklace, belt charm, or car ornament—you are bound to get noticed!"*

Length: 8 inches

TIP Use your resources. Look around your supplies to find small pieces of chain, extra beads, charms, or even single earrings. Anything goes for this charm!

YOU'LL NEED

- Pliers
- Thin brush
- 5 or 6 different types of chains in various sizes and lengths (stay within 1 to 4 inches)
- Small jump rings and eyepins
- Assorted glass beads (including heart-shaped beads)
- Assorted heart charms (including Mexican *milagros*)
- 1 large jump ring
- 36-gauge wire
- 1 large flat bead
- Acrylic paint
- Varnish

1. Start with one chain at a time. Use your pliers to separate the links, and use an eyepin or small jump ring to attach a bead to reconnect the chain. Do this

with all the chains, but make sure to place the beads in a random fashion.

2. Open the jump rings, and attach your charms to the end of each chain.

3. Connect all the chains to the large jump ring.

4. Cut a 36-inch piece of wire and double it. Connect it to the top of the jump ring, slide on the large flat bead, and wrap the wire around the top to create a loop for hanging.

5. On the flat side of the large bead, use a thin brush to write the word *suerte* (which means luck in Spanish). Let dry, add a coat of varnish, and let dry again.

Tassel Talisman

This handmade ribbon tassel design is perfect for an elongated bead. Adorn it with extra charms dangling below if you like.

Length: 5 inches

YOU'LL NEED

- Scissors
- Pliers
- Sewing needle and thread
- Glue
- Fray Check
- ⅛-inch-wide satin ribbon
- 1 large, elongated vertically drilled bead
- Charms of your choice (I used three)
- Thin or medium chain
- 1 small jump ring for each charm

1. First, make the tassel. Cut two pieces of ribbon, each 12 inches long. Fold them in half, then make a neat square knot about 1½ inches below the fold, leaving a good-size loop of ribbon above it.

2. Slip the large bead on the ribbon ends, and tie another knot below it.

3. Arrange the charms as you'd like them to hang, and cut pieces of chain for each one. (I used one ⅝ inch long for my star, one ⅝ inch long for my lucky eye, and one 1 inch long for my Buddha.)

4. Attach each of the charms to their chains with jump rings. Next, hand-stitch them to the knot of the tassel, one at a time, using several stitches to secure each one.

5. Cut a short piece of ribbon and wrap it around the knot to cover the stitches. Glue it in place, overlapping the two ends at the back, and add a drop of Fray Check.

Sparkle It! Bag

Update a plain clutch, iPod® cozy or totebag with a sparkly or colorful motif. Why should your jewelry get all the attention?

TECHNIQUES

- **Gluing**
  Petals Purse
  Vintage-Style iPod Cozy
- **Hand-stitching**
  Vintage-Style iPod Cozy
  Circles in the Square Tote
- **Plain loops**
  Petals Purse

Petals Purse

Embellish a pretty vintage bag with a little extra glitter. Gluing on a simple floral pattern is a snap, and fancying up the plain-chain handle is another quick and charming touch.

YOU'LL NEED

- Craft glue
- Toothpick
- Pliers

- Handbag with chain handle
- 5 oval rhinestones
- 1 round rhinestone for the center
- 20-gauge sterling wire
- 2 faceted Lucite beads (to match the rhinestones)

1. Choose where you want your little flower to go on your bag. Arrange the rhinestones as you like, and when you're pleased with the pattern, dab a little glue on the back of the center round with a toothpick. Press it firmly in place.

2. Working from the top, glue each oval petal on the same way. Let them dry completely.

3. Now it's time for the handle. To arrange your beads as shown, make your first cut ¾ inch above the chain's fastener on the right side.

4. Cut two 2-inch pieces of wire, and form a plain loop at one end of each piece. Open one loop and slip the last link of one piece of the chain onto it. Close the loop and add a bead to the wire. Form a second plain loop above the bead and open it out. Slip the last link of the other piece of chain onto that one and close it.

5. Make a second cut ¾ inch above the first bead and repeat step 4 with the second piece of wire to add your second bead to the chain. Remember, adding the two beads will add length, so you may want to shorten your chain a bit above the beads, too.

Vintage-Style iPod Cozy

Technology is new, but it can still have a vintage feel to it. Designer Natalie Zee Drieu decided to create an iPod cozy as if it were passed down to her from her grandmother, even though iPods were far from existence in the 1940s. Brooches were big back then, and this design takes on an organic shape for a dramatic and elegant sachet-style cozy.

TIP Work your jewelry pieces in sections so that you aren't tangled up while sewing with a long piece of thread. This design is broken up in three pieces—the main centerpiece, top left, and bottom right areas. Invisible thread is fantastic because you will not be able to see the thread through the beads. But it can also be tricky to work with because in addition to being hard to see sometimes, the thread curls up easily.

YOU'LL NEED

- Fabric pencil or chalk
- Fabric glue
- Small paintbrush
- Scissors
- Straight pins
- Sewing needle
- Invisible thread
- 1 vintage rhinestone jewel or large ornate bead for centerpiece
- iPod cozy (the pattern for sewing this cozy is available on beadsimple.com)
- 12 clear small Swarovski® crystals
- 8 light blue/green small Swarovski crystals
- 5 green small Swarovski crystals
- 3 orange small Swarovski crystals

1. Position your vintage rhinestone jewel on your iPod cozy to where you think it will look best. Mark the location on the fabric with a tiny X on your cozy.

2. Dab fabric glue on a small brush and brush the back of the rhinestone jewel. Be careful not to add too much glue or it will get messy. Place the rhinestone on your marked X on the cozy.

3. Thread your needle with invisible thread.

4. Gather your 12 clear beads and start to sew each bead around the rhinestone center jewel in a circle. Sew each bead into the cozy separately and do not string them together. This will keep each bead secure to the fabric. Cut off the end of the thread and tie a knot.

5. For the color bead decoration, you can pretty much design the motif in any way you want, depending on how small or big your cozy is. To create the same look as this cozy, start with the top left area. Gather four light blue/green beads, four green beads, and two orange beads to create the top left pattern.

6. Sew on the light blue/green beads. Work your way in rows moving down, then back up until all the beads are used. Cut off the end of the thread and tie a knot.

7. The next jeweled area is the bottom right. Gather four light blue/green beads, two green, and one orange to create a pattern in the lower right side of the design.

8. Start with the light blue/green bead, and continue to sew down and back up in the same fashion. Cut off the end of the thread and tie a knot. Your embellished cozy is ready for use.

Circles in the Square Tote

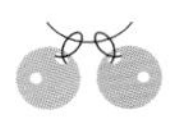

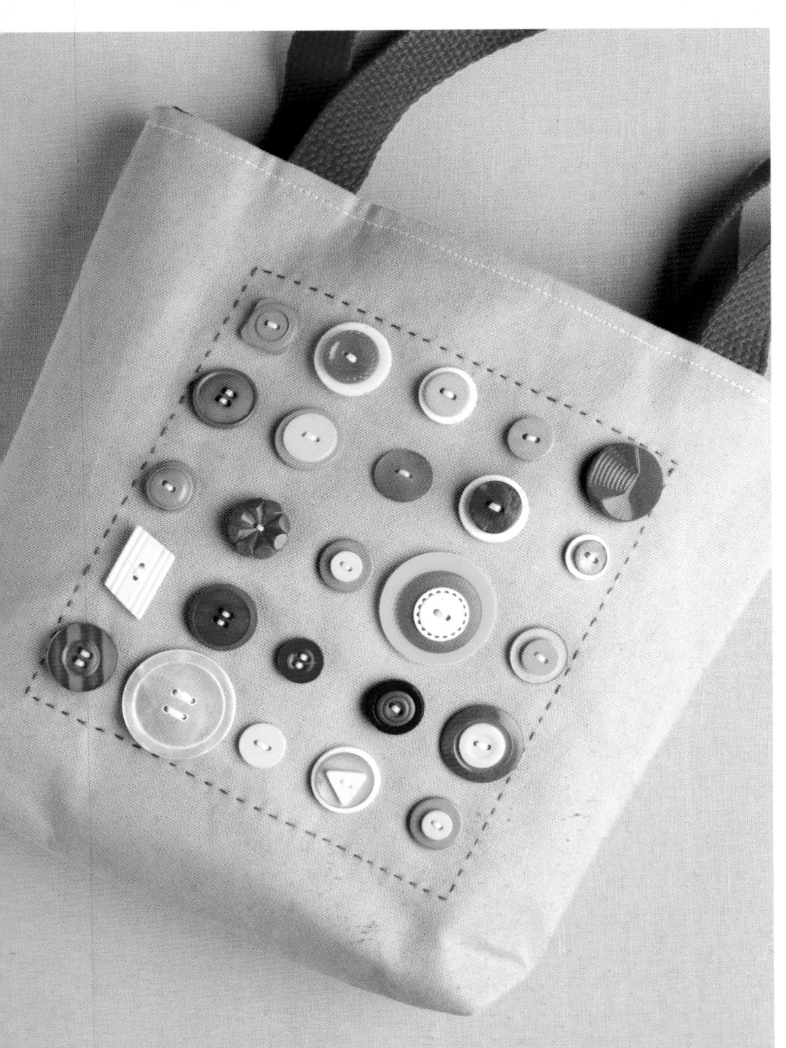

Designed by quilter Sarah Minshall, this customized tote is charmingly embellished.

TIP Any plain tote or pouch is perfect for this embellishment. Use a variety of buttons from thrift stores, garage sales, or craft sales, and feel free to stack them together to give your design a more layered look. You can also customize this project even more by creating your own tote bag—for a pattern, go to beadsimple.com.

YOU'LL NEED

- Sewing needle and thread
- Embroidery floss
- An assortment of buttons
- A plain tote bag or pouch

1. Determine a pattern for your button square. I sewed on 25 buttons (five across, five down), spacing them evenly inside a 6½-inch square.

2. Find the center button and the center of the bag. Hand-sew that one on tightly.

3. Working outward, sew on the buttons in rows to form the square.

4. Once you've added all your buttons, use a complementary colored embroidery floss to outline the square in a simple running stitch.

Beaded Belt

Making yourself a sleek, adjustable chain belt is a snap, but you can dress up the basic idea with plenty of embellishments. Another plus is that you can wear your belt as a necklace—just loop it around a few times and let the ornament fall in front or in back. Or embellish a classic ribbon belt with beads for an unexpected extra.

TECHNIQUES

- **Wrapped loops**
  Low-Slung
  Circles and Ovals
- **Plain loops**
  Low-Slung
- **S-clasp**
  Low-Slung
- **Hand-stitching**
  Beaded Ribbon
- **Machine-stitching**
  Beaded Ribbon

Low-Slung Chain Belt

Belt or belly chain? This sultry piece features black Lucite beads on one end of its chain and an S-clasp on the other. Length: 44 inches (adjustable)

YOU'LL NEED

- Pliers
- Medium- or heavy-weight chain
- 24-gauge wire
- One 18mm faceted black Lucite bead
- Three 10mm faceted black Lucite beads
- Seed beads
- S-clasp

1. Cut the chain to the length of your choosing—measure yourself at the point you want to wear it and add at least 2 inches.

2. Cut four 3-inch pieces of wire, and make a plain loop at the end of one of them. Use it to create a basic bead dangle with the largest Lucite bead.

3. Form the first half of a wrapped loop at one end of the second piece of wire. Slip the open loop onto the wrapped loop over the larger bead dangle and complete the loop.

4. Next, add a seed bead, one of the 10mm beads, and another seed bead to the piece of wire. Form the first half of a wrapped loop above it so you have a double-wrapped bead connector. Slip the open loop onto the first link in the chain you cut in step 1, then complete the loop.

5. Measure 2 inches in from the other end of the chain and make a cut there. Create a wrapped loop on both sides of a 10mm bead, and join it to connect the two pieces of chain you just cut before completing the wrap.

6. Make another cut ¾ inch from the first one, and repeat step 5 to add another 10mm bead.

7. Make an S-clasp and attach it to the last link in the chain by slipping it on before you make the final loop. Or use a jump ring if necessary.

Circles and Ovals Belt

This mother-of-pearl ovals and silver chain belt is subtle and gorgeous over a vintage dress or jeans—and the negative space looks great with a print or solid peeking through. Length: 41 inches (adjustable)

TIP Use other sizes of ovals or switch up the lengths of the chain pieces to suit your own taste. It's easy to add more segments or take them off, so you can adapt the design to your own measurements.

YOU'LL NEED

- Pliers

- 2 feet of oversize circle chain
- Eight 2-inch mother-of-pearl ovals (side drilled)
- One large lobster clasp
- One 1-inch mother-of-pearl oval
- Seventeen 24-gauge silver headpins
- 5mm jump ring

1. Cut your circle chain into nine 2½-inch segments. Arrange them on a flat surface with a 2-inch oval between each one, the clasp at one end, and the 1-inch oval at the other end.

2. Slip a headpin through one of the holes in the 1-inch oval, pointing from the center outward. Form a wrapped loop, but slip the first link on the neigh-

Beaded Ribbon Belt

Make your own embellished ribbon belt with pretty jacquard ribbon and seed beads. Queen Puff Puff designer Nicole Vasbinder suggests, "Let the ribbon's design be your beading guide."

TIP Like the Sparkle It! clothing projects, if you run your thread through beeswax twice and then give it a quick iron (on the synthetic setting) to seal it, it will strengthen your thread and also help prevent tangles. Use at least three stitches for each bead so they stay on securely. Nicole adds, "After every third bead, knot the thread. That way, in case your thread breaks, you won't lose all the beads. Pick up the beads with a beading needle rather than your fingers—it's much easier."

TIP Measure your waist or hip (depending on where you will wear your belt) and add 10 inches. This is how much of each ribbon you'll need.

YOU'LL NEED

- Beading needle
- Basting tape
- Sewing machine (recommended) or sewing needle and thread
- Assorted seed beads
- ⅝-inch-wide jacquard ribbon
- 1½-inch-wide solid grosgrain ribbon
- Polyester sewing thread
- 1½-inch center bar slider buckle

1. Lay out your seed beads on the jacquard ribbon to get an idea of your design.

2. Hand-stitch the beads onto the jacquard ribbon, making sure they are secure. Leave about 3 inches on each end unbeaded.

3. Lay the beaded jacquard ribbon centered on top of the grosgrain ribbon. Nicole found it helpful to use a basting tape like Wonder Tape to attach the jacquard ribbon to the grosgrain ribbon.

4. Using a zipper foot, machine-stitch the jacquard ribbon to the grosgrain along each edge. Make sure to backstitch at the beginning and end of each seam.

NOTE: you can hand-sew the ribbons together if you prefer.

5. Take one end of the ribbon and turn it under ¼ inch, then turn under another ¼ inch. Topstitch to secure.

6. Take the other end of the ribbon and turn it back ¼ inch. Slide it up and over the center bar of the buckle so that the center bar is sandwiched. Topstitch the ribbon to secure the buckle.

boring piece of circle chain before finishing the wrap. You now have a linked oval and chain segment—the first section of the belt.

3. Add the first 2-inch oval to the other side of the chain segment in the same way, creating a wrapped loop with a headpin. Continue adding chains and ovals until you have the desired length, but make sure you end on a piece of chain.

4. Finish by adding the clasp to the last link in the last piece of chain. Try it on and wear it out!

Sunglasses Leash

Keep your sunglasses handy with a beaded leash—
and do it up to reflect your favorite colors, too.

TECHNIQUES

- **Plain loops**
  Bits and Pieces
  Eye-Catching
- **Jump rings**
  Eye-Catching
- **Wrapped loops**
  Pink and Black
  Forever

Bits and Pieces Chain

Brown and amber chips are wired to make a long chain.

Length: 34 inches

TIP You can make all the bead links at once and then gently reopen the plain loops to join them later, if you prefer.

YOU'LL NEED

- Pliers
- 20- or 22-gauge wire
- Small beads of your choice in two complementary colors, A and B
- Two lobster clasps
- Two eyeglasses holders

1. Cut about 48 pieces of wire, each 1¼ inches long.
2. Form a plain loop at the end of one piece of wire, and put three beads on it, alternating A, then B, then another A. Form another plain loop at the other end of the wire, trimming any excess before you make the loop.
3. Make another bead link as in step 2, but slip the second plain loop onto the first bead link before you close it, joining the two links.
4. Continue making bead links, always joining them together as you go, until you have 48 links, or the total length is at least 32 inches.
5. Add a lobster clasp to each end, either by opening the outer plain loops or with jump rings.
6. Open the clasps and slip them over one end of an eyeglasses holder.

Eye-Catching Eyeglasses Chain

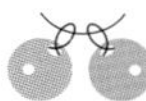

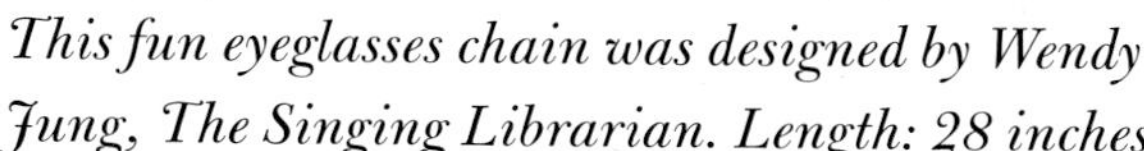

This fun eyeglasses chain was designed by Wendy Jung, The Singing Librarian. Length: 28 inches

TIP Wendy says, "If you don't want people looking at your chain more than they are looking at you, use unusual accent beads sparingly, keep the pattern near the temples more symmetrical, and the color monochromatic. If you're more interested in making a statement, put all the showcase beads at the ends near your temples and wear with no-nonsense sunglasses."

TIP The great thing about creating a chain with small sections is that if it starts to look unappealing, you don't have to scrap the whole project. You can take out the section that isn't working and move on. You may even use that section later. It's easy to fix mistakes.

YOU'LL NEED

- Pliers
- 22-gauge wire
- Small glass beads
- Unique accent beads
- Vintage beads
- Small round gold beads
- Lobster clasps
- Jump rings
- Two eyeglasses holders

VARIATION: I chose to mix up the bead pattern by alternating randomly between sections of three beads, one bead, or a vintage bead "sandwiched" between round gold beads. The order is entirely to taste. She kept the color palette simple, sticking to blue and green tones with just a pop of pink, so she knew it would all match when she started putting it together.

BONUS: You can always unclip the clasps from the eyeglasses holders and connect them to each other to make an impromptu necklace.

1. Cut wire as you go, the size depending on how many beads and the size of the beads you are using for that section.

2. Form a plain loop, place the selected bead(s), and form another plain loop, trimming any excess wire before closing the final loop.

3. Begin your next section in the same way as above, but slip the new plain loop onto the finished section's end loop before you close it to join the two sections.

4. Continue making sections, joining them as you go until you have about 26 inches.

5. Attach a lobster clasp with a jump ring to each end. Add a jump ring to the eyeglasses holder piece so that it is easy to clip your chain on and off.

6. Put the eyeglasses holders on your glasses, clip your chain on, and you're ready to go!

Pink and Black Forever Sunglasses Chain

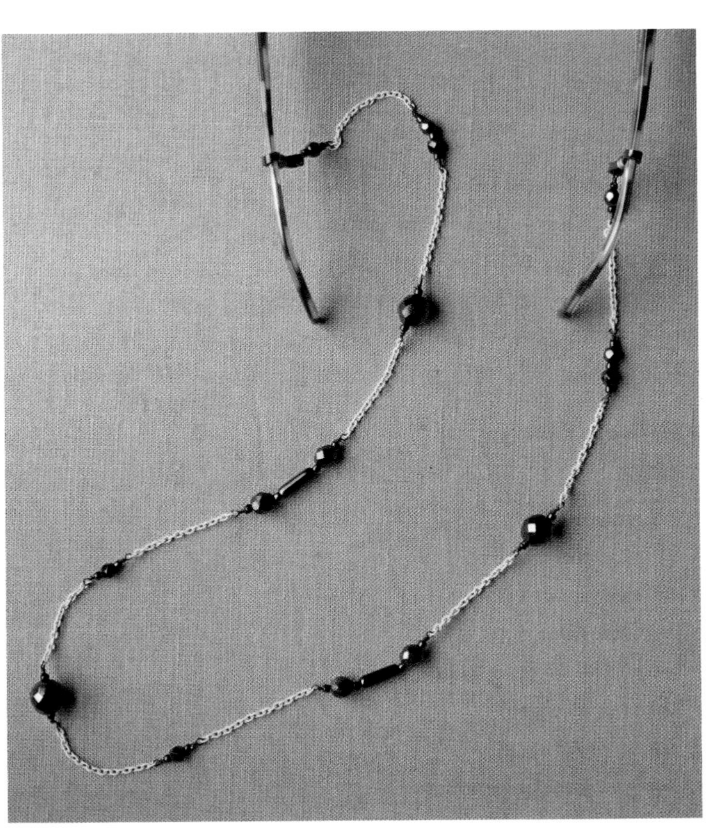

This hot-pink chain studded with black beads really pops. Use any combination of sizes in a symmetrical pattern to reflect your taste or just to take advantage of what's in your stash. Length: 29 inches

YOU'LL NEED

- Pliers
- 15 inches of pink chain (C)
- Black 24-gauge craft wire
- Assorted black faceted beads (I used eight 6mm, four 8mm, and three 12mm rounds)
- Two ½-inch black cylinder beads (CY)
- Black seed beads
- Two black eyeglasses holders (E)

1. Cut 10 pieces of chain, each 1½ inches long. Lay them out on a flat work surface, end to end, and begin planning your bead pattern.

2. For the design shown, make a series of bead connectors—each one bookended by wrapped loops to link the pieces of chain. Each larger bead will have a seed bead on either side of it, too.

3. Assemble the chain, following the pattern below, from side to side.

PATTERN: E-6-C-6-6-C-12-C-8-CY-8-C-6-C-12-C-6-C-8-CY-8-C-12-C-6-6-C-6-E

Holiday Ornaments

Create a tiny dove of peace, a wreath of vintage buttons, or a sparkling Christmas star with a handful of beads and buttons. Put your own spin on any of these ideas to make quick, thoughtful gifts or to decorate your own house.

TECHNIQUES

- **Jump rings**
  Shining Dove of Peace
- **Wrapped loops**
  Shining Dove of Peace
  Sparkling Christmas Star
- **Gluing**
  All
- **Wire looping**
  Vintage Button Wreath

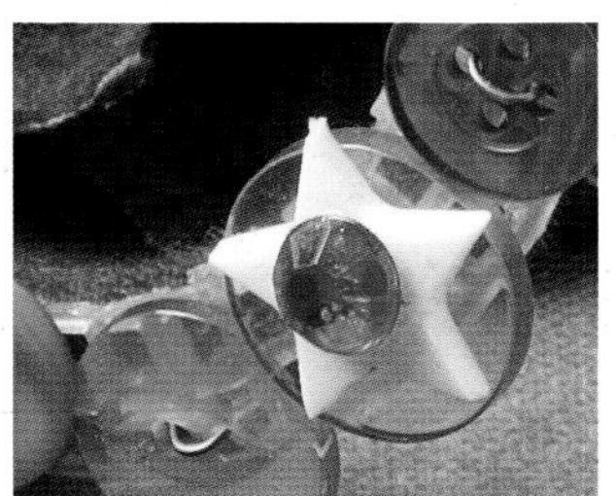

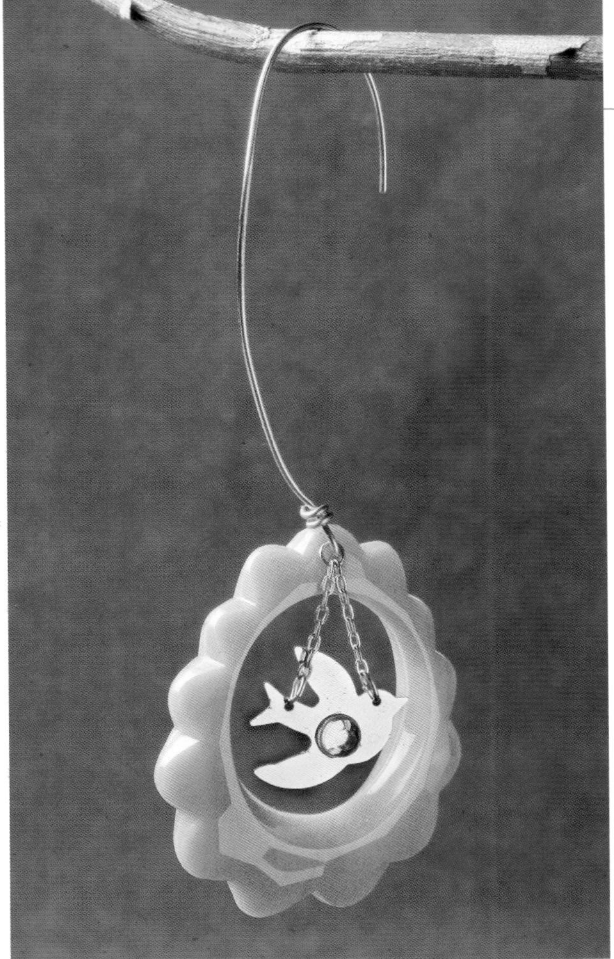

1. Glue a rhinestone onto your bird and let it dry completely. Open the jump rings and slip them through the two small holes on the bird charm.

2. Cut the piece of chain in half, slip one piece onto each jump ring, and close them securely.

3. Cut a 4-inch piece of craft wire, and thread it through the hole at the top of the open drop so 1 inch is to the back and the other 3 inches are in front. Slip the last links of the two pieces of chain onto the front tail of wire so the bird hangs in place. Adjust the chain length if it isn't right.

4. When you like the arrangement, create a wrapped coil with the wire tail from the back winding around the longer front piece. Curve the longer piece into an ornament hanger, using round-nose pliers or your fingers.

5. Hang the ornament on your tree or in your window.

Shining Dove of Peace

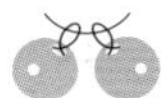  

A tiny gold bird hangs inside a vintage pink bauble. Length: 4 inches

TIP Look for lightweight sequin-style bird charms for this piece—I found mine at Berger Beads in Los Angeles. Or change the scale of the ornament and use larger elements for everything.

YOU'LL NEED

- Pliers
- Craft glue

- 1 rhinestone
- 1 bird charm
- Two 3mm jump rings
- 1 inch of thin gold chain
- 20-gauge gold craft wire
- 1 vintage or new bauble, large enough to suspend the bird inside

Vintage Button Wreath

Weave green buttons around an open mesh circle and accent them with a little sparkle.

Length: 6 inches

TIP I used buttons that were from ⅜ to ⅝ inch across and mixed them color- and size-wise around the circle. I also layered a small opaque button over a larger translucent one here and there to add interest.

TIP I used all buttons with holes instead of shanks and wired them this way: If it has two holes, come up through one from behind and down through the other to the back of the mesh again. If it has four holes, wire through two of them diagonally, the same way as if it had two.

YOU'LL NEED

- Pliers
- Scissors
- Washable fabric marker
- Sewing needle and thread
- Industrial-strength glue
- 3-inch-wide plastic mesh circle
- 24-gauge craft wire
- Green felt
- A selection of flat green buttons (I used about 20 for my wreath)
- 8 inches of ⅛-inch-wide red satin ribbon
- White ½-inch star button (flat-backed)
- 1 medium-size red rhinestone

1. For this design, you'll use the outer ring of a mesh circle (see the Vintage Button Brooch how-to on p. 146 for more on this). Carefully trim any spiky bits of plastic from the inside edge of the ring so it is smooth.

2. Next, you'll "mend" the circle at the cut. Trim any spiky plastic at the opening, as you did in step 1, so the two sides are clean-edged where they meet. Cut an 8-inch piece of craft wire and form a wrapped loop at one end. Thread the tail through one side of the opening, leaving the loop at the back, then thread the tail back through the other side, slipping the tail through the loop to catch it. Gently pull it taut, holding the two halves together. Repeat the wrapping a few more times, covering the join evenly, up and down, to unite the two pieces securely.

3. When the ring is lying flat and securely fastened, wrap the tail around one mesh grid line off to one side three or four times and leave a ½-inch tail, smoothing it flat to the back.

4. Using the mesh ring as a template, cut out a round piece of felt in the same size with your scissors. Then place the ring on the felt circle and trace around the inside of the negative space with a fabric marker. Fold the circle in half and carefully cut out

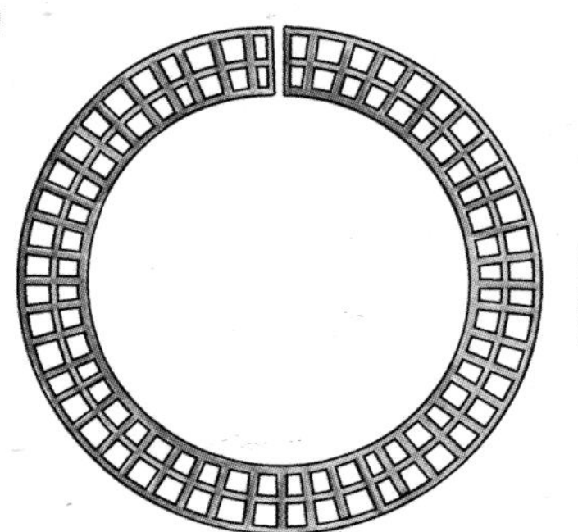

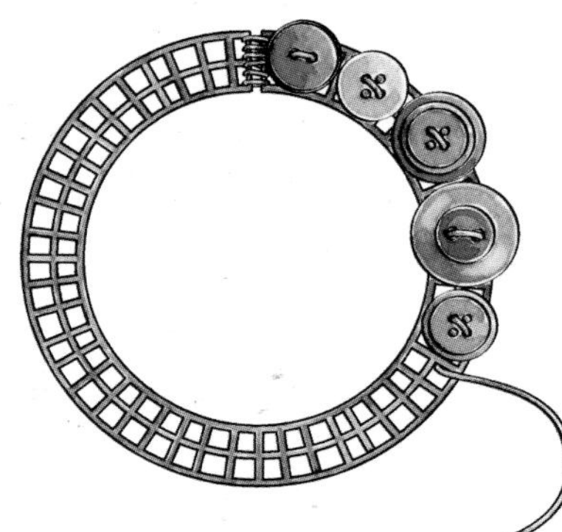

the center so it is the same size and shape as your ring. Set it aside for now.

5. Put all your buttons on a plate or tray and sort through them. Arrange them around the mesh circle so the edges touch, mixing up colors and sizes as you go.

6. Cut a 2-foot piece of craft wire. If this length gets unwieldy or kinks while you're working, cut it shorter—you can always bind off when the wire runs out and start again with a new piece.

7. Form a wrapped loop at one end, and thread the tail through the mesh circle just to the left of the mend, back to front, leaving the loop at the back. Put your first button on the wire tail. Now thread the tail back through the button's second hole so that the button covers the mend seam, and slip the tail through the loop to catch it. Gently pull it taut.

8. With your first button in place, pass the wire tail back through a hole in the mesh just to the right of your last "stitch," and choose another button to add next to your first one. Slip it on the wire and pull the wire back through the second hole to hold it down the same way.

9. Continue to add buttons, working in a clockwise pattern away from the first one you wired on, and have fun mixing in different shapes, sizes, and lighter or darker ones as you go.

10. Keep working until you reach the top of the circle again and have placed your last button and threaded the wire through to the back. Then wrap the wire securely around one mesh grid line behind

the button three or four times and leave a ½-inch tail, smoothing it flat to the back.

11. Fold the red ribbon in half so the two ends are together and flat. Slip one end through the mesh opening at the mend (either side), then secure the ribbon with a few stitches at the ends. Tug it down just slightly so the sewn bit is well below the edge.

12. Turn your ornament over, buttons side down, and put industrial-strength glue all over the back, distributing it evenly. Then press your felt ring down over it, covering the entire back, including the ribbon join. Let it dry completely, smoothing it down if it bubbles out or warps.

13. Choose a button at roughly the 5 o'clock position on the circle, and glue the white star onto it. Then glue the red rhinestone over that to cover the two holes. Let those dry as well and you're done.

Sparkling Christmas Star

This fun holiday piece was designed by writer and crafter Meredith MacDonald. Size: 5 inches

TIP You can use silver, gold, or bronze materials to create different looks. About 20g of seed beads will make eight ornaments. Mix seed beads of various colors for another effect. Or instead of a wooden charm, use a small photo and glue on a seed bead border.

YOU'LL NEED

- Paintbrush
- Pliers
- Craft glue
- Acrylic paint
- Unfinished wooden star
- Filigree backing
- Crystal cut seed beads (enough to cover the front of your charm)
- Coordinating 20-gauge wire

1. Paint the wooden charm (front, back, and sides) in your choice of colors. I used white acrylic paint from my stash.

2. While that dries, use the pliers to create a small loop at the top of the filigree backing. This will be where the hanger is attached. You can also use a regular jump ring, but I wanted mine to match with the hanger.

3. Spread craft glue on the front side of the wooden charm, and press the seed beads into it. Let dry.

4. Make the hanger by cutting a 4-inch piece of wire (or longer if you prefer). Feed it through the loop of the filigree backing, and wrap it shut using pliers. Curve the wire so it makes an upside-down J shape.

5. Glue the wooden charm onto the backing. Let dry.

6. Hang on your tree and admire the sparkling ornament as you sip hot chocolate!

Guest Designers

TANJA ALGER (p. 116) lives in Portland, Oregon, with her husband and two stepsons. In her spare time she loves to garden, draw, and look after her family's menagerie of cats and chickens.

JENNIFER BONNELL (p. 56) is a born and raised Jersey crafty girl with a penchant for all things sparkly, and the author of *DIY Girl*. She lives in Montclair, New Jersey, with her husband, their cat, and her monstrous stash of craft supplies.

CATHY CALLAHAN (p. 141) is a crafter who draws inspiration from crafts of the '60s and '70s. Her website is cathyofcalifornia.com.

NICOLA CORL (p. 154) is a hairstylist and make-up artist who lives with her husband, Neal, and three children, Henry, Maisie, and June, in Portland, Oregon. Any crafting projects are undertaken in the middle of the night!

STACY ELAINE DACHEUX (p. 90) enjoys writing, baking pumpkin bagels, and drawing pictures of lions with astronaut helmets. Her projects can be found at stacyelaine.com.

NATALIE ZEE DRIEU (p. 203) is associate editor of *CRAFT* magazine and web editor of the *CRAFT* blog (craftzine.com). Her personal blog, Coquette (coquette.blogs.com), expresses her love of fashion, style, technology, and crafts.

NANCY FLYNN (p. 35) is a writer and crafter who lives in San Francisco. She is co-editor of getcrafty.com and the author of *Jeaneology: Crafty Ways to Reinvent Your Old Blues*.

DIANE GILLELAND, (p. 135) also known as Sister Diane, organizes the Portland Church of Craft. She also produces CraftyPod, a podcast about making stuff, at craftypod.com.

When she's not crafting lesson plans, FIONA GILLESPIE (p. 119) knits, sews, quilts, and visits the second-hand and vintage shops of the world.

BETSY GREER (p. 173) is a writer, thinker, and crafter living in North Carolina. When not busy making things, she writes about the ethical side of crafty life at craftivism.com.

ALEXIS HARTMAN (p. 70) is an illustrator and self-proclaimed remedial crafter born into a very crafty family in Los Angeles. Her work can be found at greenbluegreen.com.

WENDY JUNG, (p. 209) the Singing Librarian, designs sweet and simple accessories using vintage buttons, shiny beads, and unique souvenirs from the past, found at singinglibrarian.com. She earned her moniker while working at an interior design firm, organizing their library and taking liberties with the office intercom.

In 2003 LEAH KRAMER (p. 144) created the online community craftster.org as a haven for people who love to make stuff but who also love to break the traditional rules of crafting. She's also the author of a book on kitschy crafts from the 1950s and '60s called *The Craftster Guide to Nifty, Thrifty, and Kitschy Crafts*.

FAYTHE LEVINE (p. 32) works under the moniker Flying Fish Design, in Milwaukee, Wisconsin. She also owns a brick and mortar shop called Paper Boat Boutique & Gallery, is the founder of Art vs. Craft, and is the producer and director of "Handmade Nation."

MEREDITH MACDONALD (p. 214) lives in the San Francisco Bay Area and enjoys all manner of domestic arts, especially sewing, knitting, baking, and collecting Blythe dolls. Her work can be found at paperdollygirl.com.

BETHE MACK (p. 188) is an enthusiastic crafter, part-time actor/musician, reiki healer, and chihuahua lover. She divides her time between Portland, Oregon, and the rest of the universe.

JESSEE MALONE (p. 76) resides in Baltimore City, Maryland, where she designs one-of-a-kind jewelry in her home and runs her online shop, artschooldropout.net.

SARAH MINSHALL (p. 204) is a quilter, crafter, knitter, and maker of all things fabric-related. She keeps tabs on what she makes at her blog, Hip to Piece Squares hiptopiecesquares.avenueb.org.

KATHY CANO MURILLO (a.k.a the Crafty Chica) (p. 200) is a book author, TV personality, and syndicated newspaper columnist. She is addicted to glitter and all things sparkly, and runs the website craftychica.com.

TORIE NGUYEN (p. 197) is a member of PDX Super Crafty (pdxsupercrafty.com) and the owner/designer of Totinette Accessories (totinette.com). She co-organizes the Crafty Wonderland sale in Portland and helps her husband, Quentin, with his T-shirt company, Monsieur T.

MEGAN NICOLAY (p. 190) is the author of Generation *T: 108 Ways to Transform a T-shirt* (generation-T.com) and a founding member and secret craft agent for the Department of Craft (departmentofcraft.com). She lives in Brooklyn, New York, with her sewing machines, typewriter, and her teacher man, Luke.

SHANNON OKEY (p. 195) is the author of the *Knitgrrl* series, *Spin to Knit, Felt Frenzy,* and many other crafty books. She lives in Cleveland, Ohio, where her studio is filled with sweaters just waiting to become other things.

REBECCA PEARCY (p. 49) is the designer and founder of Queen Bee Creations, a handmade accessories company. She loves sewing, knitting, gardening, cooking, and making music.

JENNIFER PERKINS (p. 170) keeps herself busy running her online jewelry company Naughty Secretary Club, being a member of the Austin Craft Mafia, hosting "Craft Lab" and "Stylelicious" on the DIY Network and producing the Stitch Fashion Show and Guerilla Craft Bazaar.

LINDA PERMANN (p. 96) is a founding editor for *Adorn* magazine. She loves making things, thrifting, and visiting national parks.

CHRISTY PETTERSON (p. 153) is a crafter, designer, and writer from Atlanta. She is co-editor of getcrafty.com, organizes a craft market called the Indie Craft Experience and creates her own line of clothing and accessories, a bardis. In between all the craftiness she enjoys working full-time in public relations.

JULIAN QUARESIMA (p. 65) is in elementary school in East Meadow, New York and loves making jewelry with his Aunt Susan.

TRICIA ROYAL (p. 55) hails from San Francisco, California. An artist, fashion designer, and writer, she is obsessed with sewing, knitting, crocheting, and thrift shopping. Her fashion-focused blog and website live at bitsandbobbins.com.

JENNY RYAN (p. 160) is a kitsch-and-cupcake-obsessed artist and crafter living in Silverlake, California, with her cartoonist husband, Johnny, and their two insane cats, Kang and Kodos. She is the owner of SewDarnCute.com and moonlights as the organizer behind Felt Club (feltclub.com), LA's popular indie craft fair.

Southern California artist LAURA STOKES (p. 148) runs Charcoal Designs, a showcase for her vintage-inspired designs.

JENN STURIALE (p. 75) crafts, tinkers, writes, and codes using fabric, paper, wire, computers, and lots of glue in Brooklyn. She is a founding member of the Department of Craft, and her work can be seen at muchdesign.com.

KAYTE TERRY (p. 39) is a stylist and crafter living in Brooklyn with her husband and her rabbit/muse, Potato. Find out more about Kayte's crafty exploits at thisisloveforever.com/blog and departmentofcraft.com.

Raised in Montana in a family of artists, CAITLIN TROUTMAN (p. 42) has been making things since she can remember. After going to school for painting, she found herself in the woodshop.

NICOLE VASBINDER (p. 207) lives in Petaluma, California, and is the designer of the Queen Puff Puff handbag and accessory line. She also teaches sewing and crafty business classes throughout the Bay Area.

JESSICA VITKUS (p. 167) wrote a recycled crafts book called *AlternaCrafts,* developed projects for the Martha Stewart Living TV craft department, and has written for several of Martha's magazines. She lives in New York's East Village with her blacksmith/sculptor/Texan boyfriend, and embroiders whenever possible.

KELLY WIGLESWORTH (p. 157) is a writer and yoga teacher living on California's Central Coast who's been making jewelry for more than 10 years. She brought her bead bag as her luxury item on the first season of "Survivor," and used the hemp rope to lash a hut together, invisible thread to catch fish, and made necklaces and bracelets for everyone with shells she found on the island.

JESSICA WILSON (p. 180) is a color junkie, a hoarder of kitsch and an erratic baker. A native Californian, she currently lives in the Los Feliz Village with her ukulele-playing better half, who often teams up with her to craft the night away.

EMILIE ZANGER is a Chicago writer and the former DIY editor of *Venus Zine*. Her day-job alter ego is a restaurant publicist, so it's no surprise that her favorite crafty pastime is concocting elaborate meals from her numerous cookbooks. Emilie and her sister (and talented co-contributor) JESSICA (p. 184) grew up in Cincinnati, Ohio.

Resources

Here are some of my favorite sources for all things beading. Be sure to check out beadsimple.com for even more suggestions.

p.s. Don't forget to support your local bead shops, too!

BEADS, TOOLS, AND SUPPLIES

Berger Beads
(vintage and new beads, rhinestones, stampings, and materials)
413 E. 8th St., Los Angeles, CA
213-627-8783
bergerbeads.net

Beyond Beads
(semiprecious, glass, and vintage and new charms)
1251 Howard St., San Francisco, CA
415-861-1865

Dava Bead and Trade
(beads and findings)
1815 NE Broadway, Portland, OR
877-962-3282
davabead and trade.com

Eloxite
(jewelry blanks, beads, and tools)
307-322-3050
eloxite.com

Fire Mountain Gems
(glass, semiprecious, charms, metal, and more)
800-355-2137
firemtn.com

M & J Trimming
(lace, ribbons, trims, and buttons)
1008 Sixth Ave., New York, NY
800-9MJ-TRIM
mjtrim.com

Metalliferous
(vintage and new beads, charms, and chain, plus tools and findings)
34 W. 46th St., New York, NY
888-944-0909
metalliferous.com

Michael Levine
(fabrics, buttons, and ribbons)
920 Maple Ave., Los Angeles, CA
213-622-6259
mlfabrics.com

Ornamentea
(beads, ribbons, charms, and miscellany)
509 N. West St., Raleigh, NC
919-834-6260
ornamentea.com

Rings and Things
(metal and findings of all kinds)
800-366-2156
rings-things.com

Rio Grande
(semiprecious, metal, and tools)
800-545-6566
riogrande.com

Toho Shoji
(beads, chain, charms, and crystals)
990 Sixth Ave., New York, NY
212-868-7465

VINTAGE, SECONDHAND, AND UNUSUAL PIECES

Search Etsy (etsy.com) and eBay (ebay.com) for specific things you're looking for, or browse a whole category.

Estate sales, flea markets, and thrift stores are an amazing resource for vintage pieces, too.

And you can find all kinds of unusual things to work with at hardware stores or in your recycling bin!

Index

Index note: page references in *italics* indicate a photograph; page references in **bold** indicate a drawing.

F

G

H

I

J

K

L

M

N

P

R

S

T

V

W